P9-APG-330

WITHDRAWN FROM

National Health Care

MONTGOMERY COLLEGE
ROCKVILLE CAMPUS LIBRARY
ROCKVILLE, MARYLAND

National Health Care

Lessons for the United States and Canada

Edited by Jonathan Lemco

Ann Arbor

THE UNIVERSITY OF MICHIGAN PRESS

SEP 2 2 1995

ABD 5448

Copyright © by the University of Michigan 1994
All rights reserved
Published in the United States of America by
The University of Michigan Press
Manufactured in the United States of America
♾ Printed on acid-free paper

1997   1996   1995   1994   4   3   2   1

A CIP catalogue record for this book is available from the British Library.

Library of Congress Cataloging-in-Publication Data

National health care : lessons for the United States and Canada /
    edited by Jonathan Lemco.
        p.   cm.
    Includes bibliographical references and index.
    ISBN 0-472-10440-3 (alk. paper)
    1. Insurance, Health—United States.   2. Insurance, Health—
Canada.   3. Health care reform—United States.   4. Medicine, State—
Canada.   I. Lemco, Jonathan.
RA395.A3N335   1994
362.1′0973—dc20   94-9075
                                                                        CIP

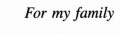

For my family

Acknowledgments

Theodore R. Marmor and Jerry L. Mashaw's article "Canada's Health Insurance and Ours: The Real Lessons, the Big Choices" is adapted from chapter 6 of *America's Misunderstood Welfare State: Persistent Myths, Enduring Realities* (New York: Basic Books, 1990), by Theodore R. Marmor, Jerry L. Mashaw, and Philip L. Harvey. Reprinted by permission of New Prospect, Inc., from the Fall 1990 issue of *The American Prospect*.

Malcolm G. Taylor's "Insuring National Health Care" is reprinted from *Insuring National Health Care: The Canadian Experience*, by Malcolm Taylor. © 1990 The University of North Carolina Press. Used by permission of the author and publisher.

An earlier version of Steffie Woolhandler and David Himmelstein's "Resolving the Cost-Access Conflict: The Case for a National Health Program" was published in the *Journal of General International Medicine* (1989). Reprint permission is granted.

Earlier versions of the articles by Raisa Deber, Edward Neuschler, David W. Conklin, and Paul W. Sperduto were published in *Canada-U.S. Outlook* (published by the National Planning Association, 1991). Reprint permission is granted.

An earlier version of the article by Bert Seidman was published in *Curing U.S. Health Care Ills* (published by the National Planning Association, 1991). Reprint permission is granted.

Morris L. Barer and Robert G. Evans's "Interpreting Canada: Models, Mind-sets, and Myths" was published in *Health Affairs* 11, no. 1 (Spring 1992). Reprint permission is granted.

Edward Neuschler's article "Is Canadian-Style Government Health Insurance the Answer for the United States' Health Care Cost and Access Woes?" is a shortened version of *Canadian Health Care: The Implications of Public Health Insurance* (published as a *Research Bulletin* by the Health Insurance Association of America, 1990).

Contents

CHAPTER 1

Introduction

Jonathan Lemco

There is a crisis in the American health care system. Costs are growing
dramatically, the uninsured or underinsured must gamble that they won't get
sick, and there is widespread dissatisfaction with the existing system. All of
the health care players agree that reforms are necessary, but there is no
consensus about what they should be. Canada's national health care insurance
system is now frequently cited as a useful model, but the Canadian system has
its opponents in Canada as well as in the United States.

This being said, there are forces lobbying for change in the United
States, and elements of the Canadian system, particularly its universality,
might well be applicable. The U. S. health care system offers state-of-the-art
technology and world-class care for those who can afford it. Indeed, there are
those who maintain that certain aspects of the U.S. system might be appropriate to a Canadian system that, its critics maintain, is characterized by reduced
access and scarce high-tech facilities.

The articles in this collection offer an overview of the relative benefits
and costs of the Canadian and American health care systems. The writers
clearly demonstrate that no single health care system is perfect but that meaningful reforms are possible. Their policy prescriptions are worthy of consideration, especially at a time when so many one-sided approaches are now on the
table. This volume attempts to provide a balanced, policy-focused discussion
of many of the most prominent health care reform strategies. There will be
change in both countries, and the more knowledgeable that decision makers
and the public are about their options, the better the chances that these reforms
will best suit the needs of health care consumers.

In the United States the current push for national health insurance reflects
the convergence of several factors, including the growing number of poor
people, whose ranks rose sharply during the Reagan presidency. This increased the burden on public hospitals and denied all but the most basic
medical services to many Americans. In addition, the cost of health care
consumed $830 billion in 1990, over 11 percent of the U.S. gross national
product (GNP), and continues to rise three times as fast as the consumer price

TABLE 1. U.S. Public Opinion on the Current Health Care System

Question	Source
Thinking about everything that has to do with health care and medicine, what do you think is the main problem facing health care and medicine in the United States today?	Survey by the Gallup Organization, January 23–February 17, 1992.
For your personal health care and that of your family, which of the following is your biggest concern?	Survey by the Gallup Organization, June 1992.

index (CPI). Business, labor, medical, and political leaders have all begun to respond. They see declining profits, worker dissatisfaction, increasing levels of poverty, and burgeoning societal problems if the crisis is not rapidly addressed. When George Bush was elected president in 1988, health care was not among the top fifteen issues of concern to Americans. In 1992 it was third in importance to the economy and the deficit, and it may soon be first (table 1). It is already the number one concern of Americans over the age of fifty-five, causing more alarm than the national deficit, crumbling roads and highways, and education. There is great concern about rapidly escalating health care costs.[1]

The poll discussed in table 1 revealed that 78 percent of the American public believe that the current health care system doesn't meet the needs of most Americans, and 74 percent say a complete overhaul is needed to cover everyone and to control costs.[2] A subsequent survey indicated that as much as 85 percent of the American public support a major overhaul of the health care system even if they will not benefit from the reforms.[3]

According to surveys, a majority of Americans favor some form of national health care. In one survey 60 percent of Americans support a national health insurance system, and nearly as many people are willing to pay six hundred dollars a year to finance it. Most said that the funds should come from higher taxes on liquor and cigarettes or on the incomes of people making more than fifty thousand dollars a year.[4] Only 5 percent are willing to accept higher payroll taxes. A subsequent poll revealed even stronger support for some form of national health care (table 2). Even the most conservative

1. See, for example, a survey published in the *AARP Bulletin* 33, no. 3 (March 1992): 14.
2. *NBC News Poll/Wall Street Journal* as discussed in the *Wall Street Journal,* March 12, 1993, A1, A4.
3. Unpublished survey by the Harvard University School of Public Health (March 18–25, 1993).
4. As reported in the *Philadelphia Inquirer,* May 16, 1992, A5.

TABLE 2.   U.S. Public Opinion on National Health Care Insurance

Question	Source
In general, do you strongly favor, favor, oppose, or strongly oppose implementation, by the United States government, of some type of national health insurance system?	Survey by the Gallup Organization, January 1992.
Do you favor or oppose national health insurance, which would be financed by tax money, paying for most forms of health care?	Survey by CBS News / *New York Times*, July 8–11, 1992.

groups in American society are expressing support for some form of national health care. In one survey, for example, 39 percent of industrial electronics distributors said that they would support national health care.[5] Fifty percent of those firms with less than one million dollars in sales would also support national health care, thus revealing a result that has been demonstrated in many other industrial sectors. That is, the smaller the firm, the more difficult it is to pay employees' health care insurance needs. Of course, larger firms are also feeling the pinch.

What are the most acute problems of the U.S. health care system? In comparison to other Western industrialized countries, the American system is more expensive in dollars and as a percentage of the U.S. gross national product. In 1970, 7 percent of national output was spent on health care. In 1992 it was 14 percent. Most observers believe that this figure will rise. There is little government control over capital expenditures for new hospitals or equipment, the result being that there is too much wasteful duplication of equipment and services. American hospital patients undergo innumerable tests and procedures. Americans undergo record numbers of caesarean sections, hysterectomies, pacemaker implants, bypass surgeries, and appendectomies. There are serious doubts about the necessity of all of these procedures.

American hospital costs and physician fees are among the highest in the world. The United States allows many of its health care providers to control utilization and set prices to a degree that is unmatched elsewhere. This being said, other nations, including Japan, much of Europe, and Canada, have longer life expectancy rates, lower infant mortality statistics, and so on. Officials in these nations pay more attention to preventative medicine than American providers do, and they provide better cost-effective care. It is also

---

5. As reported in *Industrial Distribution*, July 1992, 28.

worth noting that the United States educates and employs a very high number of expensive specialists but relatively few primary care physicians. Specialists make extremely high salaries, while general practitioners are rewarded more modestly. As many as thirty-seven million Americans lack health insurance. A disproportionate number of these are either poor or young. Although most can get treatment, it is usually on a haphazard and inefficient basis. Furthermore, a Census Bureau report noted that 3.6 percent of Americans, mostly children, are without health insurance over a twenty-eight-month period.[6] Finally, many insured Americans worry that they could lose their health coverage or feel constrained to stay at unsatisfying jobs for fear of sacrificing their health insurance. In fact, up to fifty-seven million Americans were without health insurance at some point in 1992.

U.S. hospitals are underutilized relative to other nations, and many are kept open with direct or indirect subsidies. Meanwhile, the cost of the U.S. health care administrative and support system is higher than elsewhere. Malpractice insurance costs have skyrocketed in the United States. The United States is unique among its industrialized neighbors in not supporting universal access to and financial coverage for doctor's visits, hospitalization, catastrophic illness, and long-term care. Finally, levels of public dissatisfaction with the U.S. health care system are among the industrialized world's highest.[7]

In short, U.S. health care dollars are spent unwisely, the nation's health care bill is rising too rapidly, and the burden of paying that bill is shared unequally. For example, there is great health care cost variation across the United States (table 3).

Given all of these problems, it should be no surprise that Americans will look to the apparently more successful Canadian system as a model. But could the Canadian system of reduced costs and universal access work in the United States? Canada's political history and culture are different, and its health care system may not be entirely appropriate for the United States.

It should also be stressed that, in dealing with a market as huge, complex, and diverse as health care, a very real worry is that a wave of well-intentioned reforms might make things worse rather than better. In repairing the current system's shortcomings, it is important that advantage is taken of government's known strengths, that irreversible mistakes are avoided, and that we not try to solve all of the United States' problems at once.

That English-speaking Canadians and Americans are obviously different may be best demonstrated in Canada's strict gun control laws and national health insurance provisions. Both of these are "sacred cows" in Canada,

6. As reported in *Public Perspective,* July/August 1993, 8.

7. Much of this discussion is adopted from Humphrey Taylor, "What Do Americans Want from Their Health Care System?" in *U.S./Canadian Health Care Systems: A Comparison* (Washington, D.C.: National Committee for Quality Health Care, 1990), 11–24.

largely invulnerable to government manipulation. All three major political parties and all of the provincial governments support national health insurance in Canada. Since 1966 the federal government has insisted that every Canadian should have access to health care that would not be limited by financial restrictions. Coverage is comprehensive, benefits are transferable between provinces, and the system is publicly administered.

The fact that Canada has a national single-payer health care system allows Canadians to feel morally superior to Americans, who must do without such a system. This is at the heart of the Canadian national identity and contributes to the perception, reflected in national surveys, that Canadians

TABLE 3. Average Cost to Community Hospitals per Patient, by State, 1990

State	Average Cost per Day	State	Average Cost per Day
Alaska	$1,070	Hawaii	$638
California	939	Virginia	635
Arizona	867	Tennessee	633
Nevada	854	Oklahoma	632
Utah	832	Georgia	630
Connecticut	825	New Jersey	613
Washington	817	Vermont	598
Oregon	800	North Carolina	595
Massachusetts	788	South Carolina	590
Delaware	771	Alabama	588
Florida	769	Maine	574
Texas	752	West Virginia	565
New Mexico	734	Kentucky	563
Colorado	725	Wisconsin	554
Ohio	720	Idaho	547
Illinois	717	Minnesota	536
Michigan	716	Arkansas	534
Louisiana	701	Kansas	532
Missouri	679	Iowa	495
Maryland	678	Nebraska	490
New Hampshire	671	Wyoming	462
Indiana	667	Mississippi	439
Rhode Island	663	North Dakota	427
Pennsylvania	662	Montana	405
New York	641	South Dakota	391
U.S. Average	**$ 687**		

Source: U.S. Bureau of the Census, *Statistical Abstract of the United States, 1992* (Washington, D.C.: Government Printing Office, 1992), 114.

Note: Includes nonfederal short-term general or special hospitals (excluding psychiatric or tuberculosis hospitals and hospital units of institutions). Total cost per patient is based on total hospital expenses (payroll, employee benefits, professional fees, supplies, etc.). Data have been adjusted for outpatient visits.

believe that medicare makes Canada the best country in the world in which to live. Health care is a right, not a privilege, and a two-tiered system of health care, composed of those who can pay and those who cannot, is unacceptable to the vast majority of Canadians.

On the surface it is not clear why the United States and Canada should be so different. Why should the Canadian system be more egalitarian than the American one? Both have multiparty systems based on democratic ideals. Both are federations with substantial powers granted to the provinces or states. The two differ, however, in the sort of people who settled the two countries. Without going into detail,[8] it is worth noting that the American revolution dispensed with "Toryism" and many social democratic values. By contrast, Canada has managed to accommodate certain Tory values with social democratic principles. More emphasis was placed on collective rights in English and French Canada than was evident in the United States, where individual rights are absolutely dominant.

The existence of this collectivist culture is central to the evolution of a health care system in Canada far different from its American counterpart.[9] There is an emphasis on consensus building and no institutional provision for the adversarial checks and balances present in the U.S. government. The Canadian parliamentary system, with its fusion of powers,[10] gives the party in power effective control over which policies will be adopted. The American system of checks and balances makes it much more difficult to effect such a sweeping policy change and adhere to it.

In Canada society as a whole bears the cost of caring for the sick. Each province funds a universal health care insurance scheme out of either general tax revenue or premiums paid by employers or individuals, or both. By contrast, the American system stresses economic liberty whereby federal and state governments provide a few programs, such as Medicare for people over sixty-five and Medicaid for people on public assistance. But other patients or their employers must pay their own way. In fact, there are U.S. health care

---

8. For a fuller discussion, see William Christian and Colin Campbell, *Political Parties and Ideologies in Canada,* 3d ed. (Toronto: McGraw-Hill Ryerson, 1990); and Jonathan Lemco, "The Implications of an 'Official' Language: The Cases of Quebec's Bill 101 and California's Proposition 63," forthcoming in Martin Lubin, ed., *Public Policy: Canada and the United States* (Westport, Conn.: Greenwood Press, 1994).

9. See the argument made in Robert Evans et al., "Controlling Health Expenditures—The Canadian Reality," *New England Journal of Medicine* 320, no. 9 (1989): 571–77. Note also Samuel Mitchell, "Defending the U.S. Approach to Health Spending," *Health Affairs* 7, no. 3 (Winter 1988): 31–34.

10. See Jonathan Lemco and Peter Regenstreif, "The Fusion of Powers and the Crisis of Canadian Federalism," *Publius* 14, no. 1 (Winter 1984); and Jonathan Lemco, "The Fusion of Powers, Party Discipline, and the Canadian Parliament: A Critical Assessment," *Presidential Studies Quarterly* 18, no. 2 (Spring 1988).

economists who insist that people who don't buy private health insurance are simply risk acceptant and should be free to be without health coverage.

It is not at all clear that Americans will ever favor a government-administered program that provides free health care for all of its residents. It is the conventional wisdom that they are skeptical of government's ability to operate programs effectively. Of course, the existence of government-administered Medicare and Medicaid programs force one to wonder about this point. It is also the case that Canada's government bureaucracy may not be as interventionist as its U.S. critics portray it to be. In fact, one could make the reasonable argument that in the United States third-party interference by insurance companies and utilization review firms is far more pervasive than provincial governments are in Canada. Nevertheless, Americans are said to put great stress on freedom and opportunity. Some critics maintain that they put less emphasis than do Canadians on social justice. Some argue that a Canadian type of health care system does not make available a sufficient number of choices nor the most modernized innovative technology to American health care consumers.[11] Nevertheless, there is great interest in the United States about Canada's health care system. Health care experts Robert Blendon and Karen Donelan note that their surveys reveal that "Americans preferred foreign systems to American systems."[12]

Canada's health care system falls within the administrative jurisdiction of the provinces, although each province's health care provisions must meet national standards. Between 1946 and 1961 each of Canada's provinces instituted government hospital insurance programs. Until that time neither Canada nor the United States had an effective health care delivery mechanism. Both nations had virtually the same mechanisms for training physicians, providing medical education, and paying for doctor and hospital services.

By 1961 the federal government insisted that a federal oversight authority would be needed to insure provincial equity of services and standard levels of benefits. The federal government would allocate funds to contribute to the costs of the provincial hospital plans. In so doing, a nationwide standard of health care would be guaranteed, although the provinces had to cede authority to the federal government in terms of control over their health plans. The federal government insisted that each provincial plan had to be comprehensive, publicly administered, universal, accessible, and portable. National hos-

---

11. Edward Neuschler, *Canadian Health Care: The Implications of Public Health Insurance* (Washington, D.C.: Health Insurance Association of America, 1990).

12. Robert Blendon and Karen Donelan, "The Public and the Emerging Debate over National Health Insurance," *New England Journal of Medicine* 323, no. 3 (July 19, 1990). For a fuller discussion of recent U.S. interest in Canada's health care system, see Laurene A. Graig, *Health of Nations: An International Perspective on U.S. Health Care Reform* (Washington, D.C.: Wyatt, 1991).

pital care was followed by the Medical Care Insurance Act in 1968. The same federal conditions applied, and the federal government paid half of the cost to all of the provinces by 1971.

The Canadian system, now called medicare, is rooted in the notion that health care is a right and not a privilege. Preventing a two-tiered system of health care, consisting of those who could pay and those who could not, is a top priority. The federal government has determined that the best way to avoid such a two-tiered system is to outlaw private insurance coverage for any services covered under the provincial plans. Provincial universal hospital and medical plans take the place of all the various forms of insurance—private, not for profit, and public—that had existed up to that point. The provincial governments became the single purchasers of publicly insured hospital and medical care services.[13] In short, the Canadian medicare system consists of ten separate provincial plans subscribing to minimum national standards and funded jointly by the provincial and federal governments through personal taxes, business and corporate taxes, gasoline, tobacco and liquor taxes, and property taxes and insurance. By contrast, in the United States the largest source of funds for health care is provided by the business sector.

In the United States the basic form of health coverage is the employer-sponsored group plan, but employers are not obliged to offer this. Small businesses, especially those with fewer than ten employees, typically do not. Part-time workers are seldom covered.

Employers arrange coverage through hundreds of insurance companies and other health care actors, including coalitions of doctors and hospitals. Each has its own payment rules and cost controls. The resulting paperwork absorbs billions of health dollars and drives doctors to distraction.

There is no required level of coverage. Some health plans set a lifetime maximum family payout of U.S.$250,000 or less, meaning insurance ends when the family's bills reach that level. A more common figure is $1 million. Some plans pay only part of hospital costs, typically 80 percent, leaving unlucky patients with thousands of dollars in unpaid bills.

Rates for family coverage routinely exceed three hundred dollars a month. Many employers pick up all or part of that cost; others simply pass it on to their employees, and low-income workers often opt out. Faced with a choice between insurance and groceries, they gamble that their families will not get sick.

Insurers adjust rates to reflect claims. In a small group the rate may suddenly double if one or two workers suffer expensive ailments. In some circumstances an insurer may insist that a worker in poor health be barred

---

13. Malcolm Taylor, "The Canadian Health Care System 1974–1984," in R. G. Evans and G. L. Stoddart, eds., *Medicare at Maturity* (Calgary: University of Calgary Press, 1986).

from the plan, leaving him or her unprotected. In other cases, workers find themselves locked into jobs, unable to move because a family member's illness would be counted as a preexisting condition not covered under a new plan.

For people with no coverage at work private insurance often costs more than the rent on a small-town apartment. In Washington one outfit that advertises heavily on television asks $339.50 a month for a healthy family of four. For an extra $42.50 a month it will promise not to raise the rate for two years.

Medicaid is available to welfare recipients and to certain working families with incomes well below official poverty lines. It pays doctors and hospitals at far less than standard rates, which means Medicaid patients often get a chilly welcome.

A separate program, called Medicare, provides limited coverage for the elderly and disabled and for kidney dialysis patients. It is the nearest thing to a U.S. national health plan, although most people with any money feel that they must supplement it with private "medigap" insurance.

As noted, the Canadian national health care system is frequently mentioned as a model for the United States. If the U.S. system is expensive, inefficient, and burdensome, then one remedy might be a Canadian-style system, or so certain critics maintain. What are the problems of the American system? How is it that critics see it as structurally flawed, with excessive costs, difficult access for millions, exorbitant malpractice charges, and inefficient delivery of services? Although the United States spends more than any other country in the world on health care, many Americans believe that they are not getting value for their money.

The U.S. health care system is staggering under costs that are rising faster than any other segment of the nation's economy, while thirty-seven million Americans have no health insurance. Ironically, twenty-five million of these have at least one family member with a full-time job. In 1990 the cost of health care to Americans was 11 percent of the gross national product, and it continued to rise three times as fast as the consumer price index. By 1992 spending on health care accounted for 14 percent of the national output. Costs had risen to $838.5 billion and were expected to rise to $940 billion in 1993 and $1 trillion in 1994. Fifty million other Americans, the majority of whom are members of families headed by full-time workers, have only partial insurance coverage that would not pay for a serious illness.

While nearly all of the uninsured are poor, they are not poor enough to qualify for Medicaid, the state and federal program for the poor. Today Medicaid covers only 45 percent of those below the poverty line, compared with 66 percent a decade ago. Eligibility requirements vary widely from state to state. In Alabama, for example, a family of three had to earn less than $1,146 a year to qualify for Medicaid in 1988; in Virginia the cutoff was

$3,492, far below the federal poverty line of $9,300. In addition, federal spending on Medicaid rose 29 percent in the last fiscal year, to $67.8 billion. The states and the federal government share Medicaid costs, and many state officials complain that Medicaid has imposed a crushing burden on them.

The working poor are more likely to be self-employed or to work in the fastest growing sector of the economy at low-paying service jobs—as babysitters, fast-food employees, sales clerks, or construction workers. And they are more likely to live in the South or West and to be African-American or Hispanic. Whereas 11 percent of whites were uninsured in 1991, 32 percent of Hispanics and 21 percent of African-Americans were without coverage. They tend to be sicker than those with insurance because they receive less or inferior care and often delay seeking attention for life-threatening illnesses such as cancer until the disease is advanced.

The number of uninsured will continue to grow. In 1991 one million Americans with family incomes of $25,000 to $50,000 lost their health insurance, according to the Census Bureau. This compares to 500,000 who lost coverage in 1990. As health costs rise, paying for health insurance is becoming steadily more difficult for many American families. According to a study published in December 1991 by Families USA, a Washington-based advocacy group, the average American family in 1980 paid $2,090, or 9 percent of family income, for health care coverage. Today the same family pays nearly $5,000 a year, with another $1,200 in deductibles, or 11.7 percent of family income. The report predicted that if costs continue to rise at their current rate the same family will be paying $10,806 a year, or 16.4 percent of its income, by the year 2000.[14] By contrast, Canadian families directly contribute only a small fraction of their income to health care each year (table 4). But to fund the health care system and other social services Canadians pay more in taxes than Americans, particularly those in higher-income brackets, who pay up to 25 percent more in income taxes than Americans do.

Health care insurance is also a worry for U.S. businesses. Employee medical costs of a medium-sized company in California are about 15 percent of cash flow, according to an Ontario government study. In Ontario health care costs are only 4.8 percent of cash flow of a similar business.[15] Large and small companies in the United States are beginning to take drastic measures to curb costs. In January 1993, Dupont became just the latest of dozens of manufacturers to reduce benefits for its 145,000 current and former employees. Employees would pay 20 percent of their health care costs in 1994, compared with 11 percent in 1993.

There is another factor as well. There is a 1993 accounting rule requiring

---

14. This point is discussed in *Maclean's,* January 13, 1992, 32–35.
15. See the *Financial Post,* April 6, 1992.

U.S. companies to subtract from their profits the future costs of providing retirees' health benefits. Before imposition of the rule, called Financial Accounting Standard 106, many businesses had never estimated their future health care obligations, and few had ever disclosed them. The health cost burden on many businesses has now become prohibitive. Businesses pay one third of U.S. medical bills. Health care costs also increase the federal government budget and swell the ranks of the uninsured, as more people and companies are priced out of the market for health insurance.

Overall, access to health care in the United States is dominated by budgetary concerns; the insured are treated in a timely and effective manner. The underinsured or uninsured seek care later in their illness and have poorer outcomes after seeking treatment. Income is the main determinant of access to the system. In short, the United States has a budget-driven, fragmented health

TABLE 4.   Comparative Health Data for Twenty-four OECD Countries, 1990

	Per Capita Expenditures Based on GDP Purchasing Power Parities (PPPs)	Number of Hospital Personnel per Occupied Hospital Bed
United States	$2,566	3.35
Canada	1,795	NA
Switzerland	1,436	1.91
Sweden	1,421	NA
France	1,379	1.09
Iceland	1,372	NA
Luxembourg	1,300	NA
Germany	1,287	NA
Norway	1,281	NA
Austria	1,192	0.85
Netherlands	1,182	2.13
Finland	1,156	NA
Australia	1,151	NA
Japan	1,145	0.79
Italy	1,138	NA
Belgium	1,087	NA
Denmark	963	2.83
United Kingdom	932	NA
New Zealand	853	NA
Spain	730	NA
Ireland	693	NA
Portugal	529	1.90
Greece	406	1.48
Turkey	197	1.48

Source: U.S. Bureau of the Census, *Statistical Abstract of the United States, 1992* (Washington, D.C.: Government Printing Office, 1992), 829; Health Care Financing Administration, *Health Care Financing Review* (Summer 1992): 49.

care system with the finest technological equipment in the world. Yet these incredible feats of medical care are frequently unavailable to a substantial minority of the society.

Canada's system is not a perfect one either, however, and advocates of the Canadian system in the United States would do well to investigate Canada's health care delivery problems before recommending its wholesale application to the United States. American critics of the Canadian system charge that, because the Canadian government is the single source of income for doctors and hospitals in Canada it improperly interferes in decisions that should remain between patients and their doctors, that first-rate technology is not always available, and that waits for hospital beds can be appalling. There is some truth to these criticisms. Some American doctors complain that the Canadian government spends too little on such important advances as magnetic resonance imaging (MRI) machines, computerized axial tomography (CAT) scans, and organ transplants. They note that setting limits on service has never been acceptable to Americans. Also, although there is a more than adequate supply of doctors in Canada, there is a shortage of physicians in remote areas of the country—where few want to practice. The United States has the same problem.

Furthermore, Canada's national health care plan is showing signs of strain. Per capita spending on health rose about 10 percent a year from 1980 to 1987. Canada's inflation rate, by contrast, rose about 6.3 percent per year. Cost pressures are lower than in the United States, but they are still higher than in Europe and are the second highest in the world.

In 1991 the Canadian government spent $56.9 billion on health care, a figure that many critics believe has become far too high. They are calling for cost-cutting measures and new sources of money—and even user fees. The governing Progressive Conservative party, as well as legislators in Quebec and Ontario, has recommended the imposition of these fees. Alberta and British Columbia already collect them. A recent survey revealed that a majority of Canadians would accept paying for health care if the alternatives were higher taxes or reduced services. The federal contribution for insured health services is based on a per capita entitlement, which is adjusted according to changes in GNP and calculated independently of provincial costs. Federal fiscal restraint measures have frozen per capita entitlements at 1989–90 levels for a five-year period, and all major federal transfers to the provinces are under review. The federal contribution is financed through consolidated revenues (personal and corporate income taxes, excise taxes, import duties, etc.).

Through the years Canadian hospitals and doctors have received generous increases simply by asking for them. In Ontario, for example, hospital spending has increased 10 percent or more each year between 1982 and 1992. But this is changing. In 1992 Ontario hospitals received just a 1 percent increase in their global budgets, and the provincial ministry of health was redirecting money to other types of health care.

Since 1984 health care spending by the provinces has increased 80 percent, to about $44 billion. At the same time the economy has grown less than 20 percent. The Canadian government, which once provided 50 percent of the funding for the provincial health budgets, now supplies only 35 percent. Eventually, it may leave the funding solely to the provinces.

It should be noted that Canada does not have government-run health care, or socialized medicine, as American detractors claim. Instead, a greater proportion of doctors in Canada work in private, fee-for-service practices than do their counterparts in the United States. This is because Canada has no health maintenance organizations (HMOs), for which doctors work on salaries. Most Canadian doctors are largely free of government interference.

American detractors of the Canadian system can be found in the highest levels of government. Former president George Bush claimed that Canada's "nationalized system" of socialized medicine

1. wouldn't suit U.S. tastes;
2. would force Canadians to wait six months for heart surgery; and
3. prohibited Canadians from choosing their own doctors.

All of these assertions are unfounded. Canada has nationalized or provincialized health insurance, not health care. Emergency heart patients are seen immediately, and nonemergencies are addressed within thirty days. Of course, Canadians can also see the doctor of their choice. In the United States, however, many Americans are encouraged to see the "preferred" providers approved by their health insurance providers. Former presidential candidate Paul Tsongas, congressman Newt Gingrich, and others had all made ridiculous statements about Canada's health care system in 1992.

Nevertheless, the provinces are hampered by a combination of economic slowdown, a growing federal budget deficit, and federal transfer payment cuts. The federal government imposed a five-year freeze in 1990 on its contribution to provincial health programs. The provinces, in turn, have been squeezing budgets for health and social services.

In 1971 the provinces received 50 percent of the funds needed to administer their health care systems from the federal government. In 1991 the figure was 38 percent. The provinces must come up with the balance. As a result, the provinces are being forced to pay a greater portion of health care costs through direct taxation of their own populations. Some experts warn that by the turn of the century, under existing funding formulas, federal cash transfers for health care may disappear altogether.

Some politicians and health care experts also contend that if Ottawa continues to reduce cash transfers, which are aimed at maintaining a similar level of social services in all provinces—rich or poor—the federal government will lose the power it currently has to enforce the five basic principles of medicare established by Parliament in 1966: universality, accessibility, portability, comprehensiveness, and public administration.

To cope with the financial shortfall, since 1988 nine provinces (the exception is Manitoba) have imposed ceilings on doctors' incomes, and all the provinces have stopped paying operating deficits that hospitals incur. The government measures have angered many doctors, causing some to abandon their practices and move to the United States.

Many Canadians now believe that medicare costs are out of control, that the country can no longer afford such a universal system, that the system is unduly abused, and that user fees and extra billing by doctors are a solution to rising costs. None of these assertions are entirely true but, since these points are made so often in Canada, it is not surprising that some Canadians favor a five-dollar user fee for every visit to a hospital emergency room. Yet, once they embarked on such a course, would provincial governments then be able to resist the temptation to pass on even greater costs to patients? Why not a fee for every service? The obvious response is that this would create a good system of health care for those who could afford it but a poor one for those who could not.

At the moment the Canada Health Act prevents such abuses by withholding one dollar in federal health grants for every dollar a province collects in user fees or permits in extra billing. But the federal government, instead of maintaining its cash contributions to the provinces, has been reducing its contributions, thereby losing some of its disciplinary clout. The provinces are reacting by demanding complete control over health services, which would include the right to impose user fees. If this trend continues, it could mean the beginning of the end for the existing medicare system.

So, Canada is now faced with a system with escalating health care costs and pressures to reduce spending. There is increased demand on the system by elderly people. There is talk of closing hospital beds or, in the case of British Columbia, to limit doctor's incomes and restrict the number of physicians. In fact, the Canadian Medical Association has begun to reduce the number of new doctors now allowed to practice medicine. Furthermore, the Ontario Hospital Association reported that in 1990 and 1991 a total of five thousand support jobs and thirty-five hundred beds were lost. Ironically, the provincial governments are studying U.S. cost management techniques as a way of improving the system.

Canadians will not lose their tax-financed medical benefits, but health care will become even more a provincial responsibility—a return to the division of responsibilities that existed before 1966. The danger is that each province will be free to go its own way. Some will allow user fees, others extra billing by doctors. Some provinces might refuse to treat patients from other provinces unless they pay cash. Others might eliminate certain types of treatment from the list of insured services.

Some economists predict that in seven to ten years federal cash transfers to the provinces will be eliminated. When this happens Ottawa will no longer be able to enforce national health care standards.[16] It will be powerless to withhold funds from provinces that charge user fees, allow extra billing, or impose deterrent fees.

Clearly, Canada's health care system has its share of problems. Nevertheless, the vast majority of Canadians are fundamentally satisfied with their medicare services. In fact, one poll conducted by Louis Harris and Associates revealed that 89 percent of Americans, 69 percent of British, but only 42 percent of Canadians said that their systems needed fundamental change.[17] Many more Americans said that they faced financial barriers to receiving health care than did Canadians or Britons. Only 54 percent of Americans said that they were "very satisfied" with their most recent visit to a doctor, as opposed to 73 percent of the Canadians and 63 percent of the British.[18] A majority of Americans, 61 percent, said that they would prefer a health care system like that in Canada to the one they have. Only 3 percent of Canadians and 12 percent of the British respondents said they would prefer the American system to their own. The American system was regarded as the most expensive, the least well liked, the least equitable, and the most inefficient system of the three surveyed. More recently, an Angus Reid poll revealed that 86 percent of Canadians were happy with their health care system.[19] Furthermore, in 1992 the American medical magazine *Physician's Management* surveyed Canadian health consumers and physicians on satisfaction with their health care system. The results showed that 84 percent of Canadian doctors and more than 90 percent of consumers rated the quality of care provided by the system as "good to excellent."[20]

How does the Canadian health care system compare to the American one? One can compare the two programs on at least five sets of criteria, including services and administration, funding and costs, access and rationing, quality, and malpractice insurance.

16. See, for example, Paul Boothe and Barbara Johnston, "Stealing the Emperor's Clothes: Deficit Off-loading and National Standards in Health Care," *Commentary* (C.D. Howe Institute), no. 41 (March 1993); and Paul Boothe, "Federal Budgeting in the 1990s: The End of Fiscal Federalism," in Thomas J. Courchene and Martin Prochowny, eds., *The February 1992 Federal Budget* (Kingston, Ont.: John Deutsch Institute for the Study of Economic Policy, 1992).

17. "Polls Show Discontent with Health Care," *New York Times*, February 15, 1989, A16.

18. Ibid.

19. As reported in the *Montreal Gazette*, May 14, 1991, B2.

20. *Physician's Management*, August 1992.

The Provision of Services and Administration
in Canada and the United States

By any standard Canada has an outstanding record in providing effective administration of its payment system.[21] The Canadian system is not perfect, of course, for there are variations in servicing patterns and costs that have no apparent connection to the population's needs. As in any other nation, there is some waste, inefficiency, and excessive cost. Nevertheless, the administrative side of the Canadian system works, for the most part. Its citizens are issued a health card by the government, and they present it when they receive care. Doctors run private independent practices and process claims much as retailers handle credit card transactions. The government then pays the doctor with money that comes largely from personal sales and corporate taxes. The majority of hospitals are operated by private, voluntary, nonprofit organizations. Only a few services are excluded, such as private or semiprivate hospital rooms, drugs prescribed outside the hospital, eyeglasses and wheelchairs, and preemployment and insurance examinations. Hospitals are primarily accountable to the communities they serve, not to the provincial bureaucracy.

Provincial governments have ultimate control over hospital budgets and doctors' fees according to a negotiated fee schedule but in return do not force physicians to justify every procedure and test, as U.S. doctors must do. Hospitals must operate within the parameters of an overall "global budget." All Canadians receive complete health coverage without deductibles for physician and hospital services. By contrast, Americans can participate in a wide variety of insurance plans, many of which involve deductibles, ceilings, and other limitations. Medicare and Medicaid are available for many, but not all, Americans. The fifteen hundred private companies selling a mix of insurance plans leaves thirty-six million Americans with no coverage and a similar number with inadequate coverage. For these people health care problems can be devastating financially. The Canadian system lacks an entire level of bureaucracy that Americans take for granted. Canadians spend eleven cents of every health care dollar on administration and billing, while Americans spend twenty-four cents.[22] Overall the United States spent $665 billion on health care in 1990, or $2,600 for every resident of the country. This is more than any other nation spends on health care and a far larger share of GNP—12.2 percent—than in any other country of the developed world.

Doctors are the highest-paid professionals in Canada. The mean net income of self-employed Canadian doctors (about half of them general and

---

21. For a discussion, see M. L. Barer, R. G. Evans, and R. J. LaBelle, "Fee Controls as Cost Control: Tales from the Frozen North," *Milbank Quarterly* 66, no. 1 (1988).

22. Steffie Woolhandler quoted in Constance Matthiessen, "Should the U.S. Copy Canada?" *Washington Post*, November 27, 1990, 12–14.

family physicians) in 1990 was U.S.$100,248, compared to $164,300 for all U.S. doctors and $102,700 for general practitioners and family physicians, according to the American Medical Association (AMA). The medical profession remains an attractive one in Canada, and the number of physicians per capita has grown steadily since the introduction of public medical insurance. There are even concerns that Canada has an oversupply, with about 60,000 active physicians at the end of 1990, one for every 450 Canadians.

In 1987 running hospitals cost U.S.$162 for each American and U.S.$50 for each Canadian. The overhead and billing expenses of physicians—even apart from their malpractice insurance—were about two-thirds less per person in Canada, as was the administration of nursing homes. According to David Himmelstein and Steffie Woolhandler, the U.S. system could save more than U.S.$100 billion a year by bringing its bureaucracy down to Canadian proportions. Himmelstein and Woolhandler of the Harvard University Medical School suggest that this savings would be more than enough to finance health insurance for the uninsured Americans.[23] Estimates from the Congressional Budget Office in 1991 placed potential administrative savings between U.S.$25 and $50 billion. In 1992 the U.S. General Accounting Office projected a $67 billion yearly saving in overhead costs.

U.S. hospitals spend an average of 40 percent more on each patient than do those in Canada. According to one study, adopting Canadian practices would save U.S. hospitals as much as forty billion dollars a year, while the reverse would add five billion dollars a year to Canadian hospital costs.[24]

Himmelstein and Woolhandler also note that administrative costs are U.S.$118 per person in the United States but only U.S.$6 per person in Canada. The central reason cited for this disparity in administrative waste is the wide array of private insurers in the United States, each with their own regulatory and marketing regime. As Ted Marmor, of Yale University, and his colleagues note, the U.S. experience proves that the more fragmented a health care system becomes, the more expensive it is and the less susceptible to cost control.[25] Furthermore, it appears likely that Canada's single-payer system increases the quality of health care by promoting preventative care and the appropriate use of expensive high-tech procedures.

It is also worth noting that the U.S. system is not a market-based health system, contrary to popular belief. More than 40 percent of American health care is paid for by government. The industry is heavily regulated by national and state laws, and evidence of bureaucratic and government-caused waste is extensive.

---

23. As quoted in the *Globe and Mail,* May 3, 1991, A12.

24. *New England Journal of Medicine* 325, no. 328 (March 18, 1993).

25. Theodore Marmor, Jerry Mashaw, and Philip Harvey, *America's Misunderstood Welfare State: Persistent Myths, Enduring Realities* (New York: Basic Books, 1990).

Ultimately, the administrative advantage that Canada holds relative to the United States is the result of just one "insurer" per province—the government. This means that billing is straightforward, reimbursement is quick, and paperwork is kept to a minimum. With no competition among private insurers, Canada's health care system has no advertising costs to pass on to consumers.

Affording Health Care in the United States and Canada

Health care costs in the United States since 1970 have accelerated 60 percent faster than has the rate of inflation. The factors responsible for these high costs include general inflation, the aging of the population, increasing patient demand, increasing physician supply, the implementation of inappropriate care, the practice of defensive medicine, and advances in medical science leading to expensive new technologies—all compounded by high administrative costs.[26] Since the health care sector is one of the largest sectors of the economy, high health care costs have a negative impact on the entire U.S. economy. In fact, per capita U.S. health care costs, which are already the highest in the world, are expected to double by 1997. The figure is already $800 billion more in 1993 than it was in 1988. Health insurance premiums for business are rising, on average, by 20 percent a year. This is inhibiting business investment and employment growth. The United States' largest industry group, the National Association of Manufacturers, has called rising health care costs the greatest threat to industry's economic vitality, its competitiveness, and its ability to promote employment. Medicare and Medicaid are in trouble, and physicians' fees have been increasing at double the rate of inflation between 1976 and 1981. According to one analyst, by 1999 Medicare will replace Social Security and defense as the largest and fastest-growing federal expenditure—and hence will be the largest contributor to the nation's massive deficit.[27]

Throughout the 1980s there was a great deal of attention in the United States paid to "cost containment" in health care, but the goal was never realized. Cost containment was presumed to be likely because competition would force costs down. Instead, it became apparent that there was no real competition in medicine. This is because business and government do not receive individual service; they are just buying insurance with no room for negotiation, except on the rising cost of premiums. Also, there is virtually no price competition for procedures nor any mechanism for controlling the total

---

26. This list is adapted from Henry Simmons, "Report of the National Leadership Commission on Health Care," *Connecticut Medicine* 53, no. 11 (November 1989): 659–64.

27. Henry Simmons, "Reforming the Nation's Critically Ill Health Care System," *Looking Ahead* 12, no. 4 (March 1991): 1–7.

volume of services. There is very little real competition in the U.S. system.[28] Furthermore, between 7 and 15 percent of the cost of U.S. health care is due to overhead and multiple insurers, consultants, the costs of billing, collecting and identifying services, and the profits of private insurance companies. As a result, the portion of the U.S. GNP spent on health care hit an all-time high of 12.2 percent in 1990, while Canada spent 9.5 percent. It jumped by 11 percent—to $830 billion—in 1992, making it the fifth consecutive year of double-digit increase. Average annual increases of 12 to 13 percent over the next five years are expected, or about two and one-half times faster than the GNP. If present trends continue, national spending on health will hit $1.6 trillion by the year 2000.

The Commerce Department attributed a number of reasons for the rising health care costs, including increasing reliance by medical professionals on costly, high-tech equipment; "innovative treatment" of such illnesses as AIDS and cancer; the aging of the population, which increases the government's medicare and medicaid expenditures; and the rise in malpractice suits. To this could be added such factors as expensive hospital procedures and physicians' fees, the high cost of catastrophic care, the expense of marketing in the new competitive age, the surplus of physicians, and relatively low productivity in hospitals.[29] To these should be added general economic inflation.

To control costs in Canada the provincial governments dictate hospital operating budgets, set doctors' fees through bargaining with medical associations, limit the number of specialists, allocate the purchase of expensive equipment, and restrict costly procedures such as open heart surgery to a few hospitals in major population centers. This being the case, health care costs are still about a third of provincial budgets. Between 1988 and 1992, provincial spending on health care increased by an average of 41.8 percent. An aging population, costly new equipment, and new diseases such as AIDS are aggravating the problem. Because there is no competition in the Canadian health care system—since prices, costs, markets, and profits are fixed—there is no reasonable expectation that the accelerating costs can be cut without real pain. The result is an apparently insoluble debate concerning numbers of hospital beds, doctors' salaries, service cutbacks, uncontrolled costs, mounting debts, nurses' responsibilities, growing provincial budget deficits, rising per capita expenditures, and so on. All of these will have to be resolved by political decisions.

Nevertheless, Canadian costs are still much lower than in the United

---

28. For an expanded discussion, see Sandra Hackman and Robert Howard, "Confronting the Crisis in Health Care: An Interview with Arnold Relman," *Technology Review,* July 1989, 30–40.

29. See Dean Coddington, David Keen, Keith Moore, and Richard Clarke, *The Crisis in Health Care: Costs, Choices, and Strategies* (San Francisco: Jossey-Bass, 1990).

States. The difference is due, in large part, to differences in expenditures for hospitals, physicians, and general administration. In turn, these differences relate to the U.S. multiple-payer system versus the Canadian single-payer, provincially run system. The provinces control hospital budgets and physicians' fees.[30] Public expenditures account for about 72 percent of total health care spending in Canada. Some drugs, dental care, and eyeglasses are covered by supplementary benefits programs or are paid for out of pocket. Under provincial laws private insurers are restricted from offering coverage that duplicates that of the governmental programs, but they may compete in the supplementary benefits market. Canada's provincial health ministers are now warning that Canada's medicare system is imperiled, but this is not true in any fundamental way. There is also no evidence that Canadians want to scrap their public medical care system or that it is necessary to do so to contain medical care costs. Indeed, Canada's example reveals that it is easier to control costs in a publicly administered health care system than in a privately administered one.

Ironically, this position is supported by many in the American corporate community. For example, in 1990 Lee Iacocca of the Chrysler Corporation noted that health care costs account for U.S.$700 of the cost of making a car in the United States. By contrast, the equivalent cost was just $223 in Canada, $276 in Japan, $337 in the former West Germany, and $375 in France.[31] By 1992 the U.S. cost had risen to $900. In addition, according to an Oregon state agency report, Canadian patients stay in the hospital twice as long as Americans but spend only one third as much per day.[32] In 1991 a standard quadruple coronary artery bypass cost U.S.$12,236 at a Quebec hospital but U.S.$25,439 at the New England Medical Center in Boston. Administrative overhead, physicians' fees, and hospital costs are all sharply lower in Quebec. Recovery rates from major surgery are similar, although Americans spend up to 50 percent more per capita on hospitals. On the average, in 1992, identical brand-name prescription drugs cost 32 percent more in the United States than in Canada.

As of 1990, annual health costs per capita were U.S.$1,926 in the United States and $1,370 in Canada. As noted, health costs as a percentage of GNP was 12.2 percent in the United States and 9.5 percent in Canada. As a percentage of gross domestic product (GDP) it was 9.9 percent in Canada and 13.2 percent in the United States. Life expectancy was seventy-five years in the United States and seventy-seven years in Canada. Infant mortality deaths

30. See an extensive discussion in Laurene Graig, *Health of Nations: An International Perspective on U.S. Health Care Reform* (Washington, D.C.: Wyatt, 1991).

31. As reported by *Canadian Press,* June 21, 1990.

32. *Montreal Gazette,* December 28, 1990, B8.

per one thousand births were eleven in the United States and seven in Canada.[33]

Those who argue against the Canadian national health care model say it would require a 14 percent increase in federal income tax rates for everyone. Or it would take a boost in the combined payroll taxes paid by both employers and employees from the current 15 percent to 29 percent. Or it could be paid for by a new national sales tax of 10 percent. Or, if states paid the same share of health costs as the Canadian provinces do, they would have to increase their revenues by 71 percent.

A study by Representative Richard K. Armey (R-Tex.) found that health costs would jump by $81.5 billion a year under a national insurance system covering all Americans, while a report released by Representative Fortney "Pete" Stark (D-Calif.) estimated that such a system would save $26.3 billion.

In 1991 the General Accounting Office estimated a Canadian system, with no cost sharing, would cut U.S. costs by $3 billion while providing universal coverage. But, using many of the same assumptions, the Joint Economic Committee GOP staff concluded that such an overhaul would lead to an $81.5 billion cost increase. The Congressional Budget Office estimated that savings in 1991 would have been $14.2 billion.

Health care costs are slippery figures, especially when projected into the future using hazy, perhaps biased assumptions. The U.S. population differs from Canada's in several ways—a greater number of urban poor and elderly, more drug abuse, more teenage pregnancy—that would increase Americans' costs.

Canada can provide the United States with some good ideas for improving its present patchwork health system. Unfortunately, it doesn't have a blueprint that will solve all U.S. problems. Americans have too little faith in government to trust it totally with their health, particularly if it would be almost impossible to return to the private sector. Most Americans would fear the political haggling and deal making that would be involved in incorporating all health care spending into federal and state budgets.

Rationing and Access to Health Care in Canada and the United States

All Canadians have access to health care facilities, although certain technologies and services are rationed under certain circumstances. Millions of Americans have no access to insured health services, but all Americans can gain access to the best technology and service in the world if they are insured or

---

33. Statistics taken from the Organization for Economic Cooperation and Development (OECD), the National Center for Health Statistics, and the United Nations Statistical Office.

can afford it. Ironically, while the United States has the most expensive health care system in the world, approximately 35 percent of the country's hospital beds are empty on any given day. One in four Americans is or will be either completely uninsured or significantly underinsured at some point during a year. This is a situation that affects the poor, of course, but also many in the middle class. At the same time, there may be an impending surplus of doctors. Health care in the United States is rationed based on the ability to pay.

U.S. critics of the Canadian system point to waiting lines caused by the single-payer system as a reason not to adopt a government-administered national health care system. The reality, however, is that Canada has few waiting lines and none for emergency care. A June 1993 survey by Statistics Canada revealed that 95 percent of Canadians receive necessary care within twenty-four hours. But, waiting lines do exist for specialized high-tech procedures, such as heart bypass surgery. Furthermore, there is rationing in the United States as well, although it is less obvious. Many U.S. insurance companies protect their profit margins by sometimes denying care, even when it is prescribed by a physician, increasing cost sharing, and refusing to cover preexisting conditions. In addition, relatively high copayments and deductibles force many Americans to wait months before they can afford to go to a physician, while skyrocketing insurance company premiums are pricing more and more Americans out of the health care system.

On balance, then, the evidence suggests that rationing exists in both countries at similar levels but in different ways. One study revealed that elderly Canadians have the same access as Americans to medical treatments, high-technology services, and acute-care hospitals, although Americans pay significantly more for their care.[34] Canada has explicit forms of rationing, such as limiting the number of CAT scanners, dialysis machines, or such procedures as heart surgery and hip replacements. Also, Canada has only twelve MRI machines, or one for every 2.1 million people. The United States has 1,375 machines, or one for every 182,000 Americans. It should be understood that Canada's population is one tenth that of the United States.

In all of Canada only 11 hospitals do open heart surgery, compared with 793 in the United States. Fourteen Canadian hospitals do organ transplants, and 319 do so in the United States. In addition, certain cost-control methods serve as implicit rationing mechanisms in Canada. Setting global budgets for hospitals keeps expenditures down, but it also limits the number of available services in the process. Allocating scarce health care resources is by need: Emergencies come first; perceived nonemergency cases might have to wait. Rationing in Canada takes the form of waiting time. Rationing in the United States is determined by the ability to pay. But note what is happening in

---

34. As reported in the *Toronto Star*, November 23, 1989, A30.

Canada. Canadian hospital costs are contained because the province gives hospitals only a portion of what they ask for. For an extreme example, in 1992 Ontario hospitals asked for an 8.6 percent increase in funding and received 1 percent. This has contributed to Toronto hospitals closing 3,700 of the area's 12,500 acute-care beds since 1989.

It should be noted that the solution for many wealthy Canadians on long waiting lists is to go for immediate but expensive care in the United States. Of course, this has the effect of creating a two-tiered system, one for those Canadians who won't wait and can afford to seek U.S. care and those who have no other option but to wait. So, although Canadians cannot pay a Canadian doctor to insure faster treatment, they can jump the queue by going south. In fact, in 1993 a large U.S. insurer, American Medical Security Inc., introduced a program in Ontario that would allow Canadians who wait more than forty-five days for medical care in Canada to receive their treatment in the United States. The policy covers a wide range of medical procedures and pays for the patient's airfare to the United States and lodging there. Canadians going to the United States may not always be a reflection of acute need. In 1991 the British Columbia Ministry of Health contracted with hospitals in Seattle to provide two hundred heart surgeries. It took more than a year before Canadians filled the two hundred slots, thereby putting into question whether the delays were really life threatening. In addition, several procedures in the United States are paid for by the provinces. For example, Ontario law says that the provincial government will compensate any doctor or hospital up to 75 percent of costs for operations on an Ontarian overseas. In some cases there has been 100 percent reimbursement, although critics are calling for an end to this practice. American hospitals are usually delighted to accept even partial reimbursement as payment in full rather than have empty beds. Interestingly, a few Toronto-area hospitals are now marketing their services to potential U.S. clients. They can offer lower costs while earning U.S.$80 million and creating 645 jobs. Since all Ontario hospitals have excess capacity, this is a vehicle to fill unused hospital beds without reducing access to Canadian patients.

One final point in this regard. Much is made of how Canadians will wait for nonemergency services while Americans will not. In fact, in the United States many HMOs require substantial waiting periods for medical appointments. This is used as a method of discouraging needless visits. With HMOs access to the doctor of one's choice, when one wants to see the doctor, is not always straightforward.

Quality of Care in the United States and Canada

At first glance Canadians appear to have a better quality of life than Americans. As of 1991, Canadians' life expectancy was longer, their infant mortality rate was 24 percent lower, and heart disease killed Canadians at a rate 20 percent lower than that for Americans, despite similar dietary habits.[35] A direct comparison, however, is misleading. As noted, the United States has ten times the population of Canada. Its inner cities are poorer and more heterogenous. Most important, the health of the two populations depends only in part on their health care provisions, and how health care is organized and paid for may not affect its quality. The more impressive statistics in Canada may not be telling us much about the two health delivery systems.

For example, a 1979 study by the U.S. Department of Health and Human Services estimated "that only 10 percent of premature deaths in developed countries are attributable to inadequate health services," the rest to "unhealthy lifestyles (50 percent), environmental factors (20 percent), and human biological factors (20 percent)."

Also, the United States provides more specialized high-tech procedures, such as heart bypass surgery, than Canada, but it is not clear that Americans are healthier. In fact, the Rand Corporation found that 40 percent of heart bypass operations performed in the United States were unnecessary.

It is certainly the case that both Canada and the United States have too much waste and inefficiency in their quality control systems. For example, U.S. hospitals have focused traditionally only on how health care is delivered; they are only now beginning to measure the impact of that care on patient outcomes.[36] Patients in both countries have few tools to help them assess the quality and appropriateness of their treatment. These deficiencies drive up health care costs.

This being said, Canada's system is more efficient. It spends 40 percent less per person on health care than the United States, yet Canadians visit their doctors more often. Nearly all Canadian expectant mothers receive prenatal care. In the United States only 76 percent of women who had live births in 1988 received prenatal care starting in the first trimester. The American Academy of Pediatrics estimates that only seven of every ten two-year-olds have received their immunization shots. The estimated figure in Canada is eight of ten. High vaccine costs, poor access, and parental indifference are to blame.[37]

In the United States physicals, "well-checkups," educational sessions, and so on are not covered by most insurance programs. Many health maintenance organizations actively discourage regular physical examinations. Preexisting conditions can hamper one's ability to obtain any insurance at all. In

35. Sources include the *World Almanac 1991* and the "Report of the National Commission to Prevent Infant Mortality."

36. This point is discussed in detail in Henry Simmons, "Report of the National Leadership Commission on Health Care," *Connecticut Medicine* 53, no. 11 (November 1989): 659–64.

37. Sally Squires, "U.S. Immunization Campaign Struggles," *Washington Post,* October 22, 1991, Health section, 6.

short, the Canadian insurance system allows for, and even encourages, preventative medicine. This sharply reduces long-term costs and societal instability. By contrast, the American system emphasizes a policy of treating symptoms only when they occur. The extraordinary remedies available to cure injury and disease in the United States only partially fill the gap left by the lack of emphasis on prevention. Canada's health care system relies extensively on primary-care physicians (i.e., family physicians, general practitioners, pediatricians, internists, and obstetrician-gynecologists) who provide medical care and make referrals to specialists. Primary-care physicians account for about 63 percent of all active physicians in Canada (compared to 45 percent in the United States); about eight out of ten primary-care physicians in Canada are family physicians and general practitioners (compared to about one in three in the United States).[38]

Malpractice Insurance in the United States and Canada

Malpractice litigation in the United States has forced dramatic increases in the cost of health care. Doctors pass on these costs to patients or third-party payers, and there is no end in sight. U.S. physicians are forced to practice "defensive medicine" such as performing duplicate tests and completing extensive documentation as a shield against malpractice claims. The U.S. Commerce Department estimates that this adds U.S.$15 billion to the nation's health care costs. In 1989 the average annual amount of malpractice insurance premiums for U.S. physicians was U.S.$15,500. This figure has probably risen substantially since that time. By contrast, Canadian physicians paid an average of U.S.$2,446.[39] The reasons for the discrepancy include the following:

1. There are fewer claims in Canada, in part because the loser in court pays all legal costs of the winners.
2. There are no "ambulance-chasing" lawyers in Canada because the provinces either discourage or do not permit contingency fees.
3. In Canada compensation for injury and suffering claims is lower than in the United States. The Canadian Supreme Court has set a limit on general damages at U.S.$225,000, and punitive damage awards are minimal.
4. There are fewer lawyers in Canada.
5. Finally, 90 to 95 percent of all Canadian physicians belong to the

---

38. Sources are Health and Welfare Canada and the U.S. Health Care Financing Administration.

39. As reported by the American Medical Association and the Canadian Medical Association.

Canadian Medical Protective Association, which provides legal representation. This also means that there are few insurance companies in Canada offering malpractice insurance.

The National Leadership Coalition for Health Care Reform has offered one set of remedies for reversing accelerating malpractice costs, including "instituting strict criteria for expert witnesses in malpractice suits, strengthening standards of negligence, limiting punitive damages and contingency fees, and encouraging mediation and arbitration as alternatives to lawsuits for resolving disputes."[40] These would be important steps in the right direction. But, so long as the United States retains a frequently inefficient multipayer system, malpractice insurance costs will probably remain high.

U.S. Interest Groups and Health Care

In 1992 there were 741 medical lobbying organizations in Washington, D.C.[41] These groups are divided on the merits of the Canadian health care system. Many labor and some business leaders and groups argue that the Canadian system has much to teach U.S. health care policy actors. On the other hand, vocal critics such as the AMA, the Health Insurance Association of America (HIAA), and various trade, hospital, and pharmaceutical associations point to such perceived Canadian problems as rationing, scarce resources, limited research and development expenditures, minimal levels of high technology, and rising costs.

These groups are unanimous in their opposition to a Canadian-style system in the United States. For example, the AMA insists that "Canada spends less on health care but many Canadians get less, and with government spending constraints, the quality of care and care-givers will decline."[42] Lawyers' groups lobby against any reduction in malpractice settlements, any restriction on the type of claim that can be brought to court, and any effort to curtail contingency fee cases.

The American Medical Association is a particularly well funded critic of the Canadian system. It has consistently opposed comprehensive state-run medicare programs, citing fears of government interference in the medical profession, such as limits on the amount of money doctors can earn. The AMA and other groups insist that national health insurance is a simplistic and unworkable solution that overlooks the heterogenous nature of the uninsured,

---

40. Henry Simmons, "Executive Summary, Report of the National Leadership Commission on Health Care," *Connecticut Medicine* 53, no. 11 (November 1989): 664.

41. Robert Pear, "Conflicting Aims in Health Lobby Stalls Legislation," *New York Times,* March 18, 1992, A8.

42. AMA executive vice-president James Sammons, quoted in the *Toronto Star,* June 8, 1989, A4.

tramples on the American tradition of free enterprise, and would result in the rationing of care. The AMA has sponsored its own reform program, which would expand access to health care by broadening government and employer health coverage. Most insurance companies oppose national health insurance because it would likely wipe out the health insurance business. The influential Pepper Commission of congressional leaders also rejected a Canadian-style system in September 1990 as too costly and impractical.

By contrast, some of the United States' largest corporations, including Marriott Corporation, Ford Motor Company, American Telephone and Telegraph Company, DuPont Company, and Eastman Kodak Company, have joined with a number of the nation's largest labor unions in an effort to enact some form of national health insurance. They have formed a group called the National Leadership Coalition for Health Care Reform. Organized labor has long supported national health insurance, but now business organizations, stung by the sharply rising costs of employee health insurance and the difficulty of competing with companies in other nations that subsidize health care, are calling for a government health program.

These groups and others have been joined by the American College of Physicians (ACP), the United States' second-largest physicians' organization with 68,000 members (the AMA has 300,000 members). The ACP broke ranks with the AMA and now advocates a national health insurance program. They are wary of the extent of government involvement in the Canadian system, however, and advocate a made-in-the-U.S.A. program.

Even opponents of the Canadian system acknowledge its popularity in the United States. Up to 75 percent of Americans—especially people over fifty-five—favor a Canadian-style, tax-funded health care system with equal access for all, according to polls conducted by the American Association of Retired Persons (AARP). High cost is the principal reason cited. Carl Schramm of the HIAA has noted that "from the public's perspective, there is freedom of choice in selecting physicians and hospitals and relatively few out-of-pocket expenses for health care. . . . There is no balance billing, the government pays for most health care. . . . We cannot be mistaken about the implications of all this. A move in the United States to a Canadian approach to health care financing is antithetical to our interests."[43] Given the power and influence of the groups opposed to a national health care system in the United States, it will be a formidable fight.

Remedies for the U.S. Health Care System

The National Leadership Coalition for Health Care Reform (NLCHCR) has proposed a mechanism for financing universal access to a basic level of health

---

43. As noted in an HIAA fund-raising letter to members.

services. As it is advertised, the plan would provide access to basic medical services for all Americans, curtail the escalation of health care costs, and improve the quality of care. It would be paid for by all employers and all Americans above 150 percent of the poverty level. Employers would be offered financial incentives to extend coverage to all employees. State agencies would implement the program. First introduced in late 1989, this thoughtful proposal has gained some support, but it faces a substantial degree of competition as well. Some reform proposals call for more government involvement and others for varying levels of employer financial involvement. Robert Blendon of Harvard University maintains that federally sponsored universal health insurance can be accomplished without copying Canada if the burden is shared by government, employers, and the private insurance industry.[44]

Another prominent plan has been suggested by the Physicians for a National Health Program. This Massachusetts-based group of three thousand physicians has proposed a Canadian-style system. Private insurance would be replaced by federal funding. Coverage would be universal and administered by the states. In addition, there is the Basic Health Benefits for all Americans Act, sponsored by Senator Edward Kennedy (D-Mass.) and Representative Henry Waxman (D-Calif.), which suggests that employers provide basic health coverage to those who work more than seventeen and a half hours per week and their families. Also, the Pepper Commission plan called for universal health coverage through a combined job-based and public system. What is not clear in these proposals is what range of health benefits would be provided and how costs would be controlled.

The AMA proposed that employers provide coverage for all full-time employees and their families. Medicaid would also be expanded. Other proposals call for more health care decisions to be made by consumers, forcing them to become more cost conscious.[45]

There are also a variety of "play-or-pay" suggestions whereby businesses either provide insurance that meets legislated standards (play) or pay a tax that would help support a government insurance program for the retired and working uninsured (pay). Employees would pay a 1.75 percent tax to support the system. This proposal requires an extensive degree of coordination between the federal government and the states. It restructures the relationships between insurance companies, businesses, workers, and governments. Play-or-pay proposals guarantee universal access based on employer-based coverage, with the government overseeing the health care coverage.

44. As quoted in the *Toronto Star*, June 8, 1989, A3.
45. Many of these plans are discussed in Dean Coddington, David Keen, Keith Moore, and Richard Clarke, *The Crisis in Health Care: Costs, Choices, and Strategies* (San Francisco: Jossey-Bass, 1990). See also Laurene Graig, *Health of Nations: An International Perspective on U.S. Health Care Reform* (Washington, D.C.: Wyatt, 1991), 30–35, 252–54.

Another proposal being discussed among Democrats would fund a health care system entirely through a payroll tax supplemented by increased taxes on wealthy Americans. Henry Aaron of the Brookings Institution has evaluated many of these proposals. He concludes that national health insurance in the United States would be a nonstarter because of the disruption that it would cause. Mandatory employer-financed insurance with public backup might be a better solution for the United States.[46]

The U.S. states have often been health care innovators, and some analysts suggest that their experiences might be considered for nationwide application. In Oregon every person would be covered by health insurance by 1995 if the Oregon Health Plan were to be implemented. The plan would expand the number of people on state medicaid rolls but would limit the types of services that are covered. In addition, the plan would help small businesses provide coverage to employees. Health care would be rationed, but there would be universal coverage. The Oregon proposal has been the boldest and most comprehensive plan devised by any state to address the twin problems of uncontrolled medical costs and inadequate access to health service by millions of poor people. Under the plan Oregon ranked 709 health services in terms of usefulness. The costs of these services were estimated, and a cutoff was drawn at 587 services. Everything above that figure would be treated under the state medicaid program for the poor; everything below would not. In short, coverage for lower-priority conditions was cut out, but everyone under the federal poverty line would be covered. The basic level of services was determined by a combination of expert opinion, community sentiment, legislative judgment, and fiscal reality.[47]

The Oregon plan had its detractors, who noted that it imposed severe restrictions on medical care for the poor while leaving untouched benefits for the elderly, who account for the bulk of state medicaid spending. Also, whether care was of "low benefit" would not be determined by doctors' judgments but, rather, by a politically appointed state commission and the legislature's annual budget projections.

In 1992 former secretary of Health and Human Services Louis Sullivan rejected Oregon's request for a waiver from federal rules needed to activate its plan, arguing that it violated the Americans with Disabilities Act. This action demonstrated that, as innovative as they might be, the states are not their own masters in making health policy; they need national political support. The Clinton administration's secretary of Health and Human Services, Donna

46. See Henry Aaron, "Why Bother? America Won't Buy It," *Washington Post*, September 15, 1991, C3; and Henry Aaron, *Serious and Unstable Condition: Financing America's Health Care* (Washington, D.C.: Brookings Institution Press, 1991).

47. For a fuller discussion of the Oregon plan, see Howard M. Leichter, "Rationing of Health Care: Oregon Comes Out of the Closet," in Howard M. Leichter, ed., *Health Policy Reform in America: Innovations from the States* (Armonk, N.Y.: M. G. Sharpe, 1992), 117–46.

Shalala, has pledged this support. As of 1993, the federal government has tentatively agreed to Oregon's waiver.

In Hawaii all employers provide basic medical coverage to their regular full-time employees under the state-mandated Prepaid Health Care Act. Many employers have extended the plan to their workers' families as well. Coupled with Medicare and Medicaid services for the elderly and indigent, this 1975 statute guarantees that health care coverage is provided for 95 percent of Hawaii's 1.1 million residents. Another insurance program, the so-called gap group or state health insurance program, extends services to an additional 2 to 3 percent of the state's population who are self-employed, unemployed, or employed on a part-time basis. Partly because of this coverage, Hawaii boasts the lowest costs and best survival rates for heart and lung disease in the United States. Life expectancy is the highest in the nation, at seventy-eight years.[48] Of course, there are a variety of reasons besides statewide health care that can explain low mortality rates in Hawaii, including a relatively clean environment, many young people and healthy lifestyles, and an emphasis on primary and preventative care. Also, Hawaii is rather unique in that it has few competing insurance companies: Risks are shared in a large pool, and large or small businesses get about the same insurance rates. Nevertheless, health care costs in Hawaii have been contained to 8.1 percent of the state's gross product, and the quality of care is good. It might be a model for the nation. Ironically, some state officials in Hawaii worry that a potential national health care program could replace Hawaii's program and reduce the level of coverage that Hawaiians currently enjoy.

Hawaii is able to have such near universal coverage because the law setting up its health care programs preceded by a year the Federal Employee Retirement Income Security Act, which now bars other states from requiring employers to insure workers. The law actually made buying insurance more affordable for small business, which is 98 percent of all business in Hawaii. Although it prohibits insurers from turning down a worker because of medical history or condition, the mandate also lowers the risk by drawing in healthy young people, many of whom might otherwise reject insurance for more income.

In terms of health rankings, Hawaii is ranked number one in the United States. It has the second-lowest infant mortality rate (after Vermont) and one of the lowest death rates from heart disease and cancer. Hospital usage in Hawaii is one third less than the national average, and the state has half the national average of hospital beds per capita.

It should be noted that Hawaii's system is dependent on a big tax base,

---

48. Sandra Oshiro, "Hawaii Health Care: A Model for Other States," *Washington Post*, November 26, 1991, Health section, 6.

full employment, and the continuation of current levels of government support for medicaid and medicare. This may become increasingly difficult to maintain. The state's low unemployment rate—2.8 percent in 1991—went up to 5 percent in 1992 and continues to rise.[49] Health costs in the state are also rising rapidly.

President Clinton's Plan

President Clinton has pledged to provide universal health care at an affordable price. He has focused on a version of "managed competition," a blending of market-based and government-based reform plans. Managed competition relies on market forces to make insurance companies compete on the basis of quality and cost. It uses government to rein in the remaining cost of providing medical care and to guarantee universal coverage. This reform plan has not been tried in any other country. Its central goals are to provide universal coverage, enforce a ceiling on health care spending, and offer portability of benefits. Employers would be required to pay 80 percent of the premium cost for full-time employees and their dependents. Employees would be required to pay 20 percent. To protect small businesses from bankruptcy and employee cutbacks resulting from premium costs, President Clinton plans to phase in the coverage requirement, with the smallest and financially most vulnerable firms adopting it last. The unemployed could buy health insurance, at a sliding scale based on their ability to pay, through a publicly sponsored coalition of individuals who buy insurance together. Medicaid would cover the remaining poor. Presumably, employees would be price conscious, and health insurers would be encouraged to hold down the costs of their plans to make them attractive.

There remain some questions, however, about the Clinton health plan. These include whether to let competition control costs or have the government set a national spending ceiling. Also, should there be mandated policies guaranteeing health care for all citizens, or would there be financial incentives created for employers to cover their employees? Finally, should the federal government set a standard benefits package that all health plans would have to offer, or would there be a truly competitive market for customers offering different levels of benefits?

Notwithstanding this uncertainty, the National Governor's Association, among other influential groups, has endorsed the Clinton proposal. In fact, sensing that reform is in the air, some of the most conservative groups are

---

49. For a fuller discussion of Hawaii's health plan, see Deane Neubauer "Hawaii: The Health State," in Howard M. Leichter, ed., *Health Policy Reform in America: Innovations from the States* (Armonk, N.Y.: M. E. Sharpe, 1992), 147–72.

calling for reform. In December 1992, for example, the Health Insurance Association of America, representing 270 health insurers, proposed a sweeping plan for universal coverage that would be financed partly by taxing Americans with generous benefits. In a new twist insurers would accept people with preexisting conditions. These people are usually rejected for coverage. This proposal is a signal that insurers understand that reform is coming. Since they are particularly vulnerable to restructuring, the industry wants an influential voice in the reform process; they want to be seen as working with the president.

More states have also been pushing for reform. Florida has called for universal coverage to be offered by nonprofit, state-chartered organizations called Community Health Purchasing Alliances. These institutions would collect health care premiums and sign contracts with insurers judged to offer the best quality and the best cost. This, too, is a form of managed competition that has been triumphed by the president.

Advocates of a single-payer system contend that a managed-care ceiling would be nearly impossible to enforce. Proponents of a free market have argued that imposing a limit on expenditures would hinder market forces. All critics worry that providing universal coverage will require an increased federal deficit, higher taxes, or sharp price controls on medical services. Finally, *managed competition* is an umbrella term for a variety of related options that remain to be tested. If implemented, it will be a fascinating experiment.

President Clinton and various health care reform analysts have looked to Germany as another possible model. Germany has preserved its private insurance system. It keeps costs down by emphasizing preventative medicine, tight restrictions on access to hospital care, government control over the purchase of expensive technology, and a close linkage between cost increases and wage hikes. On the other hand, employee contributions average 13 percent of income. The 10 percent of Germans at the top of the income scale may opt out of the public health system and be uninsured, or they may buy private insurance. About 90 percent of the German population is insured through 1,100 nongovernmental "sickness funds." These are large buying groups that negotiate regionally with private associations of physicians and hospitals to set fee schedules. Premiums average 12.5 percent of a worker's gross wages. The employee pays half and the employer pays the rest. The full costs of medical treatment are covered, although patients are charged small copayments for hospital stays and medicine.

Administrative costs are as high as 9 percent of costs. Most important, the German system is susceptible to rapidly escalating costs. The country's population is aging, and health care demand is soaring. The government's solutions mirror those found in the United States: higher worker contributions and capping hospital costs by prescribing specific treatments for each illness.

Germany presents an interesting model, but it has its own set of problems that mitigate against wholesale adoption by U.S. policy actors.[50]

There are no obvious solutions for the United States' health care plight. A Canadian national health insurance system, notwithstanding its serious problems in the Canadian context, might be a long-term goal. A more likely alternative could be a managed competition system leading to a made-in-the-U.S.A. national health care plan entirely consistent with U.S. political culture. There will be significant roadblocks, for there are powerful interest groups poised to fight these suggestions, but many business leaders are desperately seeking radical alternatives to circumvent accelerating costs.

As noted, the Canadian system is by no means a perfect model either. It is under severe strain with rising costs, occasional rationing, and too few high-tech facilities. But it is an effective system for the vast majority of Canadians and must be carefully studied by those who would seek health care reform in the United States.

Raisa Deber of the University of Toronto explores the ideological bases of the health care systems in both the United States and Canada. She outlines four primary motivations behind public health care policies: (1) health care as a public good; (2) a healthy labor force; (3) health care as a charitable service; and (4) health care as a right for all citizens. According to this model, the U.S. system of public health care is influenced primarily by the notion of charity, resulting in a two-tiered system of health care—private insurance for those who can afford it and public Medicaid and Medicare for the poor and elderly. Canadians, on the other hand, consider health care as a right, and they have thus developed a system for universal health care that does not discriminate between the wealthy and the poor. In theory the same services are equally available to all Canadian citizens.

There are significant discrepancies between the "demands" and the "needs" views regarding public health. The United States strongly adheres to the policy of keeping the health system subject to market forces of supply and demand. Accordingly, insurance should not cover all health service fees; the patient must meet some of the costs in order to control unnecessary demands for health care. The Canadians, however, following the needs view, object to these deterrent charges, claiming that they reduce not only unnecessary care but also *necessary* care as many poor patients are unable to meet even these nominal fees. This, of course, defeats the purpose of universal health insurance. Canadians feel that health care should be allocated on the basis of need rather than on a willingness to pay for services.

---

50. For a comprehensive discussion of the German health care system, see John K. Iglehart, "Health Policy Report: Germany's Health Care System," *New England Journal of Medicine* 325, no. 324 (February 14, 1991): 503–8.

Canada's universal health plan generated initial successes in increased accessibility to health services as the class differences in the provision of health care disappeared. But today this universal strategy meets new challenges. Canadians are now asking: How equal can health services actually be, both between and within the provinces? How can health administrators determine the appropriate level of resources to be allocated to the health plan and what types of services should be covered by universal health insurance? Some point out that the system suffers from an inefficient use of resources resulting from the increase in demand for health services now that insurance coverage extends to all Canadians. Current critics suggest the need to shift the emphasis of health care away from physicians and hospitals to other health care providers such as nurses and other professionals as well as to the development of comprehensive community health care centers; this "new agenda" for health care proposes that a greater emphasis be placed on *preventative* health care policies, such as housing developments and improved sanitation, rather than on curative practices, noting that many health problems could be prevented before requiring medical treatment. These proponents suggest that much of the current resources flooding into the health care system that are aimed at improving technology have marginal effects at best on the overall health status of the nation.

Clearly, both the United States and Canada confront challenges with regard to their respective health care systems. Deber notes that mixed systems of public and private health care coverage—like that in the United States—tend to be the most economically inefficient. Ironically, the United States spends the world's highest proportion of its GNP on health care while leaving over thirty million people inadequately covered. As the rest of the world looks toward more universal forms of health coverage, Deber argues that the United States should reevaluate its provision of health care on the basis of demand rather than on need. Canada, facing new problems with its universal system of health care, should focus attention on improving the efficiency with which it delivers health services, paying close attention to what services should be insured as well as how health providers should be most appropriately compensated.

Theodore Marmor and Jerry Mashaw of Yale University stress the advantages of what they see as the exemplary performance of the Canadian health care system. They assert that six of the American Medical Association's objections to a national health insurance plan are creations of the AMA and were designed to discredit the Canadian system. Marmor and Mashaw note that the AMA maintains that national health insurance causes high administrative costs, an exodus of physicians, interference in the doctor-patient relationship, long queues for treatment, lower-quality medical care, and rationing. Although there may be some truth to a few of these assertions, for the most part they are, according to Marmor and Mashaw, an unfounded, self-serving set of American Medical Association statements. In fact, according to the authors, although there would be obstacles, the Canadian model might have applicability to the United States.

According to Steffie Woolhandler and David Himmelstein of Harvard University, for the fifteen years following the adoption of Medicare and Medicaid programs (until 1980), America enjoyed significant improvements in its level of overall health care. Life expectancy rates increased, while mortality rates fell. Recipients of public funds for health care sought more medical care, since they could now afford it. During this period of increased access, however, medical costs skyrocketed. For the past decade policymakers have placed great emphasis on controlling these costs, yet these policies have significantly reduced the access of millions of Americans to appropriate health care. Interestingly, this article points out that American policymakers seem to be "rationing the surplus." While millions are denied health care because they cannot pay, the number of empty hospital beds grows as resources are underutilized.

There seems to exist a trade-off in attempts to cure the problems of the American health care system. Provisions for improved access to health resources necessitate higher medical costs. At the same time, attempts to constrain these costs are made at the expense of access to health care. Current measures to reduce these costs, however, have had little, if any, impact. Ironically, the administrative dollars allocated to supervisors working to eliminate the sources of these high costs more than offset any money saved by their findings. The growing bureaucracy in the medical field only worsens the problems of spiraling costs. This is like a vicious cycle for the medical field: Attempts to curb health care costs only add to them.

Woolhandler and Himmelstein recommend that America adopt a national health program (NHP) based on Canada's health care system. They offer a succinct description of Canada's program, noting particularly how this system has kept costs (both physician and administrative) down. Although the authors note some criticisms of the Canadian system, they conclude that this system of universal health care has minimized health care costs without sacrificing the quality of care to patients. Therefore, according to Woolhandler and Himmelstein, an NHP is appropriate for the United States.

Frank Puffer of Clark University compares the U.S. and Canadian systems with regard to access to care. Puffer cites the results of two surveys, one taken in each country, in examining the issue (and problems) of health care access. A survey conducted in Canada by Broyles, Manga, Angus, and colleagues supports the widely held belief that the Canadian program of universal government-sponsored health insurance has eliminated the role income plays in access to medical care. Yet a similar study conducted in the United States produced some data that may be surprising for those who consider income to be the determining factor in health care access in the United States.

Puffer contends that other factors besides income determine whether an American has access to necessary health care. He writes that the National Medical Care Expenditure Survey produces "no evidence that in the United States low income plays a negative role in access to medical care." (He admits that the survey does not address the issue of the quality of medical care in relation to income.) The government programs of Medicare and Medicaid seem to have taken care of the elderly and those on the lowest rung of the economic ladder. There is, however, still a problem of access to health care in the United States, and Puffer maintains that this problem is largely the result of access to insurance and ethnic and educational differences rather than of income variance. The U.S. survey showed that those least likely to seek medical care were the uninsured (or underinsured) and minorities, a trend that Puffer largely contributes to lower educational levels. He places a great deal of emphasis on the complexity of insurance programs. He also states that the increase in HMO programs creates problems for the uninsured, as physicians working for HMOs are less likely to treat patients who are not covered.

In an attempt to solve the problems of access to health care in the United States Puffer advocates the adoption of a Canadian-style government insurance system. The United States is still plagued by coverage gaps that do not exist in Canada. To add more government programs to try to fill these gaps would only further burden the already complicated administrative bureaucracy, and the U.S. overhead for health care is already higher than Canada's. Puffer maintains that the best solution for the U.S. health care crisis is for Americans to overcome their fears of government programs and to adopt a Canadian-style health care system.

Edward Neuschler of the Health Insurance Association of America acknowledges that many Americans are looking to the Canadian health care system as a model. Americans who support the transition to such a system regard it as one in which the government pays for all health costs, one that covers all citizens, and one that offers patients the freedom of choice of doctors and hospitals. These attributes appear to be favorable to the suffering American system. Yet Neuschler indicates that such a view of the Canadian health care system is much too narrow for the purposes of considering it for adoption.

Advocates of the Canadian system are generally discouraged with the high proportion of GNP that the United States spends on health care. Canada's lower proportional spending is thus attractive. But these statistics are clouded by the fact that Canada's economy is growing at a faster rate than that of the United States. Statistics show that the growth rates of health expenditures in both the United States and Canada are virtually the same. These findings weaken the argument that an adoption of the Canadian system would save the United States dollars. In fact, one of Canada's main problems today is in cost containment.

Canada also faces other problems that would be unacceptable to Americans, namely with regard to accessibility of health services. Since health care is virtually free to Canadians, the demand for health services is greatly inflated. There are long waits for surgical procedures, even those for life-threatening situations as well as for preventative procedures such as mammograms. Furthermore, as hospitals work to remain within their budgets, they often close hospital beds, even though these beds are much needed to provide adequate care for patients. Critics of the Canadian system suggest that it provides excess routine medical care for all Canadians at the expense of those who require more immediate, specialized care. Providers recommend that some of the excessive costs be shifted to the consumers through a coinsurance plan or a reduction in the number of services covered by the universal plan. This would discourage overutilization of resources while providing more money for the system. In this sense it seems that some Canadians may prefer a more American-style health plan.

Americans see other problems with Canada's system. For instance, it effectively discourages technological innovation, for, as hospitals are constricted by governmental budgets, the money available for innovation is minimal. Also, most Americans value their ability to choose their appropriate level of medical insurance, a freedom that would be eliminated essentially by a Canadian-like system of universal health coverage.

Neuschler suggests that, given these problems as well as the political realities in the United States, it is highly unlikely that the United States would, or even could, adopt a Canadian-style health care plan. First of all, the costs would be incredibly high—around $230 billion, which would necessarily be provided by the states. Given the Americans' suspicions of any government controls as well as their distaste for high taxes, such a plan is unattractive. Furthermore, the "success" of Canada's system depends on a particular federal/provincial relationship, which allocates a high level of provincial control over the health programs in each respective province. On the other hand, U.S. states are significantly restricted by federal regulations, a situation that would make the ability of the states to effectively manage the health care needs of that state highly questionable. Likewise, it would be extremely difficult for the federal government to secure support of all fifty states in the adoption of a new health plan such as this. Neuschler's discussion indicates that, while the United States must find some solutions to its growing problems, Canada does not necessarily provide the answers because it faces significant difficulties of its own.

Morris Barer and Robert Evans note that, as the United States ponders its health care predicament, it increasingly looks to working models of public alternatives to the American private insurance and health industries, the so-called Medical-Industrial Complex. The Canadian national health insurance program often lands on the list of possible models for the United States to emulate. Barer and Evans worry that what might be a useful comparison, beneficial to both the American and Canadian health care structures, is being sabotaged by the creation of disinformation about the Canadian system, put forth by the beneficiaries of a "free-market" private insurance industry in the United States.

The article revolves around the theory of myth, in reference to both the U.S. and Canadian systems. First, according to Barer and Evans, the United States does not enjoy the competitive, ideal free-market system that is often held up as a comparison to the "flawed" Canadian system. That ideal does not now nor did it ever exist in the form of a private health insurance system anywhere in the world. Around this central myth, regarding the U.S. model, Barer and Evans refute the accusations of free-market proponents, most notably those of Patricia Danzon, that a national plan such as Canada's harbors numerous hidden costs that make it a distasteful, if not downright inviable, option for the United States.

Interesting sidebars to their central argument of unbalanced comparison are the authors' analyses of:

> the natural struggle between payers and providers that occurs in any insurance system, and
> the unnatural struggle between ethics and economics that seems to be occurring in the current health care debate.

The Barer and Evans article seeks to avoid the derailment of suitable comparisons between the private U.S. system and the public Canadian system.

David Conklin of the University of Western Ontario argues that a broad comparison of the different systems of health care in both the United States and Canada is unrealistic and unprofitable given the unique political pressures in each country. While Canadians generally agree that health resources should be equally available to all citizens, Americans, for the most part, value their adherence to a market-based system of health care with minimal regulatory interference. Although surveys indicate that both Americans and Canadians agree that the Canadian universal health care system is preferable to the U.S. system, Americans, particularly the influential well-to-do, are unwilling to sacrifice their market system because they wish to be able to purchase the level of health care that they demand. In fact, Conklin suggests that much of the debate between these two health care systems is generated by the different expectations of those from different economic backgrounds.

Both health care systems face challenges. The United States must find better ways to deal with caring for the bottom tier of the population, as Medicare and Medicaid funds are often insufficient in providing appropriate care to this group. At the same time, Canada must look for new ways to constrain the costs of its system. Instead of performing a general, broad comparison of the U.S. and Canadian health systems, Conklin investigates eight relevant issues that may provide insight into the lessons that both Canada and the United States can learn from each other.

As Canadians look for new financial incentives to keep medical costs down, they may find the American-style HMOs and preferred provider organizations (PPOs) a valuable lesson. Similarly, they may refer to the diagnostic-related groups (DRG) system in the United States, which reimburses hospitals according to the particular benefit, by examining the ways in which the U.S. system fosters programs for ambulatory health care, home health care, care for the elderly, and private health care for some sectors.

Bert Seidman of the National Council of Senior Citizens considers many of the most prominent proposals for health care reform. He looks at how health care is financed in Canada, France, the former West Germany, Japan, the United Kingdom, and the United States and concludes that the United States is different in that it does not set a limitation on national health care expenditures. Seidman also studies how the U.S. states administer health care and then summarizes various proposals for reform, including those of both limited and more comprehensive scope.

Paul Sperduto of the University of Minnesota sees the problems of the U.S. health care system as including quality of services, malpractice suits, efficiency, and administrative costs. This study suggests that the factors must be appropriately weighed in judging the value of alternative health policies. To do so, a grading system evaluates these factors and determines an overall GPA for each of thirteen proposals presented by different groups of the health services community.

Malcolm Taylor of York University insists that changes in the Canadian health care system are inevitable. He is most interested in health issues that will face Canadians in the future, including cost containment, the aging of the population, the impending surplus of physicians, the shifting emphasis from sickness care to wellness, and the likelihood of introducing innovations in the health services delivery system. Taylor then suggests how Canadians might best meet their health care challenges.

Lee Soderstrom of McGill University and Luciano Bozzini of the University of Montreal examine the process of public decision making in Quebec's health care system. They point out that there are good reasons for public involvement in the financing and management of a health care system but that, in practice, the effects of this public involvement depend on the quality of the decisions made by the public agencies. Soderstrom and Bozzini maintain that the organizational and financial problems that persist in Quebec's health care system are in part because of public decision-making difficulties. They argue that the system would perform better if decision making were more decentralized and if available information were improved.

Several advantages of decentralized decision making are noted. Giving more power and responsibility to regional agencies produces an administration both more in touch with local conditions and more accountable to the local population. It also encourages more experimentation and local participation. Furthermore, this process would result in smaller, more efficient bureaucracies than that of the central government. Soderstrom and Bozzini acknowledge, however, that there must be an appropriate balance between regional and central decision making in order to establish national standards.

The authors then analyze the health care system in Quebec. They point out that, although finances are not a barrier to health care access, some access problems do exist, especially in regard to geography. They argue that these access difficulties are largely a result of excessive centralization and are exacerbated by insufficient information. Reform toward decentralization is already in process, with a power shift from twelve regional councils to sixteen regional boards. Yet little is being done about information problems, even though, Soderstrom and Bozzini maintain, better interpretation and dissemination of available information are feasible. They cite lack of information about the system's performance as a source of dissatisfaction with it. Finally, the authors state that decision making is shaped by public values and that this must be remembered when looking at the problems of decision making. In the area of public health there are two contradictory value systems involved. On one hand, people want and enjoy the benefits of government-sponsored health insurance. On the other hand, North American culture contains an element of distrust of excessive government involvement, which in turn constrains the degree to which governments involve themselves in health care systems. Finding a way to accommodate these contradicting values is an important element in solving the problems of public decision making in health care systems.

In this volume Raisa Deber looks at how ideology has played a role in forming the character of the Canadian and U.S. health care systems. The question is then posed: Is the Canadian model relevant to U.S. health care reformers? Marmor and Mashaw, Woolhandler and Himmelstein, Barer and Evans, and Puffer suggest that it is. Neuschler vehemently disagrees. Conklin goes on to argue that even making a comparison between two such disparate systems may be inappropriate.

This being said, most analysts agree that the U.S. health care system is in need of reform. Seidman and Sperduto evaluate many of the most prominent proposals for change.

The Canadian system is not without its problems either, and Taylor and Soderstrom and Bozzini identify some of the problems that the Canadian system faces and suggest possible remedies.

The Canadian health care system may or may not have applicability to the United States. This topic is the subject of intense debate in Washington. It is generally agreed that in both systems costs are too high, access to care can be problematic, and changes are warranted. The articles in this collection suggest real-world policy prescriptions for one of the vital and difficult problems of our era. Since the issues associated with health care reform will affect all of us in North America, it is incumbent upon our policymakers to pay particular attention to the most pragmatic and effective policy prescriptions. The evidence suggests that voters in Canada, and even more in the United States, will reward candidates who meet their health care expectations.

CHAPTER 2

Philosophical Underpinnings of Canada's Health Care Systems

Raisa B. Deber

Health care is one of the most popular and expensive programs provided by governments, and Canada and the United States are among the highest spenders.[1] Although the rhetoric may often become feverish, health care has been remarkably unscathed by the recent attacks on the welfare state. Even in the United States, where the free market is an article of faith, the government feels some obligation to insure that health care services are provided to its citizens.

Among the first health policy questions that must be addressed concerns why governments have this sense of responsibility. What is the justification for government involvement in insuring that high-quality health services be provided to all? How does the need for health care differ from the need for food, clothing, or housing? To what extent have changes in technology and/or public attitudes meant that the former answers to these questions are no longer adequate?

Justification for Public Involvement

Admittedly, good health is greatly valued and is one of the most important human concerns. But this does not indicate why health care should be seen as a political problem in need of government attention. In earlier times, for example, health was often viewed as a gift from God, and medicine was deemed an act of divine intercession. Thus, health was a matter of fate or luck or appeasing the gods, and the search for health was of necessity profoundly

---

1. In 1987 mean spending for health in twenty-three OECD countries was 7.5 percent. The United Kingdom was among the lowest spenders (6 percent), and the United States was among the highest (11.2 percent). Canada and France, at 8.6 percent each, shared third place. On average about three quarters of this spending is provided by governments—87 percent in the United Kingdom, 76 percent in Canada, and 41 percent in the United States (Schieber and Poullier 1990).

personal or religious (with or without expert help in placating the gods). Scientific medicine has transformed this view to a "modern" belief—that health is under human control and hence achievable if appropriate actions are taken. In this view a healthy population can be guaranteed by making sure that everyone who "needs" the attention of physicians and hospitals can receive it without financial or geographic barriers. Proponents of this view follow what Wildavsky (1979) has termed "The Great Equation—medical care equals health." The principal job of any health planner who accepts the Great Equation is to insure accessibility of medical services. Not surprisingly, the planners who set up Canada's health care system concentrated on this aspect of health care.

Wildavsky went on to note that "the Great Equation is wrong." But, even if we were to accept this concept, why should government care whether its people are healthy? Four possible levels of justification, which reflect varying degrees of altruism and beliefs about the role of government, are discussed next.

Levels of Justification

Public Goods

The term *public goods* is used by economists to denote a special category of benefits that cannot be rationed; if they exist, all can reap the benefit whether or not they have chosen to pay for it. For example, the army protects a nation; the government cannot decide to restrict such services to citizens willing to pay the "defense tax" and allow other citizens to be invaded. Clean air, where it exists, is available to everyone who, or everything that, breathes. Thus, there is a clear incentive for a rational individual to refuse to pay for such goods and to reap whatever benefits that others are willing to provide. This "free rider" problem leads to the underacquisition of public goods and provides a justification, on both practical and moral grounds, for governments to compel their provision and financing (Olson 1965).

The term *quasi–public goods* refers to items that could in theory be rationed but at a cost (financial and/or administrative) that makes this option impractical. For example, toll gates on city streets or admission booths controlling access to public parks are possible but not really feasible. It usually makes more sense to consider items such as streets or parks as public goods and to cover their costs through taxation. Even the libertarian is willing to admit that governments can appropriately be involved in the provision of public goods.

The term *externalities* refers either to costs that are shifted to other payers or to benefits that are enjoyed by them. An industry, for example, can choose to pollute its environment rather than to pay for the costs of cleanup, but this "savings" is accomplished by making others pay (in health or property damage). In a market setting such activities, if not regulated, would place those who operate more ethically at a comparative disadvantage. Justice would seem to require someone to play a policing role and insure that all members of society assume the costs of their own activities. Similarly, if an educated populace benefits future employers and increases the economic well-being of the entire society, the costs of education should not be paid solely by the individuals being trained, because they are not the only beneficiaries.

Traditional public health care, which deals with the prevention of epidemic diseases through the inspection of food, sewage, and water, is a clear example of a public good. As the Black Death showed, infectious diseases do not respect class distinctions. Those who do not comply with standards of hygiene can begin epidemics that can then affect their neighbors. Here the role of the state—first as an enforcer of quarantine and later as a provider of clean food and water—is obvious.

State involvement in health care generally begins with these types of activities. But, as technology evolves, public goods can become quasi–public goods (or the reverse). For example, the development of totally effective vaccines could in theory erode the justification for state involvement by turning protection against disease into a market commodity: Those who valued such protection could purchase it, and those who did not would remain at risk and take the consequences. The pure market theorist would presumably be happy to live in a plague town, content that paternalism had not interfered with consumer choices. Epidemiologists who study the factors affecting the health of populations argue, however, that this view ignores two scientific facts.

First, not all vaccinations give perfect immunity; further, medical problems can prevent individuals who would have purchased protection from being immunized. Therefore, "buyers" may not be able to purchase perfect protection. Second, the mathematics of the spread of disease indicates that the likelihood of an individual falling ill depends on the prevalence of disease in the community. If there is a high enough rate of illness, most individuals are likely to come into contact with the infection and hence to risk falling ill themselves. If there is a high enough rate of immunity, the disease is unlikely to spread, and even the unprotected are unlikely to become ill. This concept of "herd immunity" also implies that the most efficient way of protecting a community is widespread prevention. Thus, individuals who refuse to protect themselves are in effect also endangering others, while, if enough members of the community agree to immunization, the unimmunized can be free riders and enjoy no-cost, no-risk protection. Accordingly, even the most dedicated market advocates accept public health activities as an appropriate area for government involvement.

It is therefore not surprising to find that public health activities have been the traditional starting point for national involvement in health care. In addition to being easily justified in philosophical terms, public health activities also promise considerable "bang for the buck." As McKeown (1979) has shown, the increases in life expectancy over the past centuries have resulted largely from improvements in the purity of water and food, the consequent reduction in infectious diseases, and preventative improvements such as better diets (related to technological advances in transportation and refrigeration) and better housing. Medical breakthroughs, despite the attention they receive, have made comparatively minor contributions to the health of populations. This logic is now well accepted internationally. For example, the World Health Organization's (WHO) strategy of "Health for All by the Year 2000" emphasizes "primary care." WHO recommends that developing nations put their limited resources into public health (particularly sanitation, immunization, and maternal and child health) rather than into physicians and hospitals. This strategy recognizes that traditional curative medical care is, in many cases, a luxury that developing countries cannot afford.

A Healthy Labor Force

But even a population relatively free from epidemic disease is not necessarily a healthy population. Poor people generally have poorer health and thus make a less productive workforce. The second level of justification for public involvement in health matters comes from the notion of "human capital." This view assumes that the state has some responsibility to develop its human capital, both to assist in economic growth through the provision of a fit and trained labor pool and to insure a healthy military. Accordingly, health coverage in many nations was first applied to industrial workers and only gradually spread to other segments of the population. War, not surprisingly, has been a spur to national involvement in improving health services, particularly when preservice medical examinations have revealed how large a proportion of the population is deemed "unfit to serve." A similar justification could be used to provide health services to children as an investment in the future.

Under the human capital rationale it is hard to justify expenditures for groups who would not contribute to national productivity, particularly the elderly and those unlikely to enter the paid workforce (including much of the rural population).

The need to keep the population healthy to enhance the economic functioning of the state can also be interpreted in Marxist terms as an economic concession to the working class to better realize the long-run political and economic interests of the capitalist class and at the same time dull the revolutionary instincts of the working class (Swartz 1987). At this level of justification the state operates out of self-interest by investing in its future. This rationale, however, is not necessarily entirely self-interested; it has often been accompanied by moral arguments. For example, the periodic discovery of massive ill health among the poor has often been deemed "a national disgrace." Its alleviation was part of the Brave New World that the two world wars had been fought to achieve. As Taylor (1987) has noted, this moral argument was one of the major factors in convincing the Canadian government of the need for national health insurance. The addition of this moral dimension leads to the third level of justification of state involvement.

Charity and Mutual Responsibility

If we are "our neighbor's keeper," then we presumably have an obligation to insure that he or she receives medical attention when necessary. Indeed, the infrastructure of health care in Canada, like that in many other countries, grew out of a series of church- or charity-run institutions for which the state gradually took on more and more financial responsibility.

At this level of justification we may view the state as having an obligation to guarantee that the poor are cared for while allowing the rest of the population to fend for itself. This is the system of "two-tiered" medicine—a market sector for those able to afford health care and a charity sector for the rest. In such "soup kitchen medicine" the poor will neither be allowed to starve nor be encouraged to develop champagne tastes. The history of the development of health insurance in most countries is the development of plans to cover particular segments of the population and the gradual extension of coverage and benefits to cover larger and larger proportions of the population.

A Human Right

The fourth level of justification denotes health care as a "human right" to which everyone is equally entitled. This viewpoint is linked to the basis upon which one believes health services should be allocated. Contrast the assumption underlying the use of the word *needs,* as opposed to *demands* or *wants.* Is the recipient of services a "patient," a "client," a "consumer," or a "user"? Acceptance of the view that patients "need" health services if they are ill (and, conversely, that they should not receive them if health services are not needed) usually leads to arguments for some type of national health system so that all citizens will be guaranteed equal access to equal services. At this level the equitable provision of health care may take on religious or ideological overtones; Christians may note that "thou shalt love thy neighbor as thyself" (Matt. 19:19) and Socialists that health care should be distributed "to each according to his needs" (Marx 1972).

Justification for Public Involvement
in Canada and the United States

In virtually all developed nations health services are justified by some combination of the third and fourth levels, with accompanying variations in the extent to which two-tiered medicine is permitted. Movement from the third to the fourth level is accelerated by the recognition that mixed systems tend to be less economically efficient than regulated ones; once we accept that health care should be provided to everyone who needs it, we can no longer use market mechanisms because we can no longer price individuals out of the market (McLachlan and Maynard 1982). The extent to which recognition of this fact is retarded by ideological blinders varies from nation to nation, with the United States being the sterling example of the price some are willing to pay to cling to market myths. (For an excellent plea for equity, see Fein 1986.)

In Canada health care has rapidly progressed to being seen as a right. The saga of the establishment of Canada's system of medical and health insurance —now known generically as Medicare—has been told elsewhere (Deber and Vayda 1985; Taylor 1987, 1990). Because health care is constitutionally a provincial responsibility in Canada, Medicare developed incrementally from two voluntary cost-shared programs, wherein the federal (national) government provided funds to provincial plans as long as those plans complied with specified terms and conditions. The terms entrenched access to health care as a "merit good" that should, by right, be available to everyone. All provincial insurance plans had to be universal, comprehensive (covering all "medically necessary procedures"), and accessible (including a requirement that "reasonable access" not be impeded or precluded, "either directly or indirectly, whether by charges or otherwise"; in 1984 this was interpreted by the Canada Health Act as prohibiting any direct charges or deductibles for insured services). To enable Canadians to be covered anywhere in Canada the plans also had to be portable. Finally, the role of private insurers was limited by a requirement that the insurance plans be publicly administered because the private alternative was seen as more expensive and less effective. In most provinces plans are financed through general revenues, although premiums or designated payroll taxes are occasionally used to cover a proportion of the costs. Canada, however, has a single payer—the government-run insurance plan. Avoidance of the multiplicity of plans that characterizes the U.S. system has had several salutary effects: Administrative costs are far lower, there is little incentive to shift costs to other insurers, and the costs are shared across the economy rather than loaded onto the manufacturing sector.

Some of the problems of Canada's current system arose from the incremental way that Medicare was implemented. The system began by cost-sharing universal insurance for acute hospital-based treatment (1958) and added an insurance program for physician services (1966). Plans were operational in all provinces by 1972. Steering effects were immediate; there were disincentives to set up programs ineligible for federal cost-shared funds (e.g., community-based care and care by nonphysician providers). The system instead became focused around the most expensive ways of delivering care. Although the funding formula was changed in 1977, replacing cost sharing with a mixture of block grants plus tax points, the inertia has been hard to overcome.

The federal terms and conditions dictated the kinds of services that should be covered (those medically necessary), but not how they should be funded or organized. The federal steering effect did result, however, in essential similarities across provinces. Most hospitals were paid by provincial governments on the basis of negotiated budgets (in earlier years, often line by line; subsequently, through prospective global budgets; more recently, some provinces have been experimenting with modifying the global budgets to include a case-mix sensitive component). Most physicians were paid fee-for-service on the basis of provincially negotiated fee schedules, although alternative reimbursement mechanisms (e.g., capitation and salary) were often available. For the most part, therefore, physician and laboratory services have been "volume driven" and difficult to control, in contrast to the (theoretical, although not always practical) control over the budgets of institutions. Delivery systems in Canada have thus resembled those of the United States, except that public financing has insulated Canadian providers from many of the competitive pressures that have led to innovations in the United States. Hospital closures are a rarity (occupancy rates are far higher), indigent care is not an issue, and most physicians can still exercise clinical judgment independent of the patient's ability to pay. Managed care, for example, is still a rarity in Canada.

Medicare was successful in achieving its basic goal of improving accessibility: The supply of hospitals and hospital beds increased, the supply and income of physicians grew, and class differences in the utilization of services largely disappeared.

Canada's aversion to two-tiered medicine has had implications for the organization and financing of the Canadian system. Examples of its impact can be seen in policy areas such as methods of physician reimbursement and decisions about the scope of services to be insured. In the United States, by contrast, the level of government involvement is still hotly debated. In part the philosophical disputes can be seen in the extent to which we consider that the "insurance principle" should be a major determinant of health policy.

Insurance: Who Pays?

Food, clothing, shelter, and health care are all basic needs. Yet no one speaks of "food insurance." Having very predictable needs, people can reasonably expect to budget for the amounts required. The state's involvement can be restricted to situations in which an individual has insufficient income to meet basic needs. This aid can be given in kind (i.e., provision of food stamps or support of food banks) or as income supplements, which could then be used as the recipient saw fit (e.g., to buy food or to purchase symphony tickets).

Insurance, in contrast, is a response to a small but unpredictable probability of a large loss. It is difficult for an individual to budget for such expenses. If, however, the "expected value" of the loss for each individual is manageable, risk pooling would allow this loss to be spread out among a large pool of individuals (and, as in the case of life insurance, over a long period of time). Actuaries will set premiums so that the amount collected in premiums from the individuals in the plan exceeds the amount to be claimed; those insured will nonetheless gain if they place value on removing the possibility of large losses. Such insurance plans can be public or private; contributions can be collected as premiums or as taxes; benefits can be paid as services or as cash contributions toward the cost of services; and differences can exist in what is covered.

To the extent that individuals covered by insurance may behave differently than those without it (they may be more careless; they may demand more services), costs may increase. To deal with this "moral hazard" insurers may demand that clients remain financially responsible for some of the costs they incur. This responsibility may be in the form of deductibles (i.e., the client pays the first $X of expenses) and/or copayments (i.e., the client pays a fixed proportion of the cost or a fixed user fee). Such charges are often referred to as deterrent charges, aimed at limiting the "frivolous" use of services. (For an excellent discussion of the insurance issues, see Evans 1984, especially chap. 2).

How well does health care fit into the insurance model? When is health insurance necessary?

From a purely economic point of view, sometimes health insurance is not necessary. Routine health needs (e.g., checkups, well-baby visits) are often fairly predictable and can be budgeted. Indeed, most physician visits probably fall into this relatively predictable category of expenditures. If certain groups could not afford such care (e.g., the poor not being able to immunize their children), state subsidies could be provided. Routine dental care, eyeglasses, prescription drugs, and so on would therefore not appear to require insurance coverage. Catastrophic illness, in contrast, clearly meets the insurance model. As long as such illness is unlikely, a risk-pooling agreement can be mutually beneficial.

This argument suggests a limited role for health insurance, with high deductibles. Indeed, many U.S. health economists argue that routine care for the nonpoverty population does not require insurance and that public policy should accordingly discourage extensive coverage for other than catastrophic care (e.g., by restricting tax deductibility for insurance payments) (see Manning et al. 1987). But this line of argument creates numerous questions: Why do individuals continue to seek first-dollar coverage? Why is universal health/hospital insurance Canada's most popular social program? Indeed, why have most industrial countries other than the United States moved along the road to national health insurance?

In part, there is a philosophical difference in the ways in which these models view the process of seeking care. The insurance model views it as being driven by demands and largely discretionary. Hence, health care is likely to be "abused" if it is seen as "free" or if it is "underpriced." When should an individual seek out the services of an emergency room or visit a physician? What Evans (1984) terms the "naive economic view" assumes that such services would be used more appropriately if the "client" were forced to assume some of the costs of the services. This viewpoint would thus encourage direct charges to patients. In the Canadian context such direct charges are usually categorized as "user fees" levied by institutions (e.g., a cost per hospital admission, per hospital day, per emergency room contact) or "extra billing" by physicians (i.e., fees charged by physicians above and beyond the fee schedule paid by the government insurance plan).

In contrast, an assumption that health is sought on the basis of needs rather than demands would find little use for direct charges. One would point to the asymmetry of information between patient and provider and note that the patient is not ideally trained to distinguish between necessary and unnecessary care. As Evans has explained:

> The consumer/patient values health status per se, not health care, but health status cannot be bought. Rather she buys health care in the expectation that it will contribute to health status. The normal consumer sovereignty assumption is that the consumer is the best judge of the value to herself of different valued commodities or states; this includes health status. But it does not extend to health care, because that is not itself of value. There is a technical relationship, which is specific to each consumer and condition, by which health care affects health, and the expert

provider is much better informed than the consumer/patient about the structure of this relationship. (1984, 72–73)

This viewpoint suggests that deterrent charges would appear to be as likely to reduce necessary care as unnecessary care. More alarming, such deterrent effects would selectively affect those with the fewest economic resources, who are more likely to be ill (Townsend and Davidson 1982; Wilkins and Adams 1983). Indeed, deterring the poor from seeking necessary care for economic reasons would defeat the entire purpose of health insurance. If health care is a human right, then there is no place for a user-pay philosophy. As will be noted below, this philosophical dispute underlaid much of the debate over the 1984 Canada Health Act, which received unanimous approval in the Canadian Parliament. The act imposed dollar-for-dollar withholding of the federal contribution for any user charges for insured services; it led to the provinces abolishing all such direct charges to patients within the three-year grace period (Heiber and Deber 1987). The only advocates of user pay were physicians, and they were careful to indicate that no such charges should be levied if they might interfere with receipt of "needed" services. The hearings were a vigorous demonstration of the widespread Canadian rejection of the economic view of health care.

The Nature of Health Needs

As noted above, a major impetus to the provision of national health care systems has been war and the resulting discovery that the poor were much sicker than the rich. From this discovery sprang a major fallacy. It was believed that health was a kind of fixed quantity. If the poor were ill, they would need an immediate dose of medical care to fix previous deficiencies. Once that backlog of unmet needs was met there would no longer be as high a demand for health services, except at a lower maintenance level. As Aneurin Bevan, a father of the British National Health Service, wrote, "A considerable proportion of the initial expenditure . . . was the result of past neglect. When the first rush was over, the demand would even out" (quoted in Schwartz 1977, 26). The founders of Canada's health insurance system, strongly influenced by the U.K. developments, shared these ideas.

The agenda in the early days of building health services in all developed nations thus focused on accessibility—increasing the supply of hospitals, physicians, and other health professionals, often by subsidizing manpower training and facility construction, and on eliminating financial barriers to care, usually by developing systems of health insurance. It was believed that, as the poor began to be treated, the residue of unmet needs would be eliminated, and the health status of the population would inexorably rise. Class-related differences in health status would be eliminated, and the system would reach a steady state of resource consumption.

It will come as little surprise to students of health care expenditure that these forecasts were wrong. Spending did not level off. Indeed, it appeared that need was limitless. As Wildavsky has noted, "The Medical Uncertainty Principle states that there is always one more thing that might be done" (1979, 287–88). The price of benevolence, it seems, was higher than first estimated. But the very success of the accessibility policies revealed, or even created, other health policy problems, which then had to be confronted.

Emerging Health Policy Issues

Even Greater Equity

The successes of national health care programs (whether Canada's national health insurance or the United Kingdom's National Health Service) high-lighted existing inequities. The geographic areas that still had relatively low quantities of personnel, services, or facilities requested enhanced resources. If this were not feasible, there were calls for public payment of transportation. How equal could health services be allowed to be, given geographical realities? What policy actions should be taken to deal with "physician maldistribution"? Did equity require the provision of special services that were sensitive to people from different cultures, the disabled, or other disadvantaged groups?

Who Pays What?

A related issue concerned which costs should be borne by patients and which by the government insurance plan. This thrust had two prongs. First, pressure built to expand the range of services covered, a process Fried, Deber, and Leatt (1987) have termed "deprivatization." Second, attention focused on copayments and the extent to which they might be considered barriers to accessibility.

From a practical point of view the defenders of direct charges to patients faced a difficulty. If the charges were high enough to act as a deterrent, there was no guarantee that they would not deter patients from needed services. To the extent that such deterrence selectively affected the poor this policy violated equity and defeated the purpose of national health insurance. But, if the charges were set low enough to avoid deterrence, the administrative costs would outweigh the revenue gains; they would not be worth collecting. Selective charges would require means testing and administration of exemptions; this two-tiered medicine could present ideological difficulties to a universal system.

Efficient Use of Resources

Canada's universal health insurance system covered the services delivered in hospitals or by physicians. Costs to society were uncoupled from costs to patients. Not surprisingly, the Canadian system tended to overuse the insured resources, with resulting inefficiencies. A common thrust of current critiques of the present health care system is the need to deemphasize the role of hospitals and physicians.

One particularly obvious problem arose in the use of "free" acute-care facilities for long-term chronic patients. These "bed blockers" were perceived as denying the resources to acutely ill patients who "needed" the beds and as wasting medical resources. The focus on accessibility argued for providing a higher volume of "more appropriate services" for the chronically ill. Similarly, the overuse of free (to patients) insured physician services retarded the acceptance of nurse practitioners and other health service professionals (Spitzer 1984). Again, the accessibility argument suggests the expansion of funding to insure these alternatives as well.

Technology has catalyzed additional changes in the roles played by doctors and hospitals. New health professions have proliferated, and procedures formerly performed only in hospitals can now be done in clinics or at home. Sociologically, adding other members to the health team, increasing public understanding (and questioning) of medical paternalism, and increasing scrutiny of medical practice have accelerated the trend toward decreasing the autonomy of physicians (Starr 1982).

If less emphasis were placed on the hospital and the physician, though, what should take their place? One suggestion was the community health center (CHC), a community clinic in which a multidisciplinary team of providers would work together to provide comprehensive, community-based care. Such centers would be controlled by community boards, sensitive to community needs. To remove the incentives of fee-for-service medicine to overservice and deemphasize health education, these centers would be staffed by salaried providers. The community health center as envisioned in Canada's Hastings Report (1972 and 1973) was never implemented, but it spawned a series of similar approaches, particularly in Quebec (centres locaux des services communautaires [CLSC]), in Ontario (health services organizations [HSOs], CHCs, and comprehensive health organizations [CHOs]), and in Saskatchewan. Other approaches borrowed from the U.S. HMO model, which again envisioned salaried multidisciplinary teams serving a defined patient population and controlling which services that population would receive (Lalonde and Deber 1991).

As an alternative to adding on new services, however, we might focus on whether existing services could instead be eliminated. For example, is there an oversupply of physicians that must be alleviated to allow the use of physician substitutes?

Similar conclusions have resulted from a related research agenda that focused on small area variations in utilization of health services and that noted that large variations in rates of surgery, hospitalization, or other services did not seem to be related to different levels of need nor to lead to very different health outcomes (see Wennberg, Freeman, and Culp 1987; Eisenberg 1986; Vayda and Mindell 1982). The conclusion appeared to be that much inappropriate utilization was provider generated and could, in all likelihood, be curbed while improving the health status of the population. If true, this would set up a win-win situation, with the only losers being those providing (and being paid for) the excess services. The managed care movement, among others, was based largely on this premise (Lalonde and Deber 1991; see also Evans 1984, especially chap. 4).

Determining the Level of Resources

Canadian economists such as R. G. Evans (1984) have observed that health care is noteworthy for the failure of market mechanisms to function as an acceptable way of balancing supply and demand for services under a universal system. If society decides that access to health care is to be determined on the basis of need rather than on ability to pay, both overservicing of the wealthy (e.g., unnecessary surgery) and underservicing of the poor are seen as unacceptable. But there are always more health care services that could be provided, even if the marginal impact of each is small. Allowing providers to determine the appropriate level of supply may simply be handing them a blank check. As Fein has noted, "There are no monetary rewards for not filling the hospital bed, not ordering the test, or discharging the patients" in fee-for-service medicine (1986, 131). With all incentives combining to encourage more interventions, health care costs have inevitably increased. In retrospect it was inevitable that the partnership that had developed between providers and third-party payers would have to be disrupted, and some policy control given to decision makers with a broader view of overall (including nonhealth) priorities. As the biggest spenders, hospitals and physicians could be expected to bear the brunt of any control activities.

This collision between providers and payers can be seen internationally; control may be sought by private insurers and employers (e.g., in the United States) or governments (e.g., in Canada). Not surprisingly, this trend is resisted by physicians and hospitals and rarely welcomed by patients. Regardless of the level of spending, providers are likely to claim that health is underfunded, since they are rarely able to command all of the resources they could use. In the United States, however, control mechanisms tend to be directed against patients (e.g., by cost shifting), whereas in Canada the philosophy that health care provision should be needs based focuses attention on controls on providers.

The fiscal crisis of the state, however, makes the dilemma more acute. In the United States there are disputes about whether social policy can be afforded. In Canada a similar combination of economic slowdown and persistent deficits has constrained the fiscal flexibility of government. Debt service now consumes up to one third of the Canadian federal budget. The erosion of budgetary flexibility has led to a concerted attempt to shift costs among levels of government. The federal government has held the growth of its transfer payments to the province, which formerly paid about half the costs of hospital and medical insurance, to well below the rate of inflation. The provinces then seek to shift their increased costs to local government (e.g., by cutting or by altering funding formulas for services such as education). Taxpayers grumble as ever higher levels of taxes appear to buy lower levels of services. Medicare, although the most popular government program, may become vulnerable as the ability to enforce national standards diminishes.

Health Policy Challenges

Micro versus Macro Allocation Decisions

Assuming that resources are finite, there are two types of allocation decisions that must then be made. Macro allocation decisions determine how many resources will be devoted to a particular sector of the economy (such as health, education, or roads). Micro allocation decisions determine where those resources will be spent and who will receive them.

In the health arena micro allocation decisions are traditionally made by individual providers and patients making individual determinations of need. Macro decisions need not, however, be made explicitly; the free market will allow micro decisions to be aggregated into a total. Rationing occurs individually, as patients or providers decide that they do not value a particular benefit enough to pay its cost. Since the cutoff point for a poor person is usually less than for a rich one, this rule may be seen by many as inequitable. And, if all costs are guaranteed to be met through insurance—one of the underlying principles of comprehensive health insurance—the market mechanism cannot work at all. Accordingly, most systems with national health insurance are soon forced to make macro allocation decisions by setting budgetary ceilings. These decisions are difficult, contentious, and politically explosive. Providers will attempt to highlight micro decisions concerning individuals who "could have been treated were the resources available," and government will be pressured to make ad hoc decisions to increase funding for each such case

(Deber and Vayda 1985; Deber, Thompson, and Leatt 1988). Not surprisingly, governments are now trying to decouple the macro and micro allocation decisions to buffer themselves from public pressure. Devices such as budget limits, managed care, or managed competition are all attempts, of varying success, to force providers to work within fixed budgets and thereby reduce the pressure on government to increase budgets.

From an individual point of view any form of resource constraints can be seen as rationing, which is considered an anathema in a needs-based philosophy. Economists stress that scarce resources are always rationed; the only question is by what mechanism. Price rationing can be replaced by waiting lists, first come first served, or some expert triage system. Mechanic categorized "modes of rationing health services," postulating that "the process is one of movement from *rationing by fee* through a stage of *implicit rationing* through resource allocation to a final stage of *explicit rationing*. In this process the role of physician shifts from entrepreneur to bureaucratic official, and medical practice [shifts] from a market-oriented system to a rationalized bureaucracy" (1989, 21). This shift is recognized by physicians. Linton, a prominent member of Ontario's medical community, in a largely favorable assessment of Canada's health system, suggested that "the increase in demand and the explosion of new forms of technology . . . make the rationing of health care inevitable" (1990, 199) and called for public discussion on how it should best be done. These control mechanisms are politically unpopular, however, and have led to increasing challenges (particularly from providers) to the underlying philosophy, usually on the grounds of "freedom for the consumer to purchase additional care if he or she so desires." To date, these views have not attracted much public support, yet this may change if constrained resources are seen to threaten the high quality of the universal program.

The New Agenda

An even more basic challenge to health policy has come from an influential group of theorists who challenged the effectiveness of health care spending by attacking the premise that medical care guaranteed health. As noted above, McKeown (1979) made a convincing argument that the increases in life expectancy that characterized the era of modern medicine had arisen not from the one-on-one care of patients by physicians but, rather, from the community-based interventions of public health. Clean water and food inspection had virtually eliminated the epidemic diseases that had killed so many. McKeown's work was expanded by others (e.g., Fuchs 1974). The synthesis of these ideas in the Lalonde report (1974) by the Canadian Department of National Health and Welfare became an internationally influential document.

The report noted that "loss of productive years" resulted from four broad elements: human biology, environment, lifestyle, and health care organization. The report went on to say:

> Until now most of society's efforts to improve health and the bulk of direct health expenditures have been focused on the HEALTH CARE ORGANIZATION. Yet when we identify the present main causes of sickness and death in Canada, we find that they are rooted in the other three elements of the Concept: HUMAN BIOLOGY, ENVIRONMENT and LIFESTYLE. It is apparent, therefore, that vast sums are being spent treating diseases that could have been prevented in the first place. (Lalonde 1974, 32)

In its mildest form this argument suggests less emphasis on attempting to cure disease and more emphasis on attempting to restore patients to their maximum potential of functioning. Particularly given the rapid increase in the proportion of individuals over age eighty-five, stress should clearly be placed on rehabilitation and adaptation. It is not clear that the skills of physicians are the most appropriate to carry out such tasks; rehabilitation therapists, for example, might be more helpful than physicians in assisting an elderly individual to recover from a fractured hip or to cope with a chronic disability. In its moderate form this view calls for increased attention to prevention. The most sensible investment, then, might be totally outside the traditional health care system—for example, providing a maintenance person to modify a senior's residence to minimize the chance of falls by improving lighting, strengthening railings, and anchoring scatter rugs. Taken to its logical conclusion, the Lalonde viewpoint (1974) would refocus attention away from medical care to poverty, inadequate housing, and other misfortunes of the human condition.

In aggregate this line of research and advocacy, which has gained momentum under the rubrics of "health promotion," "disease prevention," and "healthy public policy," has clarified the very limited scope for influence by organized medical care and has led to what might be termed the new agenda for health care—how best to guarantee high-quality, cost-effective health care for the population (Rachlis and Kushner 1989).

It should be noted, however, that the proverb "An ounce of prevention is worth a pound of cure" has not stood up well to rigorous examination. One consideration is long time frames; the cost of a preventative intervention in a young person is incurred immediately, whereas the benefit may not be realized for thirty years. At any reasonable discount rate most such interventions are not economically attractive. In addition, the low prevalence of many diseases implies that most people will achieve no benefit because most people will never develop that disease. Accordingly, research suggests that many preventative measures may be even less cost effective than traditional curative medicine (Russell 1986). Many mass screening programs, in another example, will identify vast numbers of false positives (healthy individuals who happened to have abnormal test results) for each illness detected, driving up the cost per case to undesirable levels. It is even more alarming, depending on the sort of workup required to rule out illness among those testing positive, that these kinds of "preventative programs" may do more harm than good. As the examples of mammograms and cholesterol testing have revealed, however, such programs tend to gain high popular acceptance, and curbing them becomes politically problematic.

The new agenda suggests some massive health policy changes. If very little medical care results in measurable increases in health status, the rational conclusion is that such programs should be cut. The freed-up money might or might not then be allocated to other social programs that might have a greater impact on health status (e.g., eliminating poverty, improving housing, or providing social support to battered women). Such policy decisions should be conceptually independent of the decision to slash the amount of resources devoted to medical care services. Theorists have written that much current practice could be categorized as "flat of the curve medicine," that is, the additional resources devoted to health care have extremely little benefit (Evans 1984).

Reform from the Left

The reform agenda from the Left, then, has sought alternatives to traditional fee-for-service medicine. Resources and power would be shifted from hospitals and doctors to community- and home-based services, provided by multidisciplinary teams. Nurses, physiotherapists, and other nonphysician providers would gain more autonomy. Physicians would no longer be the gatekeepers into the system. Insured services would include all factors likely to affect health care: homemakers to allow elderly or disabled individuals to remain in their homes, respite care to aid family caregivers, improved housing, and transportation. Attention would shift from medical care to health care; we would have a "health care system" rather than a "sick care system." Emphasis would move from treatment, particularly capital- and technology-intensive treatment, to community-based programs and ultimately to prevention and healthy public policy. This agenda has been highly popular with Canadian health policy analysts, and it is increasingly being echoed by Canadian health planners (including a recent flurry of government task force reports in many Canadian provinces).

Challenges from the Right

Health policy does not exist in a vacuum. Although to a lesser extent in Canada than elsewhere, health policy has been affected by a challenge to the role of the state and the limits of its responsibilities. These attacks have several roots. The demands on democratic governments are seen to have grown beyond governments' capacity (either fiscal or administrative) to handle them (Brown 1983). Analysts speak of "the fiscal crisis of the state," or "overload."

The reform agenda from the Right thus suggested a dual attack on publicly financed health systems. From a budgetary perspective health care was an exceedingly costly spending program and continued to grow at faster rates than inflation. Some budgetary limit seemed inevitable. But, if health care was being underfunded, a natural policy alternative from this viewpoint would be greater reliance on private funds. After all, the state did not provide everyone with a Cadillac to drive or a mansion to live in or a lobster for dinner—why should health care be any different? This policy proposal was often referred to by providers as "patient participation"; it presupposed rejection of the fourth level of justification for state involvement (i.e., health care as a human right) and also, to some proponents, rejection that health care should be based on need as opposed to demand.

A second line of argument focused on the debilitating impact of the welfare state on individual initiative and suggested a drastically reduced role for public provision of services. This line of argument has been greatly strengthened by the collapse of Socialist regimes in Eastern Europe under the weight of their own economic inefficiency. The presumably adverse consequences to Western economies of a large public sector would provide further impetus to a diminished state role.

In addition, to the extent that providers of health care were seen as independent entrepreneurs, there would be opposition to the regulation of their activities, which could be described as "reducing them to civil servants." What would be the implications for the quality of the doctor-patient relationship and the quality of care in a state-run, bureaucratic system? Could patients be assured that their doctor was working in their own best interests rather than trying to cut costs, even at the expense of optimal care? Was not the solution giving a greater role to the private sector?

This line of argument to date has received little attention (and even less support) in Canada. It has been far more powerful in the United Kingdom (where Thatcher stressed her opposition to the "nanny state") and also strikes a welcome note to many in the United States.

The Debate over Direct Charges

Because most Canadians accepted the concept that those who needed care should receive it without financial barriers, the debate over whether patients should have to pay directly for their care, which culminated in the Canada

Health Act, was thus more heavily influenced by research evidence than is usually the case. Considerable attention was paid to a natural experiment studied by Beck and Horne—Saskatchewan's experiment with a modest copayment for hospital care—which found no effect on overall utilization but reduced use (of both necessary and unnecessary services) by low-income patients and increased use (because of decreased waiting times) by the more affluent. This and similar results were summarized in an influential study coauthored by three of Canada's leading health economists (Barer, Evans, and Stoddart 1979). Its title, "Controlling Health Care Costs by Direct Charges to Patients: Snare or Delusion?" reflected its forceful rebuttal of the case for user charges. In contrast, the U.S. RAND Corporation experiment of copayments was interpreted as advocating such charges (Manning et al. 1987). A striking example of Canadian-U.S. differences can be seen in the research questions addressed by the two sets of authors—the RAND sample excluded the elderly (defined as those over age sixty-two) and all with family incomes over $58,000 in 1984 dollars; this study therefore could not examine effects on overall utilization. In addition, the RAND papers initially examined only the reduced use effect; they took several years to focus on the possible adverse effects on low-income users with medically treatable conditions (e.g., their estimates eventually suggested that the adults with low incomes in the cost-sharing groups had a 10 percent excess mortality from hypertension compared to the free service group).

Few Canadian physicians viewed health care provision as being based on demand rather than need. Their arguments for direct charges were therefore based largely on presuming that government involvement in health care should remain on the third level—as charity for the poor. They therefore advocated a two-tiered, mixed system rather than a universal program; accepted a major role for government in meeting costs that patients would not otherwise be able to afford; and restricted their argument to insisting that the government program was not designed to cover the cost of all services. They saw direct charges as a mechanism for increasing the overall level of resources available to the health care sector and for bypassing macro resource allocation decisions that the government might try to make. Occasionally, they spoke of promoting "economic and fiscal responsibility"; more often, they spoke of "underfunding" and how that could be remedied by increased "patient participation."

In addition, physicians showed an ideological resistance to the transformation of the doctor-patient relationship that third-party payment had catalyzed (Starr 1982; Tuohy, in Evans and Stoddart 1986). They saw retaining direct links between doctors and patients as one method of avoiding "proletarianization," or "bureaucratization"; the ever-present fear was of physicians "becoming civil servants" in a take-it-or-leave-it situation with a monopolistic payer. They also spoke of extra billing as a "barometer of physician discontent" or a "safety valve for physicians who feel alienated and undercompensated." The alternatives—collective withdrawal of services or binding arbitration—were seen as indications that medicine had now moved from a profession to a trade union and were resisted on those grounds. Physicians referred to themselves as self-employed professionals with a "right" to establish a value for their services.

Preserving Canadian Medicare

As noted, health care, as a key component of the welfare state, could have been expected to share in the attacks from the Right. What has preserved it in Canada, to a large extent, is precisely what has made it so expensive: As a universal entitlement program, much of its service went to the middle class. Not all members of the middle class expected that they might become single parents or might need to frequent a food bank, but all suspected that they might someday become sick. Just as Social Security became a political untouchable in the United States, so did health insurance north of the border. Like aging, illness could affect anyone.

Despite the theorists, most of the public continued to equate health and medicine. National health insurance was probably the most popular government program, and politicians would tamper with it at their peril (Blendon and Taylor 1989).

Second, as Evans (1982, 1984) had pointed out, health care costs were also health care incomes, and the recipients of such incomes were vehement in their defense. The political implications could be severe. Closing a small hospital might improve patient care by making sure that procedures were done only at adequately equipped facilities (Maerki, Luft, and Hunt 1986), but it could also mean a loss of status and employment for the town in which the hospital was situated. Taking away existing benefits was far more difficult than not extending them in the first place. Accordingly, cost control as carried out in most Canadian provinces generally meant tough scrutiny over new initiatives, even those promising considerable benefit, and a hands-off approach to existing programs (Deber and Vayda 1985).

Third, a concentration on health promotion could look uncomfortably like a way to get government off the hook while blaming the victims for their own illnesses (Pederson et al. 1988).

But these academic questions have become more pressing as trends are being extrapolated. The elderly consume a much larger share of health resources per capita than do the young, and the proportion of the elderly in the population is growing. New technology makes it possible for clinicians to do more for patients, at an often vastly increased cost. Artificial organs, transplantation, and an array of medical spectaculars have attracted media attention in Canada and the United States and evoked the age-old question, "who is going to pay for this?" After all, inexpensive insurance is based on the idea that only a small proportion of beneficiaries will ever need to collect; what happens once almost everyone can expect to receive such expensive care?

In a market situation the answer to that question is simple. If an individual values a particular service enough to pay for it, he or she should receive it. Supply and demand would act to balance medical costs and benefits in the same way they operated in other sectors of the economy. A key premise of many who examine health policy, however, has been that health is somehow different—that medical services should be allocated on the basis of need rather than willingness to pay. Part of the acceptance of such paternalism in the medical market was the great asymmetry between the information possessed by the patient and by the provider. When the provider is also the expert advisor, the prospect for conflict of interest is evident; it is constrained only by concepts of "professionalism" (see Friedson 1986). Skeptics have doubted whether professional scruples could overcome financial incentives. An extreme denunciation of doctors and fee-for-service medicine was penned by George Bernard Shaw in the preface to *The Doctor's Dilemma*:

> That any sane nation, having observed that you could provide for the supply of bread by giving bakers a pecuniary interest in baking for you, should go on to give a surgeon a pecuniary interest in cutting off your leg, is enough to make one despair of political humanity. But that is precisely what we have done. And the more appalling the mutilation, the more the mutilator is paid. (1930, 3)

This distrust of market mechanisms thus works both ways: We do not want necessary treatment to be withheld, but we also do not wish unnecessary treatment to be provided. We do not get upset if an individual buys an unnecessary pair of shoes. But we tend to believe that a patient should not receive unnecessary treatment, even if he or she can afford it, and, as a corollary, that patients should receive necessary treatment even if they cannot pay the bill. As discussed, this role of guaranteeing that all who need care can get it, initially played by charities and the church, has in many countries been taken over by government. But, once it is agreed that all bills for needed services will be paid, and that the providers are the best judge of what is needed, then market controls over costs cannot exist and must be replaced by some form of regulation. To be argumentative, it could be said that the United States, almost alone among developed nations, has agreed to retain the market and sacrifice the concept that those needing health care will get it. Other nations, including Canada, have been willing to sacrifice the market and thus have had to discover alternative mechanisms for controlling resource allocations. Indeed, this is one of the dilemmas that almost all health care systems have had to face—how best to balance the desirable (but probably mutually exclusive) goals of high quality, high accessibility, and low costs.

Canadian policymakers have largely agreed that taking the government out of health care and relying on some kind of market solution is a poor policy option on two counts: It is not only politically unacceptable but it would also be even less efficient than current practice. A market situation with any aid for the poor would probably guarantee that the provision of health services would consume even more of the national product, although this money might not necessarily pass through the government. Internationally, mixed public/private systems have been both more costly and less efficient than purely public alternatives (McLachlan and Maynard 1982). In the United States government programs cover a portion of health costs for the elderly and the poor, an array of private insurers cover the middle class, and more than thirty million people have no health insurance at all (with many others underinsured). Despite these large coverage gaps, the United States spends the world's highest proportion of GNP for health care. A large proportion of this spending appears to go for shuffling paper, with little payoff in health outcomes; some observers have suggested that over 20 percent of total U.S. health expenditures are devoted to administration, marketing, advertising, and promotion (Ginzberg 1989; Himmelstein and Woolhandler 1986).

For government, however, mixed systems have the advantage that the increased costs are scattered across the population and hence make a less visible target for cost controllers. For providers the fact that mixed systems are more costly can be seen as a key advantage; those costs represent an increase in the resources available to them. For the population, however, the additional money spent does not translate into gains in health status, which one might naively expect to be the point of the whole enterprise. In the United States commitment to a free market ideology has been sufficient so that the drawbacks—worse health outcomes at a vastly inflated price—have been deemed acceptable. Canada, like most other nations, disagrees.

The acceptance of universal coverage, however, leaves little room for practice outside the universal system. If all patients participate in the plan, so must all providers. Where, indeed, would there be an incentive for a private segment operating outside the insurance system and requiring additional payment from patients? If the private plans offered services unavailable (or inconvenient) under the public plan, we have returned to two-tiered medicine. If not, why would a patient pay extra if equivalent services were available free of charge? And, if patients had no need to use out-of-plan services, how could any doctor make a living unless he or she practiced inside the universal insurance plan? Universal coverage has thus led to dilemmas around the definition of what services should be insured (since they must be provided either to everyone or to no one), and around how providers should be fairly remunerated (since, with a single payer, any offer would usually be on a take-it-or-leave-it basis if government chose to exercise its power).

Conclusion

The success of Canadian Medicare has led to a recognition of the limits of medical care in improving health. In consequence, Canadian health policy has seen a gradual shift from what we have termed the old agenda of accessibility and universality—which asked such questions as: What services are available? Where? At what cost to the patient?—to a new agenda.

The new agenda has had a different focus—on efficiency, outcome, and the appropriate role for government. From the narrow focus of health policy it asks such questions as: Who will deliver the services? How will they be organized? Which services should be provided, and which need not be? How, and how much, will providers be paid? From a wider social policy framework it asks: What is the role of government? What can government afford to pay for? Where do the responsibilities of an individual stop? Indeed, to what extent am I my neighbor's keeper?

Shifting agendas is not always a simple task. Canada's health care system has shown the limits of medical care and evoked a new set of questions. The public, however, remains attached to the old access agenda. The United States, in contrast, has not yet reached that point; much argument is still focused on how care can be provided for those with poor (or no) access to it. We have argued that much of the debate reflects a different philosophical justification for state involvement in health care, with the United States viewing it as charity and Canada as a right of citizenship. We have also noted that a market orientation is difficult to reconcile with the belief that health care should be provided on the basis of medical need rather than willingness (or ability) to pay.

Although medical care is not sufficient for health, it is often necessary. U.S. health policy, at some point, will have to deal with issues such as need versus demand and the relative balance of the marketplace and charity toward one's neighbor. Canada, in turn, will be forced to test the limits of "rights" under economic stress.

BIBLIOGRAPHY

Barer, M. L., R. G. Evans, and G. L. Stoddart. *Controlling Health Care Costs by Direct Charges to Patients: Snare or Delusion?* Ontario Economic Council Occasional Paper no. 10. Toronto: Ontario Economic Council, 1979.

Blendon, R. J., and H. Taylor. "Views on Health Care: Public Opinion in Three Nations." *Health Affairs* 8 (1989): 150–57.

Brown, L. D. *New Policies, New Politics: Government's Response to Government's Growth.* Washington, D.C.: Brookings Institution, 1983.

Deber, R. B., and E. Vayda. "The Environment of Health Policy Implementation: The Ontario, Canada, Example," in George Knox, ed., *Investigative Methods in Public Health,* Vol. 3 of *Oxford Textbook of Public Health.* Oxford: Oxford University Press, 1985.

Deber, R. B., G. G. Thompson, and P. Leatt. "Technology Acquisition in Canada: Control in a Regulated Market." *International Journal of Technology Assessment in Health Care* 4, no. 2 (1988): 185–206.

Eisenberg, J. M. *Doctors' Decisions and the Cost of Medical Care.* Ann Arbor, Mich.: Health Administration Press Perspectives, 1986.

Evans, R. G. "A Retrospective on the 'New Perspective.'" *Journal of Health Politics, Policy, and Law* 7, no. 2 (1982): 325–44.

———. *Strained Mercy: The Economics of Canadian Health Care.* Toronto: Butterworths, 1984.

Evans, R. G., and G. L. Stoddart, eds. *Medicare at Maturity.* Calgary: University of Calgary Press, 1986.

Fein, R. *Medical Care, Medical Costs: The Search for a Health Insurance Policy.* Cambridge: Harvard University Press, 1986.

Fried, B. J., R. B. Deber, and P. Leatt. "Corporatization and Deprivatization of Health Services in Canada." *International Journal of Health Services* 17 (1987): 567–84.

Friedson, E. *Professional Powers: A Study of the Institutionalization of Formal Knowledge.* Chicago: University of Chicago Press, 1986.

Fuchs, V. R. *Who Shall Live? Health Economics and Social Change.* New York: Basic Books, 1974.

Ginzberg, E. "Harder than It Looks." *Health Management Quarterly* 11, no. 4 (1989): 19–21.

Hastings, J. E. F., chairman. *The Community Health Center in Canada.* 3 vols., Ottawa: Information Canada, 1972 and 1973.

Heiber, S., and R. B. Deber. "Banning Extra Billing in Canada: Just What the Doctor Didn't Order." *Canadian Public Policy* 13 (1987): 62–74.

Himmelstein, D. U., and S. Woolhandler. "Cost without Benefit: Administrative Waste in U.S. Health Care." *NEJM* 314, no. 7 (1986): 441–45.

Iglehart, J. K. "The United States Looks at Canadian Health Care." *NEJM* 321, no. 25 (1989): 1767–72.

———. "Canada's Health Care System Faces Its Problems." *NEJM* 322, no. 8 (1990): 562–68.

Lalonde, M. *A New Perspective on the Health of Canadians.* Ottawa: Information Canada, 1974.

Lalonde, M., and R. B. Deber. *Managed Care in Canada: The Toronto Hospital's Proposed Comprehensive Health Organization.* Toronto: Canadian Hospital Association Press, 1991.

Linton, A. L. "The Canadian Health Care System: A Canadian Physician's Perspective." *NEJM* 322, no. 8 (1990): 197–99.

McKeown, T. *The Role of Medicine: Dream, Mirage, or Nemesis?* Oxford: Basil Blackwell, 1979.

McLachlan, G., and A. Maynard. *The Public/Private Mix for Health: The Relevance and Effects of Change.* London: Nuffield Provincial Hospitals Trust, 1982.

Maerki, S. C., H. S. Luft, and S. S. Hunt. "Selecting Categories of Patients for Regionalization: Implications of the Relationship between Volume and Outcome." *Medical Care* 24, no. 2 (1986): 148–58.

Manning, W. G., et al. "Health Insurance and the Demand for Medical Care: Evidence from a Randomized Experiment." *American Economic Review* 77, no. 3 (1987): 251–77.

Marx, K. "Critique of the Gotha Programme." In R. C. Tucker, ed., *The Marx-Engels Reader.* New York: W. W. Norton, 1972.

Mechanic, D. "The Growth of Medical Technology and Bureaucracy: Implications for Medical Care." In *Painful Choices: Research and Essays on Health Care.* New Brunswick and Oxford: Transaction Publishers, 1989.

Olson, M. *The Logic of Collective Action.* Cambridge: Harvard University Press, 1965.

Pederson, A. P., et al. *Coordinating Healthy Public Policy: An Analytic Literature Review and Bibliography.* Branch Working Paper HSPB 88-1. Ottawa: National Health and Welfare Canada, Health Services and Promotion, 1988.

Rachlis, M., and C. Kushner. *Second Opinion: What's Wrong with Canada's Health Care System and How to Fix It.* Toronto: Harper and Collins, 1989.

Russell, L. B. *Is Prevention Better than Cure?* Studies in Social Economics. Washington, D.C.: Brookings Institution, 1986.

Schieber, G. J., and J. P. Poullier. "Overview of International Comparisons of Health Care Expenditures." In *Health Care Systems in Transition: The Search for Efficiency.* OECD Social Policy Studies no. 7 (Paris, 1990), 9–16.

Schwartz, H. "The Infirmity of British Medicine." In R. Emmett Tyrrell, Jr., ed., *The Future That Doesn't Work: Social Democracy's Failures in Britain.* Garden City, N.Y.: Doubleday, 1977.

Shaw, G. B. *The Doctor's Dilemma, A Tragedy.* In *The Works of Bernard Shaw*, vol. 12. London: Constable, 1930.

Spitzer, W. O. "The Nurse Practitioner Revisited: Slow Death of a Good Idea." *NEJM* 310, no. 16 (1984): 1049–51.

Starr, P. *The Social Transformation of American Medicine.* New York: Basic Books, 1982.

Swartz, D. "The Politics of Reform: Conflict and Accommodation in Canadian Health Policy." In *Health and Canadian Society: Sociological Perspectives*, 2d ed., 568–89. Markham, Ont.: Fitzhenry and Whiteside, 1987.

Taylor, M. G. *Health Insurance and Canadian Public Policy: The Seven Decisions that Created the Canadian Health Insurance System and Their Outcomes.* Kingston, Ont.: McGill-Queen's University Press, 1987 (abridged and revised as *Insuring National Health Care: The Canadian Experience* [Chapel Hill: University of North Carolina Press, 1990]).

Townsend, P., and N. Davidson. *Inequalities in Health: The Black Report*. Harmondsworth, Middlesex: Penguin Books, 1982.

Vayda, E., and W. R. Mindell. "Variations in Operative Rates: What Do They Mean?" *Surgical Clinics of North America* 62, no. 4 (1982): 627–39.

Wennberg, J. E., J. L. Freeman, and W. J. Culp. "Are Hospital Services Rational in New Haven or Over-Utilized in Boston?" *Lancet* (May 23, 1987): 1185–89.

Wildavsky, A. "Doing Better and Feeling Worse: The Political Pathology of Health Policy." In A. Wildavsky, ed., *Speaking Truth to Power: The Art and Craft of Policy Analysis,* 284–308. Boston: Little, Brown, 1979.

Wilkins, R., and O. Adams. *Healthfulness of Life*. Montreal: Institute for Research on Public Policy, 1983.

CHAPTER 3

Canada's Health Insurance and Ours: The Real Lessons, the Big Choices

Theodore R. Marmor and Jerry L. Mashaw

As medical costs continue to escalate and more Americans find themselves without insurance, Canada's approach to financing health care has taken center stage in the debate in the United States. Congressional committees have invited Canadian experts to testify, and political organizations have sent parades of representatives on crash study tours to Canada. Leaders of the Chrysler Corporation—particularly its flamboyant chairman, Lee Iacocca, and Joseph A. Califano, Jr., a board member and former secretary of Health and Human Services—have lauded Canada's success. All three major television networks, National Public Radio, the major national newspapers, and *Consumer Reports* have recently done stories on Canadian national health insurance. But the best evidence of the seriousness with which Americans are taking the Canadian model is a concerted attack against it, being financed, until a few months ago, by the American Medical Association (AMA).

In 1989, under the innocent title "Public Alert Program," the AMA committed $2.5 million to "telling millions of Americans the facts about the Canadian health care system." In a campaign reminiscent of its 1948 attack on President Truman's national health insurance plan, the doctors' association placed advertisements in major media and supplied press kits for a blitz of editorials, opinion pieces, and reports about Canada. Similar essays began appearing in national and local papers by people identified as, for example, "a surgeon from White Plains."

The AMA quietly canceled the effort after a financial scandal forced the head of the campaign to resign and early reports indicated that the advertisements were irritating audiences, including Canadian physicians. The message, however, has already had an effect. Millions of people have heard that Canadian health care doesn't work well and that, even if it did, it couldn't work in the United States.

The first part of the message is plainly false. Canada's national health system has managed to insure all citizens for a comprehensive range of medical and hospital services, all the while containing medical costs. Contrary to reports, serious limitations on medically necessary services are not common. Moreover, the system is vastly more popular among Canadians than America's health system is among its citizens. Universal access, controlled costs, good care, a satisfied public—when taken together, no fair-minded American can help but be impressed, particularly because so many experts have been telling us that we could not possibly achieve all these goals together.

The second prong of the AMA attack is more serious. Major social programs can seldom be bought off the rack from abroad. Can we really learn how to solve our medical care problems by studying Canada?

Canada is not the only country that has provided universal health care at a lower proportionate cost than the United States spends for more restricted coverage. France and the former West Germany have universal health insurance at a cost of between 8 and 9.5 percent of gross national product (GNP). Britain, Japan, and Australia provide it for between 6 and 8 percent of GNP. The United States, by comparison, spends 11.5 percent of GNP on health—more than any other nation—yet ranks below all of the advanced nations except Spain on measures of infant mortality and life expectancy. For all the money spent, we have approximately thirty-five million people totally without health insurance and other undetermined millions whose health insurance is inadequate. Surely we are doing something wrong.

When other countries are doing things we would like to do, it makes good sense to set aside national pride and learn from abroad. But we need to be careful in drawing lessons, particularly because the pressure groups in the United States with the largest stake in the status quo have powerful incentives to distort other nations' experiences and slant information to their own purposes. With admirable frankness, Carl Schramm, president of the Health Insurance Association of America (HIAA), the trade association for private health insurance companies, told *Consumer Reports* that, under a Canadian approach to health care financing "we'd be out of business. It's a life-and-death struggle." Conceding it cannot make a credible case that Canadian health insurance is a failure, HIAA claims instead that American politics would never permit us to enact and carry out a Canadian-style program. Of course, the insurance industry would do its best to make sure that was true.

But if ever there were an opportunity for cross-national learning by American policymakers, it is Canada's path to national health insurance (NHI). We share with Canadians a diverse population with a similar distribution of living standards, increasingly integrated economies, and a tradition of fractious, constitutional federalism. Until Canada consolidated its national insurance in 1971, our patterns and styles of medical care closely resembled each other. Canadian regulators even used our Joint Commission on Hospital Accreditation to judge their own hospitals until well after World War II. If public financing of medical care has come to work well in Canada, it is reasonable to think it would work well in the United States, too.

In fact, Canada's health system raises three separable issues for the United States. The first is whether Canada really has an exemplary medical care system, well worth importing if only we could. A second question is whether Canada's program, no matter how desirable, is politically feasible in the United States. Are the two nations just too different? Is it too late to do what the Canadians did more than twenty years ago? And, third, even if the Canadian model is desirable and politically acceptable, can the United States successfully adapt it to American circumstances?

Canada's Exemplary Performance

Health insurance in Canada is actually provided not by the national government but by Canada's ten provinces. The Canadian federal government conditionally promises to repay each province a substantial portion of the costs of all necessary medical care, now roughly 40 percent. The federal grant is available as long as the province's health insurance program is *universal* (covering all citizens), *comprehensive* (covering all conventional hospital and medical care), *accessible* (no limits on services or extra charges to patients), *portable* (each province must recognize the others' coverage), and *publicly administered* (under control of a public, nonprofit organization).

Annual negotiations between provincial governments and the providers of care determine the total budgets of hospitals and the level of physicians' fees. As in the United States, most hospitals are nonprofit community institutions. Unlike U.S. hospitals, however, they never worry about itemized billings. Instead, they receive their annual budget in monthly installments. Their budgets are adjusted each year, taking into account inflation, new programs, and changes in their volume of services.

As in the United States, physicians practice in diverse individual and group settings, and most are paid on a fee-for-service basis rather than by salary. The provincial medical associations determine the structure of a binding fee schedule and negotiate with their governments, usually on an annual basis, a percentage increase in the total pool of money budgeted for paying physicians. In most provinces, if the fees billed to the provincial insurance fund exceed the budget ceiling, the government grants less than it otherwise would at the next round of negotiations. Escalating physician costs—largely because of increases in procedures per patient—have led most Canadian provinces to explore more explicit limits on total payments to physicians. Quebec and British Columbia have already set global budget caps—which, if exceeded, result in reduced physician fees—and other provinces, despite predictable physician outrage, are likely to follow suit.

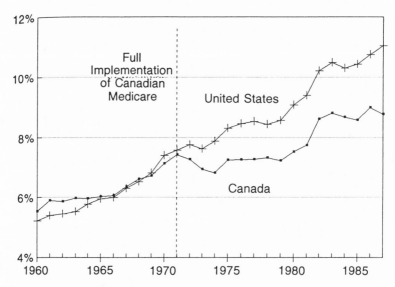

Fig. 1. Total health expenditures, Canada and the United States, 1960–87 (percentage of GNP). (Source: For the United States, Division of National Cost Estimates, Health Care Financing Administration, "National Health Expenditures, 1986–2000." *Health Care Financing Review* **8 [1987]: 1–35, and** *Statistical Abstract of the United States,* **yearly. For Canada, Health and Welfare Canada, "National Health Expenditures in Canada, 1975–1987" [Ottawa, Ont.: Health and Welfare Canada, 1987] and Canada, Department of Finance, "Economic Review," April 1985.)**

As figure 1 shows, the growth patterns of Canadian and American health care expenditures were nearly identical until 1971, when Canada fully implemented its national insurance plan. From then on, American health expenditures have continued to rise at a considerably faster rate than in Canada (or, for that matter, any other developed democracy). The gap now amounts to nearly three percentage points of GNP. It appears that America's higher payments to doctors, increased administrative expenses, and larger hospital outlays account for about equal shares of this large difference in spending. Few Americans would regard Canada's lower physician payments as harmful; fewer still would regret cutting administrative costs. Some, however, might wonder whether the Canadians spend too little on hospital care while we spend too much. Hospital technology is where the biggest questions about the Canadian system arise. Nonetheless, compared with other countries in the world, the oddity is America's lavish spending on technology, not Canada's more limited expenditures.

Cost control is not the only test of a good health care system. Neither is universal access. A good system should provide high-quality care, timely treatment, good working conditions for health care professionals and other workers, and ultimately a satisfied and healthy citizenry. On these questions, it is time to separate myth from fact.

Myth 1: NHI leads to bureaucratic red tape and high administrative costs. Doctors and hospitals in Canada receive all their payments from one source, a provincial ministry. They do not have to keep track of the eligibility requirements or complicated definitions of insured services in hundreds of insurance plans. Canadian patients never have to file claims, much less deal with incomprehensible forms. Americans, by contrast, have to file multiple, complicated claims, as do most physicians. One reason both patients and doctors in the United States fear any further government role in health insurance is their frustrating experience with the existing publicly funded programs Medicare and Medicaid. A federal agency recently estimated that about one million Medicare enrollees a year find filing claims so complicated or time consuming that they do not seek reimbursement, losing about $100 million in benefits to which they are entitled. In some states many physicians say they will not treat Medicaid patients or do not bother to seek reimbursement for treating them, because the meager payments do not even cover the administrative overhead. American providers typically wait 60 to 120 days and often longer for reimbursement from public programs. Canadian providers, in contrast, receive payment in about 30 days.

Because of the simplicity of the Canadian system, administrative costs are negligible by American standards. Moreover, the gap between U.S. and Canadian administrative costs has been widening steadily since Canada completed its program. (See fig. 2.) This six-to-one ratio clearly understates the real difference in cost. It does not count the paper-shuffling burden borne by American patients. Nor does it include the large proportion of recorded payments to doctors and hospitals that are really administrative overhead required by our complex financing arrangements. "An increasing share of the sums Americans *think* they are spending on hospital and medical care," the Canadian economist Robert Evans notes, "are going in fact to pay for administrators, accountants, lawyers, public relations specialists, and other forms of personnel whose services are not usually considered as contributing to the health of patients."

Myth 2: NHI interferes with the doctor-patient relationship. One advertisement in the AMA series asks, "Elective surgery—should it be up to you?" The ad implies that Canada reduces the ordinary citizen's freedom of choice in medical care. It is a thinly veiled message to those Americans with either broad insurance coverage or ample funds to buy whatever care they desire. Seeking allies, the AMA represents Canadian-style reform as a threat to America's affluent and insured.

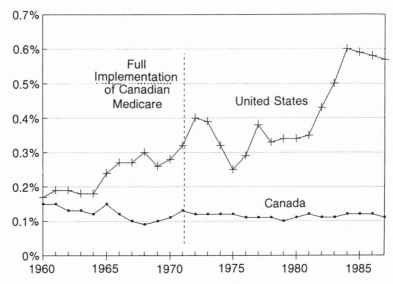

Fig. 2. Cost of health insurance administration, Canada and the United States, 1960–87 (percentage of GNP). (Source: For the United States, Division of National Cost Estimates, Health Care Financing Administration. "National Health Expenditures, 1986–2000." *Health Care Financing Review* 8 [1987]: 1–35, and *Statistical Abstract of the United States,* yearly. For Canada, Health and Welfare Canada, "National Health Expenditures in Canada, 1975–1987" [Ottawa, Ont.: Health and Welfare Canada, 1987] and Canada, Department of Finance, "Economic Review," April 1985.)

That same message, of course, will hold little appeal to the millions of Americans without the money or coverage to get elective surgery. Nor is it likely to appeal to Americans whose choice of doctor is limited by their health maintenance organization (HMO) or by lower reimbursement for visits to out-of-plan doctors (under so-called preferred provider organizations, or PPOs). An increasing number of companies are trimming their health care costs by adopting these alternatives. Under the rubric of "managed care," many such plans limit elective surgery, require second opinions, or require approval by an insurance company administrator.

In Canada, by contrast, citizens have no restrictions on their choice of physicians, and their physicians do not have to obtain approval from administrators for treatment they recommend. If freedom of choice is the deciding criterion for many people, it actually works in favor of the Canadian model, not the forms of health care that are now growing most rapidly under the aegis of market-oriented reform in the United States.

Myth 3: NHI leads to long queues for treatment. Another ad in the AMA series pictures a worried woman and warns, "In some countries she could wait months for her surgery." Every country, including the United States, has waiting lists for elective procedures and sometimes even essential ones. The important question is the impact on the patients' well-being. Americans being treated in hospital emergency rooms, particularly in big cities, often wait for hours for critical care. Private hospitals routinely turn away uninsured patients, dumping them on the public sector. These "economic transfers," estimated at 250,000 annually in the United States, often result in serious delays in treatment, cause long-term harm, and have cost some patients their lives, though federal law now requires hospitals to guarantee that patients are in stable condition before transfer.

When most Canadians are sick or injured, they are cared for in a timely manner. Indeed, the overall rates of hospital use per capita are considerably higher in Canada than in the United States. Nonetheless, there have developed long waiting lists for some services, particularly for open-heart surgery and magnetic resonance imaging, the newest radiological procedure for diagnosis. These delays typically reflect managerial problems and labor bottlenecks more than chronic shortages of facilities. If they involve patients in urgent, life-threatening condition, there is political outrage. Open-heart surgery is currently the most controversial example. Government officials in British Columbia watched their waiting list for cardiac surgery grow to more than five hundred during 1990 and, in response, purchased surgery from Seattle hospitals with excess beds and heart surgeons. This incident is the sort that opponents of the Canadian system cite as illustrating its failure. But such cases reveal as much about American slack as Canadian restrictiveness—and they bring us to the next myth.

Myth 4: National health insurance lowers the quality of medical care. As table 1 shows, some expensive, high-technology items are less available in Canada than in the United States. It is unclear, however, whether the rates of

TABLE 1. Comparative Availability of Selected Medical Technologies (units per million persons)

	United States	Canada	Ratio of U.S. to Canada
Open-heart surgery	3.26	1.23	2.7:1
Cardiac catheterization	5.06	1.50	3.4:1
Organ transplantation	1.31	1.08	1.2:1
Radiation therapy	3.97	0.54	7.4:1
Extracorporeal shock wave lithotripsy	0.94	0.16[a]	5.9:1
Magnetic resonance imaging	3.69	0.46[a]	8.0:1

Source: D. A. Rublee, "Medical Technology in Canada, Germany, and the U.S." *Health Affairs* (Fall 1989), 180.

Note: U.S. data from 1987, Canada for 1989 except where indicated.

[a] 1988.

investment in such technologies in the United States represent a standard for judging other countries. Many analysts believe the United States has overinvested in and overused some technologies. Hospitals competing for market share have installed equipment that stands idle much of the time or, even worse, is being used without good medical justification to generate reimbursement from insured patients. The fundamental patterns of investment in the United States have been distorted by differences in insurance coverage. There is no incentive to invest in preventive care if the health benefits are high but reimbursement is uncertain. There is every incentive to invest in high technology if health benefits are uncertain but reimbursement is assured.

Canada has a full range of high-technology facilities, but there is considerably less abundance and little competition for market share. Expensive capital equipment is first approved only for specialized medical centers, and subsequent diffusion is closely controlled by provincial ministries of health. This control results in lower rates of cardiac surgery, magnetic resonance imaging, lithotripsy, and some other complex services. In some cases, these lower rates are probably appropriate: The additional use in the United States reflects incentives for overtreatment. In other cases, Canadians are not receiving services that would have some health benefit at a high cost (instead, choosing to provide other forms of care and reserving more national income for other purposes). Of course, no nation can provide every service that would conceivably give someone benefit. The question is whether the Canadians are making a reasonable choice and providing medical care of high quality.

The quality of a nation's health care is never simple to measure. The United States certainly offers medical care of higher quality than does Canada if quality is defined as easier access to complex technologies regardless of their effectiveness. And American medical care may be the best in the world if quality is defined by the technologies and facilities available to the most privileged members of a population. But, if we define quality by some measure that reflects both the effectiveness of treatment and the respect and consideration shown to patients—all patients, not just the affluent and insured—America ranks lower than other countries in the West, including Canada, that have national health insurance.

There is certainly no evidence of any Canadian disadvantage if our standard is the actual health of the public, though medical care is only one of the many factors affecting health and by no means the most important. (Canada actually has a clear advantage in life expectancy and infant mortality but probably for reasons unrelated to its system of health care finance.) And, if consumer satisfaction is our basis for judgment, both polls and political behavior give a big edge to Canada.

According to a ten-nation survey published in *Health Affairs,* Canadians are the most satisfied and Americans the least satisfied with their country's health care system. While only 10 percent of Americans surveyed say their health system functions "pretty well," 56 percent of Canadians thought their health care system works well. Eighty-nine percent of Americans say their system needs "fundamental changes" or "complete rebuilding."

The higher levels of satisfaction in Canada suggest the importance of the distributive dimension of health care quality. Major aspects of American medical care—the widespread inability to obtain health insurance, the limited extent of immunization, the large number of pregnant women without regular medical attention, and the risk of bankruptcy from illness—would be considered intolerable in other comparably wealthy nations. Canada has fewer centers of technological excellence, but the average level of care is, by any definition, at least the equal of that in the United States.

Myth 5: NHI leads to rationing. Critics warn that Canada "rations" medical care. If, by rationing, they simply mean limiting services, every country in the world rations health care. The question is how and how much. The United States limits services by ability to pay and, accordingly, shows significant differences in access to health care by race, class, and employment circumstances. By contrast, Canada and most other developed countries attempt to provide more uniform access to the entire population. Medical care then depends more on a professional assessment of medical need than on insurance status.

Rationing, in this context, is another name for allocation. Whether it is objectionable depends also on the extent of free choice and the distribution of control. Americans in HMOs and other systems of "managed care" face systems of corporate rationing; the rules for rationing are matters of business strategy. To be sure, some employees in the United States are offered a choice among such plans, but they are hardly in a position to know much about how the HMOs control their spending. They have no way of knowing, for example, whether an HMO might deny them referral to a specialist in the event of a rare disease or difficult procedure. Because Canadians have free choice of physician, they do not have to worry about that kind of rationing. And, while the rationing choices of an American HMO are private, Canada's choices about spending on hospitals and other health services are publicly debated and democratically decided. If Canadians come to feel that they should spend more on high-technology services, their system allows them to do so more efficiently and equitably than does ours.

Myth 6: NHI causes an exodus of physicians. Some Canadian physicians were coming to the United States long before Canada introduced national health insurance. Emigration did not increase significantly afterward. The numbers of emigrants to the United States has always been small, never enough to offset a steady increase in the number of Canadian physicians. The ratio of physicians to population has steadily increased in Canada and has actually grown closer to the U.S. level. In 1987 the United States had 234 doctors per 100,000 people, while Canada had 216.

Stories about deep discontent among Canadian physicians are much exaggerated. Physicians were the highest-paid professionals in Canada prior to the introduction of universal medical insurance; they still are. When national health insurance began, the provincial governments accepted the existing fee schedules of provincial medical associations, although in most provinces payments were initially set somewhat below 100 percent to reflect the elimination of doctors' risks of unpaid debts. Since that time, provincial medical associations and ministries of health have negotiated changes. Because much of the bargaining for resources and control gets carried out in the public arena, these negotiations are contentious. Provincial ministers of finance typically forecast imminent bankruptcy; medical associations threaten dire service cutbacks if they don't get more money; and the media, always hungry for conflict, seize on the extremes of these positions. These controversies sell newspapers; they do not mean that the system is about to collapse.

Is It Politically Feasible Here?

Skeptics claim that the United States and Canada are too different to borrow from each other. Americans are allegedly too individualistic to accept a government program. Skeptics also argue that the United States, with its elaborate checks and balances, cannot adapt programs from a parliamentary system.

But the same arguments could as easily have been offered in 1935 against Social Security or at other times against other national programs. In fact, Canadian doctors remain in individual practice, and Canadians choose freely what practitioners to consult. It is unclear that America's current system represents any higher level of individualism.

Moreover, just as the Canadians have set up their program on a federal basis, so might we. The impediments to borrowing the Canadian model do not lie much in the structure of government. They lie in the power of the opposition. America's political leaders have traditionally allowed the providers and insurers of health care to control the substance of policy and boundaries of debate. Is it true, as Stanford economist Alain Enthoven argues, that borrowing from Canada is "off the radar screen of American possibility"? A good many people have an interest in maintaining that assumption and thereby contribute to keeping fundamental changes off the radar screen and off the agenda.

We are hardly sanguine that Canadian-style reform is likely in the near term. Nevertheless, the Canadian approach has growing support from unlikely quarters. Like Chrysler's Lee Iacocca, many large employers see themselves threatened in international and domestic markets by the high costs of insuring their employees. The small business community is pleading for government help because its health insurance costs are even more onerous. In 1989 the U.S. Chamber of Commerce, eschewing free market ideology and its usual preference for state and local authority, called for federal legislation guaranteeing small employers health insurance options at reasonable rates. Employers large and small see a clear likelihood that they will soon be required to pay for health insurance for both their own employees and others currently uninsured. All around the country, state governments are seeking the equivalent of universal health insurance.

The opposition of private insurance companies to health insurance reform is changing, too. Making money on health insurance is not easy these days. Relentless medical inflation, costly technology, a growing number of doctors, and an aging population have put the insurance industry repeatedly on the wrong side of the cost curve. More important, consumer hostility to insurers is fueling demands for legislative action. The insurers are seeking a solution that will bring insurance to the uninsured, make less visible the industry's practice of "skimming" (competing for the healthiest customers and ignoring or pricing out the less healthy), and yet leave the future administration of health insurance to them rather than to the state. They fear a political choice between a universal, mandated private insurance program, with substantial regulation of terms and rates, and a state-run insurance scheme that eliminates their role entirely.

Of course, no one should be misled about the recent, death-bed conversion of the health insurers to industry reform. They are as resistant as ever to a Canadian-style plan and have fully participated in the mythmaking about Canada's supposed unsuitability to American circumstances. After all, administrative costs to citizens and policyholders are income to the industry. But this truism should not obscure the defensiveness of the health insurers, their inclination to discuss reform, and the greater likelihood in the present climate that they might be forced to accept terms that publicly they say are unacceptable.

Finally, U.S. physicians are increasingly aware that they cannot avoid regulation. Their actions and decisions are already being scrutinized and limited by hospitals, insurance companies, and governmental agencies, all seeking to control costs. Looking at Canada's Medicare, they should be struck by the independence of Canadian physicians, the preservation of fee-for-service practice, and the reduction of bureaucracy, particularly as it affects physicians' everyday practice. If they can overcome their reflexive rejection of government, American physicians will find that a Canadian-style alternative has considerable advantages for their profession—and for their patients.

The obstacles to reform of American medical care, nonetheless, are enormous. Medical expenditures now divided among the government, employers, private insurance companies, and consumers would have to be converted or channeled into publicly controllable funds. American politicians would have to be willing to put aside their fixation with where costs are counted and deal with real issues of public economics—how much is spent overall, for what, and on whose behalf. The complaints of pro-market commentators would have to be answered, a task that is much harder now than during the fight over Medicare, because free-market ideology has gained influence in economics and policy analysis. Ideology would have to be countered with pragmatic argument, illusion with fact—and all this would have to be done by politicians who were elected by running against government.

Yet there are the makings of a political compromise here. The public wants broadened, simplified, and stable coverage at reasonable out-of-pocket cost. Firms want to reduce their costs of insuring employees and, at the very least, to avoid paying for the health insurance of the unemployed and uninsured. Insurers fear that they may be in a new ball game in which, at best, they will be the unwelcome administrators of so-called managed care and, at worst, they may be excluded from the market. Perhaps they could manage everyone's care on behalf of state insurance schemes. Or, at least, some insurers might play this reduced administrative role, as was the case in Ontario during the mid-1960s. In short, although movement toward something like Canadian national health insurance may appear ideologically a large step, most of the pieces needed for a state insurance program are already in place, and interest group politics might join with popular sentiment to permit such a move.

What would it take to make the Canadian model work in the United States? Part of the answer lies in distinguishing the necessary from the incidental elements of the Canadian success story. We see two essential elements.

Near universality of coverage: Canadians in each province are in the same boat, all insured on the "same terms and conditions." Universality has made it politically impossible to deal with cost pressures by cutting the benefits or eligibility of some people.

Clear concentration of responsibility: Canadians lodge financing responsibility in a ministry of health or its equivalent. Financing medical care under concentrated rather than fragmented auspices eliminates the administrative costs of multiple payers. Furthermore, it creates more leverage in bargaining with providers. Concentrating responsibility also means leaders cannot disguise costs by shifting them to other groups of patients. All this adds up to clear political accountability: Canadians know whom to hold accountable for the cost and quality of their health care.

What sorts of changes could be made in these elements without losing what has been necessary for Canada's relatively successful experience?

Modified Universalism

Canada's universalism is strong in two ways. Every Canadian belongs to the same provincial health insurance plan as his or her neighbor and enjoys the same coverage under the plan. Private insurers are legally forbidden to sell coverage duplicating publicly insured services, though they may provide supplementary coverage for such things as private rooms in hospitals or out patient prescription drugs.

To maintain the "equal terms" of access, Canadian doctors have been barred since 1984 from charging patients anything above the government's fee schedule (a practice known as "balance billing" or "extra billing"). In these respects, Canada is probably more egalitarian than any other comparable industrial democracy.

Perhaps not all of these features of Canadian universalism are necessary to an acceptable and workable form of health insurance. Canada itself did not start with such a firmly egalitarian version. The Hall Commission of 1964–66, a governmental commission that helped to lay the foundations of Canada's current program, defined universal as no less than 95 percent of the citizens within each province. The political force of universality arises not from complete inclusiveness but, rather, from the breadth of the constituency affected. (Our public water supply is closely monitored, even if a few people drink bottled water exclusively.)

There is consequently no reason for American reformers to insist on Canada's very strong contemporary form of universal enrollment. Universal health insurance means providing insurance to all, not necessarily requiring that everyone share exactly the same system. About a tenth of the former West German population opts for more expensive commercial insurance without impairing the rest of the system. There is a zone of adaptation and compromise between identical treatment and unacceptably different treatment. What is essential is that the health insurance boat include most Americans on roughly comparable terms, not that all the boat's cabins be the same size or have the same view.

U.S. public schools are a good analogy. Where state and local arrangements keep public schools strong, the competition of private alternatives does not undermine public support and school quality. But the balance is delicate and easily upset. We cannot force Americans to use public health insurance any more than they use public schools. But we should worry a lot if many citizens take up the private option. The public program must be sufficiently attractive that most citizens will want to be included.

Would it be acceptable to permit physicians or other medical professionals paid on a fee-for-service basis to bill for more than the insurance program provided? The answer here is clear. The capacity to contain medical costs depends on establishing firm limits. Balance billing allows providers to escape those limits; it reintroduces barriers to access that universal health insurance is meant to lower. No successful national health insurance program has permitted this practice for long. Canada found over time that balance billing became a serious problem in many communities, threatening both the uniformity of citizen treatment and access to treatment itself.

Concentrating Financial Control

Cross-national evidence suggests that it is the *concentration* of financial responsibility, not its precise location, that is crucial to countervailing inflationary health pressures. It so happens that Canada, by constitutional requirement, had no choice but to use provincial governments to administer health insurance. Great Britain, by contrast, concentrates financial responsibility in the national ministry of health, and Sweden does so in each of its county councils. The lesson for the United States is that there are options here.

The more difficult question is whether Canada's public financing and direct governmental administration are required for political accountability. Public financing—through earmarked provincial premiums and various federal and provincial taxes—makes Canadian outlays for health care highly visible. At the same time, Canadian provinces could, and some did, use existing health insurance companies as political buffers between physicians and government. In Ontario in the mid-1960s, private companies served as "post office" intermediaries for the flow of funds and the processing of claims. Such a buffer seemed terribly important then, a concession to the deeply felt hostility of many Canadian doctors to government medical insurance. In fact, the provinces that used financial intermediaries at the outset gave them up within a few years. They made administration complicated and expensive, and, once their role in moderating conflict was no longer necessary, they seemed useless (except to the insurance companies).

One can certainly imagine the use of such intermediaries in the United States. This, after all, has been the pattern with our own Medicare since 1965—an arrangement that draws upon private expertise and "economizes" on the number of public employees. The Canadians, we should clearly note, found such indirect management cumbersome and more expensive than direct administration. But contracting out of financial tasks is certainly, on the Canadian evidence, compatible with political accountability. Were this a vital element in an American compromise, giving some limited role to the health insurance industry would not be devastating.

In the United States of the 1990s, the crucial political problem facing national health insurance advocates may not be the clout of the health insurance industry but, instead, the public's hostility toward increased taxes. It is worth pondering whether it is possible to have the right level of countervailing power without the fusion of taxing power and negotiating responsibility in a single public agency. What would be lost if, for example, state regulatory authorities set the terms of medical care finance, negotiated with hospitals and physicians, and required that employers finance health insurance directly or pay into a state fund a fixed amount per employee?

In the former West Germany, national and state governments constrain the negotiations among physicians, hospitals, and the thousands of sickness funds without channeling social insurance financing through the public budget. But the United States lacks the German history of lifelong membership with one health insurance institution and the tradition of "corporatist" bargaining between payers and providers.

Financing medical care out of general tax revenues, as in Great Britain and Canada, does seem to reinforce constraints on medical inflation. Other government departments are dependent on the same tax revenues and are, in effect, organized constituencies for controlling health costs. Although contrary to the "privatization" mythology of recent years, there is a strong positive relationship between public finance of health care and cost control.

Important as it is to concentrate taxing, negotiating, and budgeting power, concentration alone will not constrain health costs. The political will to restrain health care costs is itself a necessary ingredient for success. In the early years of Canadian hospital insurance, budget overruns were very common, and the provincial governments typically covered the deficit. In later years, deficits were much less generously treated and hospital administrators who did not play by those rules often lost their positions. Some version of a spending target—with serious consequences for missing the mark—is crucial for the containment of health care costs. That is not a matter of administrative architecture or policy technique.

American health economists have persistently advised that making patients pay a portion of their hospital and doctor bills is essential to cost containment. Cost sharing by patients is said to make them cost conscious and more restrained in their use of medical care. Cost sharing, of course, adds millions of additional payers to the system of financing, with all the extra administrative costs that entails. Moreover, cost sharing threatens equity of access by raising the price of medical care to patients who may not be able to afford it. But the real lesson from abroad is that significant patient cost sharing is unnecessary to control medical inflation. With negligible cost sharing, Canada and Western Europe all achieve greater cost control than the United States.

The message conveyed to the American public since 1975—that less reliance on government is the key to controlling medical costs—needs to be challenged. That is partly why the Canadian example has become so important. Canada's experience shows that the choice Americans have given themselves, increasing access *or* controlling costs, is false. We have another alternative. The reality, bluntly put, is that as a nation we cannot afford to do without sensibly structured national health insurance. That is what the public says it wants. And it is what the country genuinely needs.

CHAPTER 4

Resolving the Cost-Access Conflict: The Case for a National Health Program

Steffie Woolhandler and David U. Himmelstein

Almost everyone agrees that U.S. health care is in crisis. Conservatives tend to focus on the problem of skyrocketing health costs, while liberals concentrate on the thirty-seven million Americans who are uninsured and often denied access to care. Both sides perceive the goals of cost control and improved access as irreconcilable. In this article we review evidence that recent policy initiatives have exacerbated both problems and fostered bureaucratic domination of medical care. We argue that a national health program (NHP) incorporating key features of the Canadian system can simultaneously improve access, contain costs, and reverse the trend toward bureaucratization.

Access in the 1980s

The United States has the world's most technologically advanced and expensive health care system (1). Yet we are the only developed country other than South Africa that fails to guarantee all citizens access to medical care. For about fifteen years, from the start-up of Medicaid and Medicare until the early 1980s, access to care, morbidity, and mortality steadily improved, but costs soared. Between 1965 and 1980 the proportion of black women receiving early prenatal care increased 50 percent, the number of poor people who hadn't seen a physician in more than two years was halved, and the proportion of health care costs paid out of pocket declined from 52 percent to 28 percent (2). Meanwhile, the infant mortality rate fell 4.6 percent per year, and overall death rates decreased 21 percent (2, 3). Unfortunately, during those fifteen years real per capita health spending, corrected for inflation, doubled (2).

Since 1980 government and corporate policies have given priority to slowing cost increases. While these policies have yet to contain costs, their toll has already been high in terms of restrictions on care and inequalities in health. Decades of steady social and health progress have been halted and, in some cases, reversed.

Access to care is worst for the poor, who are least likely to be insured and most in need of services. As the ranks of the poor have swelled (4, 5), the number of people without private health insurance has increased dramatically —47 percent between 1980 and 1985 (6). At the same time, the proportion of poor families covered by Medicaid dropped from 67 percent ten years ago to 46 percent in 1985 (7), as the average income eligibility standard fell from 55 percent to 47 percent of the poverty line (8). As a consequence, the number of people without health insurance increased more than 40 percent between 1978 and 1986 to 37 million (9–11), including 9.5 million women of child-bearing age (12). Fifty-four percent of the uninsured live in families headed by a full-time worker (9), and 13.5 percent of all employed persons are uninsured (10). In 1984 twelve million workers earning less than ten thousand dollars per year had no health insurance (9), nor did nearly one third of all students over the age of eighteen and more than a third of the poor (10).

For those with some insurance gaps in coverage, deductibles, and copayments may still impede access. For instance, five million women age 15–44 have private policies that do not cover maternity care (12). More than twenty million people have health insurance so inadequate that a major illness would cause financial ruin (13). The elderly are particularly vulnerable since Medicare pays only 49 percent of their medical expenses (14), about the same proportion covered by insurance before Medicare's enactment. Today the elderly spend 15 percent of their income on health care, while low-income elderly devote 25 percent of total income to health care (15).

The number of underinsured, like the number of uninsured, is rising. Many employers anxious to limit benefit costs have reduced the comprehensiveness of private health insurance coverage and/or increased copayments (16). Between 1985 and 1986 alone, the Medicare first-day deductible for each hospitalization rose 23 percent, largely due to the diagnostic-related groups (DRG) program, and over the past decade Medicare copayments have risen 50 percent faster than the elderly's incomes (15). Many states have severely constrained Medicaid patients' choice of providers through "managed care" initiatives (17)—despite evidence from a large, randomized, controlled trial that the health of the sick poor deteriorates in health maintenance organizations (HMOs) (18). Overall, for the first time in fifty years the proportion of health costs paid by insurance is declining, and the proportion paid out of pocket is rising (19).

These dry insurance statistics have very real and distressing human consequences—elderly patients forgoing vital medications because Medicare doesn't cover outpatient prescriptions; urgent surgery delayed until "insurance problems" can be cleared up; patients "lost to follow-up," at least partly because of the costs of care. A million families are denied care annually when they are sick because they cannot pay; eighteen million more experience financial difficulty in obtaining care (12). Half of the families dropped from Medicaid in the early 1980s were left without insurance coverage (8). Their use of inpatient services dropped 71 percent, while their physician visits declined 38 percent (8). The most dramatic consequences of a "negative wallet biopsy" are seen in public hospital emergency rooms in which thousands of uninsured patients are "dumped" each year from private hospitals unwilling to provide uncompensated care (21–23). Many of these transferred patients suffer shocking neglect.

Inadequate insurance coverage combined with funding cuts for public health programs has also undermined prevention. After decades of steady improvement the proportion of pregnant women receiving prenatal care during the first trimester has stagnated since 1980, at 62 percent among African-Americans and 79 percent among whites (24). For teenagers early prenatal care rates are even lower (25, 26). Among children less than two years old, 10 percent of African-Americans and 16 percent of Hispanics haven't seen a doctor in more than a year (7). Forty percent of children age one to four years and 80 percent of minority toddlers have not received a full series of vaccinations (27). Half of people with a diastolic blood pressure greater than 105 have not seen a doctor within the past year, and two thirds of all hypertensives are poorly controlled (28), in many cases because they cannot afford medications (29). Half of all women have not had a breast exam within the past year, and one in five has not had a Pap test for at least five years (30)—often because of lack of health insurance (31). Nearly 20 percent of people with serious or chronic illnesses had no physician visit in 1986, and overall the proportion of people without a physician visit increased 70 percent from 1982 to 1986 (20). Forty-three million Americans could identify no regular source of care in 1986, an increase of 65 percent over 1982 (20).

These barriers to access and inadequacies in prevention almost certainly contribute to the United States' poor record on infant mortality, life expectancy, and other measures of health status. For instance, a recent 118 percent increase in reported measles cases signals that falling immunization rates have begun to take their toll (32). Despite our vast wealth, the U.S. infant mortality rate ranks only seventeenth lowest among nations (24, 33), and the rapid improvements of the previous decade have stalled during the 1980s (2, 7, 24). High postneonatal and maternal mortality rates for African-Americans have not fallen over the past five years, after decades of steady decline (2, 7, 24). These data for African-Americans must illustrate socioeconomic as well as racial disparities, since vital statistics data are not routinely categorized by income or social class (34). Overall U.S. death rates are higher than in many other affluent countries and have commenced an almost unprecedented upswing (35, 19).

Much of the illness among minorities and the poor is due to medically preventable and treatable conditions (36–38). Most of the excess mortality among African-Americans is due to heart disease, strokes, cancer, diabetes, and infant mortality—things physicians can do something about. But only if the patients get to their offices.

To summarize: about one quarter of Americans are inadequately insured, and the number has been rising; they are often denied care or are reticent in seeking it because they cannot pay; their health is worse and their death rates higher than the affluent and well insured; and our national health statistics reflect the deepening access crisis. We are rationing health and health care based on ability to pay. Some form of rationing would be necessary if health resources were in short supply, but the United States faces a growing surplus of hospital beds and physicians (39, 40). In effect, health policy has focused on "rationing the surplus," an exercise that might be comical if its consequences were less dire.

The Cost Crisis and the Bureaucratic Squeeze

Health policy in the 1980s has been characterized by a virtual obsession with cost control. An exposition of the resulting welter of programs, strategies, and incentives is beyond the scope of this article, but a few key trends are discernible.

First, costs have not been contained (41). Expressed in constant dollars (i.e., adjusted for the consumer price index), health expenditures are rising more rapidly during the 1980s than they did in the late 1970s (19, 41–43). Costs continue to spiral upward, despite declining hospital occupancy rates, cuts in federal and state programs, increasing insurance copayments, and rising HMO enrollments.

Second, most cost-containment strategies have constrained clinical services through administrative limitations or financial barriers. Yet, the bureaucratic apparatus needed to erect, maintain, and police these disincentives to care is itself extremely costly (44). Thus, the Medicare DRG program has forced hospitals to spend billions on new billing computers, DRG coordinators, and other administrative appurtenances needed to guarantee financial survival (45, 46). The risk of undercare inherent in DRGs has spawned an army of vigilant overseers (PROs), whose demands for copies of medical records have forced hospitals to spend as much as $75 million annually on photocopying alone (47). Similarly, HMOs spend large sums enforcing disincentives to care (and excluding nonmembers entirely), resulting in administrative costs approximating those in fee-for-service practice (48; and D. Willis, C. Brudevold: pers. com.). By 1983 bureaucratic costs accounted for 22 percent of U.S. health spending (44), a proportion that continues to increase

(49). The number of health administrators is rising three times faster than the number of physicians or other health care workers (2, 50–53). In 1985 health insurance overhead alone consumed $106 per capita, as much as research, public health programs, and new health facility construction combined (41).

Third, recent policies have provided incentives for health institutions to act in a more "businesslike" way. Unfortunately, sound and compassionate clinical decisions sometimes lose money for a hospital or HMO. Policies that encourage a more businesslike approach reward institutions willing to bend clinical practice to financial exigency and thus guarantee administrative intrusion into clinical decision making (54–56). In this context each institution pursuing its own "rational" interests leads to irrationality in the system as a whole. Thus, research has linked increasing competition with higher hospital costs (57), longer lengths of stay for surgical procedures (58), and higher death rates (59). The fiscal laxity of the past has given way to intensive efforts by hospitals and HMOs to streamline their operations and especially to monitor and regulate medical practice. Hospitals and HMOs are identifying high-cost and low-profit physicians, patients, and services. Dumping these money losers (e.g., sicker patients likely to have longer lengths of stay and the more experienced surgeons who tend to care for them [60, 61]) benefits individual hospitals and HMOs but worsens the overall quality of care (62) and raises system-wide costs.

The resulting spectacle of bureaucracy gone wild occasionally reaches epic, almost comedic, proportions. Some HMOs have reportedly placed their enrollment offices on the upper floors of buildings without elevators to discourage the infirm. In our hospital a zealous administrator fearing loss of reimbursement outlawed the occasional practice of allowing an inpatient to enjoy a holiday dinner at home with family. He sacrificed his Thanksgiving patrolling the hospital lobby and turned back a single patient: a young woman hospitalized for anorexia nervosa.

Incentives meant to increase competition have also resulted in a sharp increase in advertising. Aggressive marketing by an insurer, HMO, or hospital may increase its market share, but the costs of TV commercials, full-page newspaper ads, and "free" health spa memberships (offered by one Boston-area HMO) must ultimately be subtracted from the money available for clinical services.

The failure of cost control to date suggests that any savings from reduced clinical care have been more than offset by growth in the bureaucracy needed to "beat" and police the system. Apparently, achieving cost containment through further pursuit of current strategies will require ever more stringent financial and administrative disincentives to care and ever greater bureaucratic domination of medical practice.

Joining the Canadian Club

If the failings of our health policies are widely acknowledged, the feasibility of solutions is as widely disputed. The extension of access seems to conflict with the imperatives of cost containment. Yet experience in other countries suggests that universal access to comprehensive care can be achieved at acceptable cost. Canada is a particularly useful example.

Patients there face few financial barriers to care (63, 64), costs are moderate (65, 66), and the quality of care is comparable to that in the United States. Moreover, until the mid-1960s the health care systems of the United States and Canada were quite similar.

Shortly after the passage of the U.S. Medicare and Medicaid programs, the Canadian Parliament enacted legislation offering federal matching funds for provincial health insurance plans meeting the following criteria (67):

1. Universal coverage "that does not impede . . . whether by charges made to insured persons, or otherwise; reasonable access."
2. Portability of benefits from province to province.
3. Insurance for all medically necessary services.
4. A publicly administered nonprofit program.

The resulting provincial programs pay for about 90 percent of all hospital and medical care. Private insurance has little role since by law it can only cover services not covered by the public plans (e.g., some long-term and dental care).

Funding comes principally from progressive taxes, though some provinces charge mandatory premiums, which really amount to a regressive form of taxation. Thus, all Canadians are covered for essentially all acute care services, and payments for these services come from a single government insurance fund in each province.

Most Canadian hospitals are private, not-for-profit institutions. Each hospital receives an annual global (lump-sum) budget to cover all operating expenses. Capital funds (i.e., for new buildings or machines) also come from the insurance fund but are allocated separately, based on hospital requests and provincial health planning goals (68). Patients are billed only for luxury items such as elective private rooms.

Most Canadian physicians are paid fee for service based on fee schedules negotiated between the provincial governments and medical societies. A minority are employed in salaried positions. Physicians can bill only for their personal services—i.e., they cannot be reimbursed for the costs of CAT scanners or other expensive machinery in their offices nor for the work of physicians' assistants or other physician extenders. A recent law has essentially banned "balance" billing (69); physicians must accept the fees from the insurance fund as payment in full. Physicians may affiliate with any hospital willing to grant them privileges.

The Canadian system has proven extremely popular with patients (67), who have free choice of providers with virtually no out-of-pocket costs. Access to care for the poor improved dramatically with the institution of universal coverage (63, 64). Most measures of health status are at least as good as the comparable U.S. figures.

Cost increases have been modest. While the United States and Canada devoted similar proportions of GNP to health care in the 1960s, by 1985 health care accounted for only 8.6 percent of GNP in Canada and 10.6 percent in the United States (19, 66).

Medicine remains a desirable and prestigious profession in Canada. Indeed, there are many more applicants per medical school slot than in the United States (4.7 vs. 1.8) (70, 71). Physicians have objected, often strenuously, to the elimination of balance billing and other constraints on fees. Physician incomes, however, are high (4.8 times the average industrial wage, similar to the U.S. figure), and income differentials between primary care and procedure-oriented specialties are relatively small. There is less bureaucratic intervention in clinical practice than in the United States, and billing is considerably simpler. Fewer than four hundred physicians chose to emigrate in 1985 (72).

The Canadian approach has encountered several problems. Some providers argue that constraints on capital spending have resulted in inappropriate rationing of high-technology equipment and services. Certainly, expensive technologies such as CAT and magnetic resonance imaging (MRI) scanners have diffused more slowly than in the United States, and fewer coronary artery bypass operations are performed (though it is unclear whether optimal rates are closer to the Canadian or U.S. figures). But the lengthy queues for services that have plagued the British National Health Service are not a feature of the Canadian NHP.

Fee-for-service reimbursement encourages excessive interventions and generates pressure for cost increases from physicians and regulation from government. In the face of rigid fee controls physician visits and referrals have increased. Government has responded by limiting the total pool of money available for physician payment, and some provinces have placed caps on physicians' incomes.

The geographic maldistribution of physicians continues. In response, some provinces have offered fee premiums for physicians in underserved rural areas, while British Columbia has virtually banned the establishment of new practices in overdoctored areas.

Though some provinces have introduced innovative long-term care programs (73), the provision of these services remains uneven. Additional problems include insufficient preventive activities, which are reimbursed but scarcely encouraged, and the failure of the Canadian system to deploy physicians' assistants, nurse practitioners, and other nonphysician providers.

While a health care system cannot be transplanted from one society to another, the United States can learn much from Canada (74). Coverage of all provincial residents under a single program has saved billions of dollars annually by greatly simplifying billing and administration (44). The monopsony payment system also aids in cost containment by facilitating enforcement of overall spending limits (75). Public administration has proven much more efficient than private insurers. Insurance overhead consumes only 2.5 percent of funds, similar to the U.S. Medicare program but less than a third of the percentage taken by private U.S. insurance firms (44).

Canada handles hospital capital allocation more efficiently than the United States. In the United States capital payments are folded in with operating reimbursement, creating undesirable economic incentives. Coupling operating and capital budgets encourages undercare in prospective payment systems such as DRGs, since money not spent on patient care can be used for institutional expansion. Conversely, such combined budgets encourage excessive interventions in fee-for-service settings, since the higher charges mean higher capital payment. Combining operating and capital payments under either fee-for-service or prospective reimbursement undermines health planning, since wealthy hospitals can expand while financially strapped institutions cannot—regardless of health needs. In contrast, the Canadian system of capital payments rewards neither skimping on care nor excessive intervention. It allows funds for expansion and modernization to be directed to areas of greatest need, preventing overbedding and encouraging the regionalization of services (68).

The Canadian experience also suggests that detailed administrative oversight of day-to-day clinical practice is not necessary if financial incentives for both insufficient and excessive intervention are minimized. Indeed, mounting costs in the United States, despite increasingly stringent administrative control of medical practice, may indicate that such oversight costs as much as it saves.

In summary, Canada's NHP has virtually minimized financial barriers to care at acceptable costs while maintaining clinical standards on a par with the United States. These apparently conflicting goals have been reconciled through a system that cuts administrative waste and cost, allows the enforcement of system-wide spending limits, and facilitates health planning.

The adoption of similar measures in the United States is fraught with political difficulty. The insurance industry will vigorously oppose the elimination of most billing and the substitution of public for private administration. Similarly, some hospital administrators, particularly at financially successful insitutions, may oppose global budgeting (which would eliminate many administrative jobs) and stringent health planning. About two thirds of the American people, however, have supported a universal, comprehensive, publicly funded and administered NHP in every opinion poll over the past twenty years (76, 77). The same proportion voted in favor of the statewide NHP referendum in Massachusetts in 1986, a major impetus to that state's recently passed (though seriously flawed [78]) universal health insurance bill. Employers whose health insurance costs have been skyrocketing also have strong reason to favor a Canadian-style NHP that would sharply cut employee benefit costs. Finally, many physicians may find a public service–oriented NHP preferable to the status quo.

Conclusions

In the United States recent health policies have restricted access and fostered bureaucratic dominance of clinical practice. Patients are being denied health care in the face of a growing surplus of health resources. Meanwhile, costs continue to escalate despite, or perhaps because of, the growing bureaucracy charged with restricting care.

We believe that it is possible to guarantee all Americans free access to high-quality care at acceptable cost. This will, however, require an NHP that greatly streamlines administration, establishes a single source of payment for virtually all services, and encourages health planning. Such a national health program is technically feasible but politically difficult. Without it we will continue to wrestle with an insolvable contradiction between cost and access.

REFERENCES

1. Organization for Economic Cooperation and Development. "Measuring Health Care 1960–1983: Expenditure, Cost and Performance." (Paris: OECD, 1985).
2. National Center for Health Statistics. "Health United States 1985." DHHS pub. no. (PHS) 86-1232. Public Health Service. Washington, D.C.: U.S. Government Printing Office, 1985.
3. National Center for Health Statistics. "Health United States 1980." DHHS pub. no. (PHS) 81-1232. Public Health Service. Washington, D.C.: U.S. Government Printing Office, 1980.
4. Axinn, J., and Stern, M. J. "Age and Dependency: Children and the Aged in American Social Policy." *Milbank Mem Fund Q* 63 (1985): 648–70.
5. U.S. Bureau of the Census. *Money Income and Poverty Status of Families and*

Persons in the United States: 1985 (advance data from the March 1986 current population survey). Current population reports, series P-60, no. 154. Washington, D.C.: U.S. Government Printing Office, 1986.

6. Health Insurance Association of America. *1986–1987 Source Book of Health Insurance Data*. Washington, D.C.: Health Insurance Association of America, 1987.

7. Hughes, D.; Johnson, K.; Simons, J.; and Rosenbaum, S. *Maternal and Child Health Data Book*. Washington, D.C.: Children's Defense Fund, 1986.

8. Rowland, D.; Lyons, B.; and Edwards, J. "Medicaid: Health Care for the Poor in the Reagan Era." *Ann Rev Public Health* 9 (1988): 427–50.

9. Issue Brief: Employer-Sponsored Health Insurance Coverage. Washington, D.C.: Employee Benefit Research Institute, 1986.

10. Sulvetta, M. A., and Swartz, K. The Uninsured and Uncompensated Care. Washington, D.C.: National Health Policy Forum, 1986.

11. U.S. Congress, House Subcommittee on Health and the Environment, testimony of N. M. Gordon (Assistant Director for Human Resources, Congressional Budget Office), April 15, 1988.

12. Gold, R. S.; Kenney, A. M.; and Singh, S. *Blessed Events and the Bottom Line: Financing Maternity Care in the United States*. (New York: Alan Guttmacher Institute, 1987).

13. Farley, P. J. "Who Are the Underinsured?" *Milbank Memorial Fund Q* 63 (1985): 476–503.

14. Rice, T., and Gabel, J. "Protecting the Elderly against High Health Care Costs." *Health Affairs* 5(3) (1986): 5–21.

15. Blumenthal, D.; Schlesinger, M.; and Drumheller, P. B. "The Future of Medicare." *N Engl J Med* 314 (1986): 722–28.

16. "Salaried Employee Benefits Provided by Major U.S. Employers: A Comparison Study, 1979 through 1984." (Lincolnshire, IL: Hewitt Associates, 1985).

17. Squarrell, K. I.; Hansen, S. M.; and Neuschler, E. "Prepaid and Managed Care under Medicaid: Characteristics of Current Initiatives." Washington, D.C.: National Governors' Association, 1985.

18. Ware, J. E.; Brook, R. H.; Rogers, W. H.; et al. "Comparison of Health Outcomes at a Health Maintenance Organization with Those of Fee for Service Care." *Lancet* 1 (1986): 1017–22.

19. National Center for Health Statistics. "Health United States 1987." DHHS pub. no. (PHS) 88-1232. Public Health Service. Washington, D.C.: U.S. Government Printing Office, 1988.

20. *Special Report: Access to Health Care in the United States: Results of a 1986 Survey*. (Princeton, NJ: Robert Wood Johnson Foundation, 1987).

21. Himmelstein, D. U.; Woolhandler, S.; Harnly, M.; et al. "Patient Transfers: Medical Practice as Social Triage." *Am J Public Health* 74 (1984): 494–97.

22. Schiff, R. L.; Ansell, D. A.; Schlosser, J. E.; et al. "Transfers to a Public Hospital: A Prospective Study of 467 Patients." *N Engl J Med* 314 (1986): 552–57.

23. Reed, W. G.; Cawley, K. A.; and Anderson, R. J. "The Effect of a Public Hospital's Transfer Policy on Patient Care." *N Engl J Med* 315 (1986): 1428–32.

24. Hughes, D.; Johnson, K.; Rosenbaum, S.; Butler, E.; and Simons, J. *The Health*

of America's Children: Maternal and Child Health Data Book. (Washington, D.C.: Children's Defense Fund, 1988).

25. Hughes, D.; Johnson, K.; Rosenbaum, S.; et al. *The Health of America's Children: Maternal and Child Health Data Book.* (Washington, D.C.: Children's Defense Fund, 1987).

26. Geronimus, A. "The Effects of Race, Residence and Prenatal Care on the Relationship of Maternal Age to Neonatal Mortality." *Am J Public Health* 76 (1986): 1416–21.

27. Johnson, K. *Who Is Watching Our Children's Health? The Immunization Status of American Children.* (Washington, D.C.: Children's Defense Fund, 1987).

28. *Blood Pressure Levels and Hypertension in Persons Ages 6–74 Years: United States, 1976–80.* Washington, D.C.: National Center for Health Statistics, Advancedata #84, October 8, 1982.

29. Shulman, N. B.; Martinez, B.; Broga, D.; et al. "Financial Cost as an Obstacle to Hypertension Therapy." *Am J Public Health* 76 (1986): 1105–8.

30. *Provisional Data from the Health Promotion Disease Prevention Supplement to the National Health Interview Survey: United States, January–March 1985.* Washington, D.C.: National Center for Health Statistics Advancedata #113, November 15, 1985.

31. Woolhandler, S., and Himmelstein, D. U. "Reverse Targeting of Preventive Care Due to Lack of Health Insurance." *JAMA* 859 (1988): 2872–74.

32. Center for Disease Control. "Measles—United States, First 26 Weeks, 1985." *MMWR* 35 (1986): 1–4.

33. Grant, J. P. *The State of the World's Children 1986.* Oxford: Oxford University Press (for UNICEF), 1985.

34. Terris, M. "Desegregating Health Statistics." *Am J Public Health* 63 (1973): 477–80.

35. *World Health Statistics 1984.* Geneva: World Health Organization, 1984.

36. Woolhandler, S.; Himmelstein, D. U.; Silber, R.; et al. "Medical Care and Mortality: Racial Differences in Preventable Deaths." *Int J Health Services* 15 (1985): 1–22.

37. U.S. Department of Health and Human Services. *Report of the Secretary's Task Force on Black and Minority Health.* Washington, D.C.: U.S. Government Printing Office, 1985.

38. American Cancer Society Subcommittee on Cancer in the Economically Disadvantaged. *Cancer in the Economically Disadvantaged: A Special Report.* (New York: American Cancer Society, 1986).

39. "Hospital Occupancy Rate Hits a Record Low at 63.6%." *Mod Healthcare* (Apr. 25, 1986): 11.

40. Iglehart, J. K. "The Future Supply of Physicians." *N Engl J Med* 314 (1986): 860–64.

41. Waldo, D. R.; Levit, K. R.; and Lazenby, H. "National Health Expenditures, 1985." *Health Care Financing Rev* 8, no. 1 (1986): 1–21.

42. Reinhart, U. E. "The Money Illusion in Health Care." *Mod Healthcare* (Oct. 10, 1986): 138.

43. "Health Costs Continue to Spiral." *Medicine and Health* (Oct. 27, 1986).

44. Himmelstein, D. U., and Woolhandler, S. "Cost without Benefit: Administrative Waste in U.S. Health Care." *N Engl J Med* 314 (1986): 441–45.

45. "Hospitals' PPS Paperwork Forcing Personnel Additions." *Mod Healthcare* 14, no. 15 (1984): 16.

46. Jackson, B., and Jensen, J. "Hospitals Turn to New Software, Hardware to Cope with DRGs." *Mod Healthcare* 14, no. 12 (1984): 109–12.

47. "Hospitals Not Liable for PRO-Related Copying Costs, Court Rules." *Medicine and Health* 40, no. 41 (1986): 1.

48. Baldwin, M. F. "Health Maintenance Organizations: IPA-Model Growth Leads Expansion." *Mod Healthcare* 17, no. 2 (1987): 46.

49. "Data Bank: Annual Increases in Health Care Expenditures According to Type of Service, 1980–85." *Mod Healthcare* 17, no. 2 (1987): 70.

50. *Statistical Abstract of the United States, 1986.* Washington, D.C.: Bureau of the Census, 1985.

51. *Health United States 1979.* DHEW pub. no. (PHS) 80-1232. Hyattsville, MD: National Center for Health Statistics, 1980.

52. U.S. Bureau of the Census. *Employment and Earnings, January 1986.* Washington, D.C.: U.S. Government Printing Office, 1986.

53. U.S. Bureau of the Census. *Employment and Earnings, January 1987.* Washington, D.C.: U.S. Government Printing Office, 1987.

54. Robinson, M. L. "New Regs Spur Monitoring of M.D.s." *Mod Healthcare* 12, no. 12 (1982): 20.

55. Johnson, R. L. "Hospital Boards Should Abandon Medical Staff Self-Governance." *Mod Healthcare* 13, no. 7 (1983): 134–40.

56. Wallace, C. "Fixed Payment Rates Force Hospitals to Reassess ICUs." *Mod Healthcare* 13, no. 5 (1983): 46–48.

57. Robinson, J. C., and Luft, H. S. "Competition and the Cost of Hospital Care, 1972 to 1982." *JAMA* 257 (1987): 3241–45.

58. Robinson, J. C.; Luft, H. S.; McPhee, S. J.; and Hunt, S. S. "Hospital Competition and Surgical Length of Stay." *JAMA* 259 (1988): 696–700.

59. Shortell, S. M., and Hughes, E. F. X. "The Effects of Regulation, Competition, and Ownership on Mortality Rates among Hospital Inpatients." *N Engl J Med* 318 (1988): 1100–107.

60. Rhodes, R. S.; Krasniak, C. L.; and Jones, P. K. "Factors Affecting Length of Hospital Stay for Femoropopliteal Bypass: Implications of the DRGs." *N Engl J Med* 314 (1986): 153–57.

61. Del-Guercio, L. R.; Savino, J. A.; and Morgan, J. C. "Physiologic Assessment of Surgical Diagnosis-Related Groups." *Ann Surg* 202 (1985): 519–23.

62. Fitzgerald, J. F.; Fagan, L. F.; Tierney, W. M.; and Dittus, R. S. "Changing Patterns of Hip Fracture Care before and after Implementation of the Prospective Payment System." *JAMA* 258 (1987): 218–21.

63. Enterline, P. E.; Slater, V.; McDonald, A. D.; and McDonald, J. C. "Distribution of Medical Services before and after 'Free' Medical Care—The Quebec Experience." *N Engl J Med* 289 (1973): 1174–78.

64. Siemiatycki, J.; Richardson, L.; and Pless, I. B. "Equality in Medical Care under National Health Insurance in Montreal." *N Engl J Med* 303 (1980): 10–15.

65. Health and Welfare Canada. *National Health Expenditures in Canada 1970–82*. Ottawa, Ont.: Department of National Health and Welfare, 1984.
66. Health and Welfare Canada, Health Information Division. *National Health Expenditures in Canada 1975–85*. Ottawa: Department of National Health and Welfare, 1987.
67. Vayda, E. "The Canadian Health Care System: An Overview." *J Public Health Policy* 7 (1986): 205–10.
68. Detsky, A. S.; Stacey, S. R.; and Bombardier, C. "The Effectiveness of a Regulatory Strategy in Containing Hospital Costs: The Ontario Experience." *N Engl J Med* 309 (1983): 151–59.
69. Iglehart, J. K. "Canada's Health Care System." *N Engl J Med* 315 (1986): 202–8, 778–84.
70. Ryten, E. "Medical Schools in Canada." *JAMA* 258 (1987): 1093–97.
71. Crowley, A. E.; Etzel, S. I.; and Petersen, E. S. "Undergraduate Medical Education." *JAMA* 258 (1987): 1013–20.
72. Relman, A. S. "The United States and Canada: Different Approaches to Health Care" (editorial). *N Engl J Med* 315 (1986): 1608–10.
73. Kane, R. A., and Kane, R. L. "The Feasibility of Universal Long-Term-Care Benefits: Ideas from Canada." *N Engl J Med* 312 (1985): 1357–64.
74. Lee, S. "Health Policy, a Social Contract: A Comparison of the U.S. and Canada." *J Public Health Policy* 3 (1983): 293–302.
75. Evans, R. "Canada: Patterns of Funding and Regulation," in *The Public Private Mix*, ed. G. McLaughlin and A. Maynard. (London: Nuffield Provincial Hospital Trust, 1982), 369–424.
76. Navarro, V. "Where's the Popular Mandate?" *N Engl J Med* 307 (1982): 1516–18.
77. Pokorny, G. "Report Card on Health Care." *Health Management Q* 10, no. 1 (1988): 3–7.
78. Himmelstein, D. U., and Woolhandler, S. "Canada Shows the Way" (letter). *New York Times*, May 9, 1988, 18.

CHAPTER 5

Access to Health Care in the United States and Canada

Frank W. Puffer

If someone familiar with the general nature and culture of Western industrialized countries, particularly their systems of higher education, but totally ignorant of their health care delivery systems were to look at unlabeled descriptions of the various health care delivery systems that have evolved in these countries, he or she would probably have a pretty easy time picking the one used by the United States, but a far tougher time selecting the Canadian scheme. This reflects both the fundamental gap between the United States and the rest of the Western world with respect to health care delivery and the strong imprint U. S. culture and political beliefs have had in shaping a very distinctive system for providing health care to its citizens. The U.S. health care system is similar in many ways to its system for the provision of higher education. Both are highly fragmented systems that mix private and public provision of service in a complex web of government regulation at all levels of government. There is substantial variation in quantity of service, and probably quality as well, in the various states and regions of the United States. The quality of the best is extremely high indeed. The United States, without doubt, has numerous world-class institutions, attracting people from all over the globe for training in the latest and best techniques. But that quality at the top fails to translate into high average quality, at least as judged by broad comparative measures of outcomes.

Access to these services is market based, more so in health care than higher education, but there are a great number of seemingly uncoordinated programs in place to attempt to offset the failures of the market in providing equal access. Yet, in spite of these programs, or perhaps to some extent because of them, access to both health care and higher education seems to many, to depend to a large extent on the usual things that determine who gets what in a mixed market system—wealth, brains, determination, and political muscle. And, while we seem quite willing as a society to accept that one's access to television sets, automobiles, and nice homes in the suburbs should be determined this way, we are less comfortable with doing the same with higher education and health care. In the case of higher education it is still generally accepted that brains can be used to determine access, but with respect to health care our feeling is that one shouldn't have better access to medical care just because he or she is smarter, richer, works harder, is the right color, or has good political connections.

Canada, on the other hand, along with the rest of the Western world, has accepted the idea that access to health care is a fundamental right of its citizens and has established over the years a system that differs in many substantial ways from various European schemes but shares with them the notion that government should take on the role of providing universal access to an appropriate level of medical care. This, in itself, is no assurance that access will in fact be equitable. In Britain, for example, there has been a long debate over the role social class and geographic region play in determining effective access. But, nevertheless, there is a government commitment to the provision of access for all citizens that is missing in the United States.

The two systems we have to compare thus differ in many ways. The U.S. system can be characterized as one in which a great deal of money on average is spent, the basic method of obtaining health care is fee for service through a variety of private health insurance plans, and the government, while accepting no general responsibility for the provision of health care, has an assortment of plans—Medicare and Medicaid being two of the most important—that facilitate access for special groups. These plans, in turn, give the government an interest in the operation of the health care system and thus justification for substantial regulatory intervention.

The Canadian system is far simpler, even with its basis in provincial plans. Everyone has access to health care, and under the plan income and wealth should play no role in obtaining medical services. There may still remain cultural and educational impediments to access, but these would be expected to be of a much smaller magnitude than the financial barriers of a market system.

The question to be addressed here is whether or not in reality the two systems perform differently with respect to access. At first glance the impression is that access must be much more equal in Canada than in the United States. But, if one looks at the groups that one would expect to suffer most under a market-based system, the poor and the elderly, the United States has programs (Medicaid and Medicare, respectively) that pump a great deal of money into the health care system to provide access for these two groups. In addition, equality of actual use is furthered by the fact that people in general don't particularly want to consume medical care services. Even if they can afford it, few people want to spend their vacations in intensive care units. Thus, it is at least possible that the combination of targeted governmental programs and a natural reluctance to consume medical care services may make access, as measured by actual use, more similar in Canada and the United States than would at first appear.

The rest of this chapter will look at the question of comparative access by comparing the results of two large surveys on health care access that were done within a year of each other during the late 1970s in the United States and Canada. While they did not use the same survey instruments, there are enough similarities to allow a fairly detailed comparison. There are a number of ways this comparison could be done, but here the United States data have been reanalyzed to provide results as comparable as possible to a pair of careful studies done on the Canadian data. The analysis was then extended to consider some issues, such as insurance coverage and racial discrimination, that the original Canadian studies didn't address.

At first glance it would appear to be relatively straightforward to determine whether or not a particular group of people are getting more or less than their share of medical care resources. Suppose, for example, we were interested in the effect poverty has on the availability of health care resources. It would be tempting to look at measures such as physician visits per year or number of hospital days and compare the averages for those below the poverty line with the averages for the rest of the population. In fact, some of the early studies of access did this, but there is a serious problem with the approach. It implicitly assumes that the two groups have the same need for medical care. If we were to actually compare the average number of physician visits for U.S. adults living in poverty with higher-income adults (using data to be discussed later), we would find that the poor adults make about 4.8 visits per year to doctors, while the rest of the adults make 4.2 visits. This, however, does not necessarily mean that the poor have better access to doctors than those better off, since the poor are on average less healthy than the rest of the population. The poor health of those with low incomes should lead them to need more contacts with doctors, and thus we can't tell from the data whether or not the 0.6 extra visit per year that the poor enjoy is enough to compensate for their greater need or not.

The problem, then, is to take the differences in the health of the groups we are comparing into account and distinguish between health-related and other differences in use. Some of the earlier attempts to correct for the need for health care across income or social classes analyzed ratios of use-to-need measures such as doctor visits per disability day. A good example of this approach is Le Grand's study of the influence of social class on the access to medical care in the United Kingdom. The measure of need he employed was the age-sex standardized count of the number of those in the social class reporting either chronic or acute illness. His health care use measure was the cost of providing health care to each of the social classes, which he based on physician contacts and hospital stays. He concluded that there was evidence of larger expenditures per illness for the upper classes, although he admitted that he had to make a number of difficult-to-validate assumptions in his calculations.

A potential solution to the sort of difficulties Le Grand and others had is to obtain comprehensive data on a large sample of individuals to sort out the effects of health-related variables from other factors. To continue with our example, if health-related variables are associated with the number of doctor visits while the poverty status of an individual had no additional explanatory effect, we might then conclude that poverty does not have an effect on access to physicians.

The problem now shifts to the question of how to measure health status. There are two approaches we might try here. One would be to have physicians do a careful study of each person in our sample and, after assessing blood pressure, X rays, physical mobility, etc., come up with some sort of objective measure of health. The difficulty with this is that it is very expensive, and, in addition, people are not all willing to cooperate. In the Canadian survey, which will be discussed shortly, a number of physical measurements were taken, but some procedures, like the taking of blood samples, noticeably reduced the participation rate in the study and thus led to an increased likelihood of nonresponse bias in the results.

The other approach to measuring health status is more straightforward. You simply ask people how healthy they are. Questions are framed concerning acute and chronic illness, general health status, days absent from work, etc., and these are used as measures of health status. An advantage of this approach is that it reflects an individual's own perception of the state of his or her health, and this may be a better indication of motivation for seeking medical care than the more objective physical examination. For example, suppose we have two individuals, both suffering from hypertension. If one of two sees this as a serious chronic illness, while the other feels it not worthy of any attention, we would expect the first to be more likely to see a doctor than the second. From a physician's point of view both should be seeing a doctor, but, since the decision is not the doctor's but, instead, the individual's, the different views of the two about the seriousness of their common illness should not lead us to conclude that one is somehow being denied access to medical care because he or she does not visit a doctor.

The problem becomes more difficult if there are group biases in the perception of health status. Suppose that it is relatively common for low-income people to view hypertension as benign, while higher-income people are more likely to see it as a serious health problem. Then, even if the incidence of hypertension were the same in the two populations, those with the higher incomes would be more likely to seek medical care than those with low incomes. There is quite a bit of evidence that differences in perception of health risks exist along class and racial lines. Berkanovic and Telesky, for example, have looked at the perception of health status by American minority groups and found significant differences. For the purposes of the present study, however, the differences in use of health care resources that result from such group differences in the evaluation of health status will not be interpreted as differences in access. If a poor person does not seek medical care for hypertension because he or she views it as an unimportant health problem, while a rich person does seek such care, since he or she sees it as a serious problem, their behavior indicates more a difference in education than access. There would only be an access problem if both the poor and rich individuals perceived themselves as being in equally poor health as a result of their similar hypertension and the two received different amounts of medical care.

Imagine a society in which the poor suffered from worse-than-average health but perceived their health as better than average, while the rich enjoyed better-than-average health but viewed their health as worse than average. If, as would be almost certainly the case, the rich saw doctors more often than the poor, we would not interpret this as unfair access. It would still be a serious social problem, but not one that would be solved by attempting to improve equality of access. Instead, one would want to establish educational programs to help everyone make more informed assessments of their own health status.

Another dimension of access to health care is that of the role played by geographic factors. Shannon and Dever have looked at a variety of factors, such as the distance to one's health care provider and the regional distribution of physicians per capita. While their results are expressed in the form of tables rather than statistical hypotheses, the factors that they and other medical geographers focus on have been incorporated as important explanatory variables in other more comprehensive studies.

Aday, Fleming, and Andersen have done a number of investigations of access to medical care in the United States, relying on the analysis of comprehensive survey data. They looked at tabulations of a number of measures of health care access, trying to explain them as a function of various socioeconomic and health status variables. A distinction is made between potential access and realized access. Potential access has to do with whether or not the individual has a regular source of health care, the convenience of the sources of care, and whether or not the individual has the ability to pay for health care. Realized access is closer to the notion of access used in this chapter in that it is concerned with the actual use of physician and hospital services along with one's satisfaction with those services and whether or not there were any unmet needs.

The analysis by Aday, Fleming, and Andersen of their 1982 survey data led them to conclude that about 14 percent of the population could be considered to be in trouble with respect to their access to health care. A disproportionate number of this group were poor minorities, the unemployed, those with public insurance, and those with no insurance at all.

While Aday and her colleagues relied on the tabulation of data obtained from an exceptionally comprehensive survey, others have explored the issue using more powerful multivariate techniques on other data sets. An example of this was one of many studies done of the 1978 U.S. National Medical Care Expenditure Survey (NMCES), that of Monheit et al., on the question of the effect of unemployment on health insurance and access to medical care. They used the statistical technique of logit analysis to investigate the probability that unemployed workers would lose health insurance coverage, explaining it as a function of a number of socioeconomic and health factors. Unemployment did not appear to lead to much loss in insurance coverage, nor did it seem to affect medical care use. Yet those unfortunate enough to not have insurance appeared to have serious access problems, regardless of their employment status.

Another study based in part on a sample from the National Medical Care Expenditure Survey was Puffer's comparison of access in the United States and the United Kingdom. The statistical tool used was ordinal probit analysis, which, like multiple regression, permits one to sort out the effects of a number of different influences on a single variable. The study concluded that income had a relatively small effect on access to medical care in the United States, with the possible exception of lower-income people in relatively poor health.

There have also been a number of studies of access to health care in Canada. Taylor mentions investigations by Beck and by Enterline et al., both of which conclude that with the introduction of Medicare in Canada low income is no longer a barrier to health care access. The high-income households appear to have decreased their use of health care resources, while the low-income households have made substantial increases.

Neither of these studies, however, drew on a national sample. For the clearest picture of access at the national level the most important work is that of Broyles, Manga, and colleagues (to be referred to subsequently as Broyles-Manga) in their analysis of a set of data from the Canada Health Survey. The Canada Health Survey was originally intended to be an ongoing monitoring of the general health status of Canadians, but budgetary difficulties resulted in it being a onetime survey. Nevertheless, a wide range of data was collected on nearly twenty-four thousand individuals fifteen years of age or older during the period from July 1978 to March 1979. A variety of measures of health status, the amount of use of different health care resources, health risk factors, and socioeconomic characteristics were among the information obtained. In addition, physical measures such as blood pressure, height, weight, and blood analysis were also obtained, but with considerably reduced participation.

The question Broyles-Manga were attempting to answer was the degree to which income was a factor in the use of health care resources. To do this they looked at both contacts with physicians and stays in hospitals. Within each of these categories they attempted to find out what factors led to any use of the resources at all and, then, looking at those who had some contacts with doctors or stays in hospitals, what factors led to the number of doctor contacts or hospital nights. Although they reported their findings in two separate articles, the methodology was the same in both. Their approach was to first employ discriminant analysis to determine the factors influencing use or non-use of hospitals or doctors. Then, using the subset of the sample that reported some use of the resource, they used regression analysis to determine the factors that influenced the amount of use, as measured by the number of hospital nights or doctor contacts. Table 1 summarizes their main results.

Most of the variables used in the analysis are qualitative variables that indicate the presence of a particular attribute. Thus, "Female" indicates the female gender, "Female (20–24)" indicates a woman twenty to twenty-four years old, "White collar" indicates a person working in a white-collar occupation, and so forth. "Income quintile 1" is the lowest of the five, while "Prescription drug user" indicates that the person is currently taking a drug prescribed by a physician. The four variables describing the number of health-related incidents are, in order, accidents during the year, number of previous bouts of illness, number of days during the year that illness caused a cutting back on activity, and number of current health conditions. The final two variables, "Physician ratio" and "Bed ratio," are the number of physicians and hospital beds per capita in the province in which the individual lives.

The entries in table 1 indicate the direction of effect and statistical significance of each of the variables. For example, having a white-collar job is associated with a reduced probability of being hospitalized, and the effect is statistically highly significant. On the other hand, those with white-collar jobs do not differ significantly from the excluded group, those without any occupation, in the number of nights spent in the hospital once they are hospitalized.

The two articles go into considerable detail in their analyses of the coefficients of all of the variables, but it may be useful to point out a few of their findings. Looking at income as a variable, we would expect to find no effect if access is not dependent on ability to pay. In the case of the amount of hospital use, however, income does appear to be a factor. Individuals at the low end of the income scale, other things equal, will spend more time in a hospital bed than their wealthier neighbors once they are hospitalized in the first place. One might speculate that this reflects generally more severe health problems facing those with lower incomes, but in any case it is the wrong sign to indicate any discrimination in access against low-income individuals. Thus, the Broyles-Manga results are consistent with the notion that Canada has eliminated the positive role of income, or ability to pay, as a factor in determining access to medical care for these two important sources of care.

There is also some evidence that an increased ratio of physicians per capita can lead to a decreased probability of hospital use. This may be, as Broyles-Manga suggest, the result of increased early intervention by physicians, which mitigates the need for hospitalization, or it may simply reflect regional variations in the style of medical practice. The results, however, are not consistent with supply-induced demand for medical care. Higher bed or physician ratios are not associated with increased utilization.

TABLE 1.   Factors Determining the Use or Nonuse of Hospitals and Doctors and Amount of Use if Not Zero, Canada, 1978–79

	Use or Nonuse		Amount of Use	
Variable	Hospital	Doctor	Hospital	Doctor
Female	0	+++	0	++
Female (20–24)	++	0	0	0
Female (25–44)	++	0	0	0
Female (45–64)	0	0	0	0
Female (65+)	0	0	0	0
Age (20–24)	0	++	0	0
Age (25–44)	0	0	+	0
Age (45–64)	0	–	++	0
Age (65+)	0	0	++	+
White collar	——	+	0	——
Blue collar	–	0	0	–
Prescription drug user	+++	+++		+++
Married	++	+++	–	0
Previously married	+	++	0	0
No. of accidents	+	+++	0	+
No. of previous illnesses	+	+++	+	++
No. of disability days	+++	0	++	+++
Disabled			0	
No. of current illnesses	++	+++	+	++
Physician ratio	–	0	0	0
Bed ratio	0		0	
Urban center	–	+	0	0
Major city	–	+	0	0
Income quintile 1	0	0	+	0
Income quintile 2	0	0	+	0
Income quintile 3	0	0	++	0
Income quintile 4	0	0	0	0

Source: Manga, Broyles, and Angus 1987; Broyles et al. 1983.

Note: +++ or —— = *t*-ratio of 5 or greater; ++ or —— = *t*-ratio of 3 to 5; + or – = *t*-ratio significant at 5 percent level; 0 = not statistically significant.

Other things equal, older people do not appear to be more likely to use hospital or physicians' services than younger people, but, if they do use them, they are likely to have more physician visits and stay more days in the hospital. While this may seem at variance with our general feeling that older people need relatively more medical care, that need is due primarily to their poorer health, rather than age itself.

The health status variables give the expected results, with the puzzling exception of the insignificant effect of the number of days of disability due to illness on the decision to use or not use a doctor. This may be a typographical error in the article, since other similar studies show disability days to be a very important predictor of physician use.

Although Broyles-Manga have made an important contribution to our understanding of access under the Canadian health care system, there are some objections that can be raised about the details of their analysis of the data. The first is that the two-stage process of discriminant analysis of the use/nonuse question, followed by regression analysis of the amount of use by users, is likely to suffer from selection bias, which will be discussed briefly later.

The second problem is the inclusion in the data set of cases for which there were missing values. If, for example, the occupation of a person was not known, he or she was assumed to be in the excluded category, which in this case was no occupation. This assigns a number of cases to categories in which they don't belong and may affect the results. As an example of the sort of problem that could occur, if a variable such as the family income was unknown, the individual would implicitly be assigned to the highest income quintile, quintile 5, which is the excluded category. To the extent that low-income families are assigned inadvertently to quintile 5, they mask the behavior of the true quintile 5 individuals and blur the distinction between the behavior of the different income levels. From the description of the Canada Health Survey there were a substantial number of missing values for some items, but whether or not there are any problems resulting from this is difficult to say. Also related to income is the problem that income quintiles do not take into account the size of a family. At a given level of income a larger family is in a relatively poorer economic status than a smaller one.

A final concern is the inclusion of the prescription drug utilization variable as an explanatory variable. Since it is unlikely that one would be taking a prescription drug without having some contact with a doctor, this variable would seem to be caused by the doctor contact, rather than the other way around.

While it was not possible to have access to the original Canada Health Survey data set, which would have permitted a direct test of whether or not these objections have any effect on the results, it was possible to take the corresponding data set for the United States, the National Medical Care Expenditure Survey, and see what difference correcting each of these problems made in the results for the United States. The procedure was to first replicate the methodology and variables of the Broyles-Manga studies using U.S. data in place of the Canadian data. Then the data were analyzed again, this time using a two-stage procedure that should correct for selection bias and associated econometric problems, dropping prescription drug use as a variable, omitting cases with missing variables, and adjusting income for family size. In addition, explanatory variables that were not included in the Canada study, such as perceived general health status, race, and insurance coverage, were included as additional explanatory variables. Table 2 reports the results of a

TABLE 2. Factors Determining the Use or Nonuse of Hospitals and Doctors and Amount of Use if Not Zero, United States, 1977

	Use or Nonuse		Amount of Use	
Variable	Hospital	Doctor	Hospital	Doctor
Female	+	0	0	0
Female (20–24)	+ +	+	0	+
Female (25–44)	+ +	+ + +	0	+ + +
Female (45–64)	0	+	0	+
Female (65+)	—	0	0	0
Age (20–24)	0	—	0	0
Age (25–44)	—	——	0	—
Age (45–64)	0	——	+ +	0
Age (65+)	0	—	+ +	0
White collar	—	+ + +	0	0
Blue collar	0	+ + +	0	—
Prescription drug user	+ + +	+ + +		+ + +
Married	+ + +	+	—	0
Previously married	+ + +	0	0	0
No. of disability days	+ + +	+ + +	+ + +	+ + +
Limited activity	+ +	+ + +	—	+ + +
Physician ratio	0	+ + +	0	+ +
Bed ratio	+ +	+ + +	0	0
Urban center	—	0	0	+ + +
Major city	—	0	0	+ + +
Income quintile 1	0	—	0	0
Income quintile 2	0	—	0	0
Income quintile 3	0	0	0	0
Income quintile 4	0	0	0	0

Notes: To make the relative effect of income levels clearer, all income quintile *t*-ratios are with respect to the average level of income, not the excluded category of high income.

+ + + or ——— = *t*-ratio of 5 or greater; + + or —— = *t*-ratio of 3 to 5; + or — = *t*-ratio significant at 5 percent level; 0 = not statistically significant.

Broyles-Manga-like analysis of the U.S. data, while table 3 gives the results of the expanded analysis.

The analysis leading to the results reported in table 2 differs from the Broyles-Manga analysis in two respects. First, the use/nonuse analysis was done using logit rather than discriminant analysis, but the results of the two

TABLE 3. Factors Determining the Use or Nonuse of Hospitals and Doctors and Amount of Use if Not Zero, Augmented Analysis, United States, 1977

Variable	Use or Nonuse		Amount of Use	
	Hospital	Doctor	Hospital	Doctor
Female			0	0
Female (20–24)			0	+++
Female (25–44)			0	+++
Female (45–64)			0	+
Female (65+)	+++	+++	0	0
Age (20–24)	++	++	0	0
Age (25–44)	−	0	0	—
Age (45–64)	—	0	+	+
Age (65+)	—	+	+	++
White collar		+++	−	+
Blue collar	−	0	−	0
Married	0	++	0	++
Previously married	+++	+	0	++
No. of disability days	+++			
Log disability days	+++	+++	+++	+++
Limited activity	++	+++	0	+++
Physician ratio	0	0	0	++
Bed ratio	+	+	++	0
Urban center	−	0	0	++
Major city	0	0	0	++
Poverty	0	0	0	0
Poverty × 1.25	0	−	0	0
Poverty × 2	0	—	0	0
Poverty × 4	0	0	0	0
Health fair or poor	++			
Health good		+++	0	+++
Health fair		+++	0	+++
Health poor		0	0	+++
Insured always	+++	+++	0	+++
Insured sometimes	+++	+++	0	+++
Minority	0	——	++	—

Notes: To make the relative effect of income levels clearer, all poverty *t*-ratios are with respect to the average level of income, not the excluded category of high income.

+++ or —— = *t*-ratio of 5 or greater; ++ or — = *t*-ratio of 3 to 5; + or − = *t*-ratio significant at 5 percent level; 0 = not statistically significant.

techniques are usually very similar. Logit, however, usually performs better in this sort of data analysis. Second, Broyles-Manga compensate for a statistical problem that the current study leaves unresolved. The problem arises from the fact that both the Canadian and U.S. surveys were not simple random samples but, instead, had a complex multistage sample design. In order to make the most accurate population estimates from such data, the raw data have to be weighted and the estimation procedure has to take account of the sample design. While the weighting problem can be dealt with in a straightforward manner, allowing for the effect of the sample design on the estimates is quite difficult. Broyles-Manga chose to use a computer package that provided estimation techniques that could take account of the sample design effects, but at the cost of leaving the selection bias problem unaddressed. The analysis reported in table 3 corrects for the selection bias but does not deal with sample design problems. The effect of the nonrandom sample design is to lead one, in general, to underestimate true standard deviations when using conventional statistical tools and thus overestimate the statistical significance of parameter estimates.

The data used for the estimates in both table 2 and table 3 come from the U.S. 1977 National Medical Care Expenditure Survey. This survey, like the Canada Health Survey, gathered information on a variety of health status, health care use, and socioeconomic variables. It did not include any physical measurements but did gather very detailed medical care use and cost data. The sample size was 40,320 individuals.

The questions asked in the U.S. and Canadian surveys were quite similar, with the main differences, for our purposes, coming in the health status measures. In place of the four Canadian variables, which count incidents of various health-related events, the U.S. survey had the number of days of disability due to illness and the presence or absence of an activity limiting physical disability. The ratios of physicians per capita and hospital beds per capita were not part of the NMCES data. Bed and physician ratios for the nine U.S. census regions were calculated and assigned to each individual case depending on the region of residence. Broyles-Manga did the same thing with provincial data to generate their equivalent variables.

While there are a number of differences between table 1 and table 2, only one is of particular interest, the role of income in affecting access. What we find in table 2 is that if one uses the same basic technique that was used on the Canadian data, there is apparently evidence that in the United States low income plays a negative role in access to medical care. The income quintile coefficients indicate significantly less use of medical care by those in the lowest two quintiles. It turns out, however, that on reexamination of the data in the better specified model reported in table 3, income does not appear to play as significant a role in access to health care.

The results reported in table 3 come from a modified analysis of the U.S. data to take into account some of the potential problems in the Broyles-Manga analysis. A two-stage procedure, suggested by Heckman as a means of correcting for sample selection bias, is used to estimate the coefficients of the equations. This consists of using probit analysis for the use/nonuse relationship, after which the inverse Mills ratio is calculated and used as an explanatory variable in the subsequent amount of use regression, which is estimated using the subset of all nonzero users of physicians or hospitals, respectively. The standard errors for the regression coefficients are calculated using robust techniques to compensate for the heteroskedasticity of the residuals.

The dependent variable for amount of use was changed to the log of the number of hospital nights or doctor contacts, since both have highly skewed distributions. In addition, the prescription drug use variable was dropped. The income quintile variable was replaced by an income categorization that takes family size into account. Each family income is calculated as a multiple of the amount of income that represents the poverty line for a family of that size. The variable "Poverty" indicates a family income at or below the poverty level. "Poverty $\times$ 1.25" is a family income between the poverty line and 1.25 times the poverty line, etc. The excluded category is income more than four times the poverty level.

Three additional types of variables are added. One is a self-rating of overall health. The "excellent" category is the excluded one. The insurance variables indicate health insurance status. "Insured always" means that the individual was covered for the entire survey year, while "Insured sometimes" indicates coverage for only part of the year. The excluded category consists of those who had no insurance coverage at any time during the year. Finally, "Minority" includes those considered to be nonwhite in response to a question on racial background.

The most important result shown in table 3 is the lack of indication of barriers to access for the very poorest when we adjust income for family size. Those just above the poverty line, though, suffer from a relative lack of access to physicians. Nevertheless, the amount of use of physicians or hospitals by those who do manage to see a physician or are admitted to a hospital appears basically to be unaffected by income.

We have to be careful not to read too much into this result. What the analysis is telling us is that there is not a strong enough pattern overall to justify rejecting the hypothesis of equal access to medical care for the poor. Yet it is quite possible that there are other types of access problems that cannot be uncovered with the survey data. There is no way of knowing from these results if the poor receive the same quality of care as others do or if the care is unequally distributed among the poor.

Critics of the British health care system argue that the class differences between the providers of health care and their often lower-class patients may lead to communication problems and other difficulties that can make a given office visit or hospital stay less effective than it would be for people in the middle and upper classes. There may be some effects along those lines in the United States as well. It may also be that the health status measures, which attempt to serve as a proxy for true need, are biased in that they do not pick up differences in the severity of illness in the different income categories.

Nevertheless, there is no indication of a major access problem. If one were to do the same analysis on access to higher education, there is little doubt that income would show up as an important variable influencing access, as it would with access to almost anything else that is desirable in our socio-economic system. To a first approximation, the U.S. policy of targeting health care dollars with Medicare and Medicaid has managed to produce generally equal overall access to medical care by income level.

What is most disturbing in the table 3 results is the strong negative effect lack of insurance coverage and minority status have on access. Those who have insurance are considerably more likely than those without insurance to have seen a doctor or be hospitalized. Since we are controlling for health status, this is not a result of the uninsured being healthier than those with insurance. Instead, it suggests a substantial barrier to access to health care for the uninsured. While many medical care providers have tried to provide care for the uninsured, it is clear that overall the programs have fallen short of need, and insurance status remains an important determinant of access.

If we look at the amount of use of medical care resources by those uninsured who manage to have any access in the first place, we find that again insurance status makes a significant difference. Since the uninsured are less likely to be able to get in the door at the doctor's office or the hospital, it is likely that those who do come under a physician's care or undergo hospitalization are experiencing more severe illnesses than their insured counterparts. Nevertheless, the insured who see a doctor have significantly more physician contacts than the uninsured. The only bright spot for the uninsured is that it appears that, once an uninsured individual is finally admitted to a hospital, his or her number of "bed days" is not significantly different from that of the insured. This may in fact reflect less care for the uninsured, however, since it is likely that the uninsured who are actually hospitalized are there for more serious conditions.

The picture with respect to minorities is somewhat different. While the uninsured are less likely to have access to either physician or hospital care, the problem of minorities is with physician access and is in addition to any access problems caused by lack of insurance, ill health, or poverty. Minorities, other things equal, are significantly less likely to have any contact with a physician, and, even if they do have contact, they have significantly fewer physician visits than nonminorities. Thus, a smaller proportion of the minority population, adjusting for other access-related characteristics, has any contact with doctors, and, when we look at those who have established contact, we find that the initial contact results in significantly fewer additional visits to the doctor.

The minority situation with respect to hospitalization reflects this lack of access to physicians. While minorities are not significantly more likely to be hospitalized than the rest of the population, their hospital stays tend to be longer. One could speculate that the longer hospital stays reflect a lack of early intervention by physicians. It seems plausible to expect more frequent physician contact to head off the development of at least some serious health conditions, and it is clear that minorities are not receiving the same volume of physician services as the rest of the population. It should be mentioned that this relative dependence on hospitalization in place of physician contacts is not the same thing as a relatively high use of hospital emergency rooms instead of physicians' offices. The physician contacts are all outpatient contacts in any medical setting, while the hospital use is admission for overnight or longer.

The supply of physicians and hospital beds also has an effect on utilization of medical services. Unlike the Canadian case, however, in which Broyles-Manga found evidence of some degree of substitution between physician and hospital services, for the United States an increased availability of doctors or hospital beds is associated with significantly more use of that resource without any indication of a decline in the other. If more hospital beds are available in a region, the likelihood of hospitalization and the number of hospital nights per capita go up, other things equal. Yet this greater use of hospitalization is also associated with a greater use of physicians, so we are not seeing a substitution of hospitalization for physician care. Instead, there is more use of both resources. This finding may simply reflect substantial differences in medical practice styles in different parts of the country, or it may be evidence that the medical resource supply is to some extent creating its own demand.

What are the policy lessons from this comparative analysis? First, it is clear that the current concern about lack of health insurance is well placed. Insurance status is a much better indicator of reduced use of health care resources than income or relative poverty. In spite of the apparent success of the government in offsetting the general effect of income on access to medical care through its targeted programs, there are still many people not covered by public or private insurance, and that lack of coverage makes a substantial difference in their access to medical care. For Canada this is a nonissue. The availability of universal health care insurance makes sure there are no subgroups without coverage. In the United States, however, the targeting of special programs to particular groups, who are seen through the political process to be in need, has left a number of coverage gaps that, taken together, create a serious access problem.

The response from most of those who are proposing reforms in the U.S. health care system is to add additional insurance programs and governmental regulation to try to extend coverage to almost everyone. There are at least two problems with this approach. The first is that the new programs will almost inevitably leave some people uncovered; even if we mandate risk pools and legislate coverage for small businesses, that only reduces the size of the uninsured population. Second, although the number left without insurance may then eventually be small enough that there is no political problem, there will still be an issue of fairness.

But, even if one of the new insurance programs was an everyone-not-otherwise-covered program, we are still left with the serious problem of the administrative burden created by the multiplicity of public and private programs. Woolhandler and Himmelstein found that the administrative overhead of the U.S. medical care system was far greater than that of Canada's, something that goes against the conventional wisdom of the market system being more efficient than any governmental structure. The problem, of course, is that the government is very much involved in the health care system but, since it is philosophically opposed to such involvement, tries to do it in a piecemeal fashion that is almost hopelessly complex and still manages to leave people without coverage. In fact, the government may actually contribute to the misery of the uninsured by driving the cost of medical care up through its demand for services and shifting some of the cost to nongovernmental programs through its attempts at cost containment.

It seems unlikely that without reform the plight of the uninsured will over time get better on its own. A number of factors make the outlook unfavorable. Among them is the sustained high rate of inflation in medical care costs, which has made health insurance increasingly more expensive in real terms. In the absence of some subsidy health insurance is now even harder to afford than it used to be, which is likely to reduce coverage, and the financial risks of not having insurance are greater as well, because of the relatively higher cost of medical care.

The increased role that HMOs play in providing medical care also puts pressure on the uninsured. Blumenthal and Rizzo, in their study of uninsured persons, found that physicians working for HMOs are significantly less likely to treat uninsured patients than other physicians. This is not surprising, since the HMO is set up for its own members, but it has the effect of concentrating the care for the uninsured, who include almost all of those who cannot pay, on a decreasing fraction of available physicians. The AMA, in its recent proposal for improving access, encourages the provision of voluntary care to fill the gaps in insurance coverage. The growth of HMOs may make this more difficult.

In addition to the insurance coverage problem, there is a racial access problem, which has had far less attention. Lewin-Epstein's recent study examines the sources of health care for low-income minority and white populations. It finds relatively high dependence on hospitals and their staffs as a source of health care among low-income African-Americans and raises concerns about the quality of such care. The use of emergency rooms and outpatient departments in place of the physician's office leads to discontinuities in care, unless special efforts are made.

The proposals for reform of the U.S. medical care system are largely silent on this issue of race. A lot more research needs to be done on this topic, and it would be very interesting to see if Canadian minorities also have access problems, but Lewin-Epstein suggests that some of the difficulties the U.S. minorities have lie in the quality and coverage of the private health insurance policies held by minority members and in the administrative complexity of the insurance programs, particularly those managed by the government. To get the most out of any insurance program one has to possess a good understanding of benefits and eligibility, and this puts minorities, who on average have poorer education and less social integration, at a disadvantage. There might well be considerable alleviation of this differential racial access problem with the adoption of a Canadian-style health insurance system. If one no longer had the task of figuring out who would accept his or her insurance, what it would cover, how he or she and/or the provider would get paid, and how the inevitable errors would be corrected, even those with insurance would have better access.

Fuchs and Hahn, in their article "How Does Canada Do It?" argue that the Canadian health care system of universal insurance allows Canadians, in effect, to have their cake and eat it. A Canadian citizen receives more health care services than his or her U.S. counterpart while at the same time paying substantially less for that care than the U.S. citizen pays for his or her lesser amount of care. This is accomplished with a system that still manages to generate physicians' incomes not far below those of U.S. physicians and that seems to enjoy far greater popular support from its citizens and health providers than does the U.S. system. The excess in administrative costs of the U.S. system over the Canadian system is so high that the General Accounting Office estimates that the adoption of the Canadian system by the United States would save enough in administrative costs to fund the entire cost of coverage for the currently uninsured and still leave enough money to enhance the program.

The approach used by the United States in providing health care for its citizens has not been successful in equalizing access. The lack of health insurance and minority status are significant factors limiting access to the full range of health care services that the United States has to offer. It seems unlikely that attempts to add still more patchwork programs to the current overly complex system would really solve the access problem. It is far more likely that we would simply have more administrative costs, adding to the incredible overhead burden we currently carry.

An alternative direction is that suggested by the Canadian system. The provision of universal health care insurance would obviously eliminate insurance coverage as a barrier to access and clearly eliminates a great proportion of the administrative overhead our current system creates. It seems possible to provide the same level of medical care that we currently enjoy and in addition, through the utilization of administrative savings, expand coverage to those with limited access without increasing the total cost.

The Canadian system also provides us with a model in a culture that is probably as close to our own as any other country in the world (although many of my Canadian friends would strongly deny this). This is important in that a society's approach to dealings with difficult allocation problems is greatly influenced by cultural values. The British approach to kidney transplantation and dialysis of severe rationing on the basis of age would be a disaster in the United States, since it is tailored to British values, traditions, and attitudes toward medicine and would shock and horrify many Americans, who do not share those values. Calabresi and Bobbitt explore the effect of cultural differences on national policy and make a strong argument for caution in trying to transplant what works in one culture to another quite different one. Thus, the relative similarities of Canadian and U.S. cultures give some assurance that what works in Canada is likely to succeed in the United States.

Taylor, in his review of the Canadian health care system, quotes survey results that show a rather high degree of satisfaction among Canadians with their system in comparison with the lower satisfaction Americans have with their health care system. This again suggests that a move in the Canadian direction would be welcomed in the United States.

It is equally clear, however, that it would not be easy to make the change to a Canadian-style system in the United States. There are a number of objections to the Canadian system that have been raised by both Canadian and U.S. observers, and in addition we have the serious problem that the very large number of people currently engaged in administering the U.S. system provide a potentially formidable lobby against any changes that would drastically reduce the number of their jobs. It is all well and good to say that there are administrative savings to be made. It is quite another thing for any government to actually make the cuts in the face of organized opposition, and the track record of U.S. administrations is not encouraging.

A recent article by Walker typifies some of the concerns raised by opponents of the Canadian health care system. Walker raises a number of points that deserve attention. While he concedes that there are major differences in administrative costs between the systems, he views the savings as coming at a considerable cost and uses the example of Galbraith's call for elimination of waste and duplication by standardizing a single provider of soap rather than have the multiplicity of suppliers we do now. The savings in the case of standardization of soap come at the price of the suppression of competition, which in turn throttles the incentive to reduce costs and make innovations in the product.

Yet soap and health care, at least health care as currently provided in the United States, are not the same thing. If we were to make soap available the same way we currently do health care, we would have long lines at the supermarket checkouts as the cashiers made sure our soap insurance cards entitled us to the particular type or amount. In addition, although I am un-aware of any data to support it, I suspect that soap use does not lead to quite as many bankruptcies as health care use or to as much concern over its purchase because of financial problems. It is difficult to accept an argument that a change in the health care system is equivalent to the regulation of a currently freely operating product market. We already have the U.S. government mas-sively involved in the health care system. The question is what sort of changes in that involvement would be beneficial, not whether or not there should be any involvement at all.

Another concern raised by Walker is that of the difficulties of having a sole provider of an essential service. He points to the increase in health care provider strikes in Canada, linking them to the negotiations with the largely unionized health care providers. This is a serious concern that arises in a number of occupations. Those working for police and fire departments, the military, and public utilities, for example, create great hardship if they go out on strike, and, as a society, we have developed a number of ways of trying to resolve such problems. The success we have had generally in keeping strikes to a minimum in these essential sectors suggests that equal success might be achieved in the health care field as well. And, of course, we already have quite a bit of experience in similar sorts of negotiations with our health care providers over such things as Medicare reimbursement.

A final concern that Walker touches on, but which others have empha-sized, is that Canadian medicine is rather "low tech" compared to that in the United States, in the sense that the latest expensive diagnostic equipment is less available and there is less capacity for doing certain complex procedures such as transplants and cardiac surgery. Related to this is a concern that universal health care would somehow reduce the amount and success of medical research and innovation.

There are a couple of responses to this. The first is that the numbers indicate that we could afford to continue our current style of medicine and extend it to the rest of the population, which currently has reduced access, without increasing the total cost. Even more money would flow to physicians and other health care workers, and even the group that would suffer, the unemployed health care administrators, would not have to worry about not having access to medical care.

It is also possible, however, to make a case for saving money on health care. The international comparisons on length of life and infant mortality seem to show that the United States does not have the world's best health care system. It is quite possible that the allocation of money away from the more expensive and dramatic procedures and diagnostic techniques and toward less spectacular interventions might both increase the overall health status of the population and reduce the fraction of GNP spent on health care. The United States, as a nation, may not want to reduce health care expenditures, but a reallocation of these expenditures may have substantial payoffs. One can be a strong believer in the general efficiency of market systems and at the same time be very skeptical of the notion that the current U.S. system has done the optimal job of enhancing the health status of its citizens.

Finally, with respect to medical innovation, it is not clear that a universal insurance scheme would choke off research in our medical schools and pharmaceutical companies. Universal access to medical care would seem to expand the markets for some products, particularly those that could be demonstrated to have some degree of cost efficiency. An increased emphasis on cost efficiency may well hurt the manufacturers of some types of diagnostic and procedure-related equipment, but this doesn't seem to be a particularly bad thing.

Overall, it appears that we in the United States have a lot to learn from the Canadians. From the point of view of access, their system is clearly superior, and it has considerable support from its citizens in comparison with ours. This does not mean that we should simply adopt the Canadian system in all its details. The U.S. system has a number of unique strengths that should be taken advantage of and preserved in any reform. For example, our extensive experience with HMOs may suggest ways of organizing our health care system that would enhance the final result.

It is the lack of universal health insurance that is the key factor in limiting access to health care in the United States. Its adoption in the United States would substantially equalize access, and, judging from the Canadian experience, we could then have our cake and eat it too.

BIBLIOGRAPHY

Aday, L. A., Fleming, G. V., and Andersen, R. *Access to Medical Care in the U.S.: Who Has It, Who Doesn't.* Chicago: University of Chicago Center for Health Administration Studies, 1984.

American Medical Association. *Health Access America*. Chicago: AMA, 1990.

Beck, R. G. "Economic Class and Access to Physician Services under Public Medical Care Insurance." *International Journal of Health Services* 3 (1973): 341–55.

Berkanovic, E., and Telesky, C. W. "Mexican-American, Black-American, and White-American Differences in Symptoms, Disability and Physician Visits for Symptoms." *Social Science and Medicine* 20 (1985): 567–77.

Blumenthal, D., and Rizzo, J. A. "Who Cares for Uninsured Persons? A Study of Physicians and Their Patients Who Lack Health Insurance." *Medical Care* 29 (June 1991): 502–19.

Bonham, G. S., and Corder, L. S. *National Medical Care Expenditure Survey Household Interview Instruments: Instruments and Procedures 1*. U.S. Department of Health and Human Services, Public Health Service. Washington, D.C.: Government Printing Office, 1981.

Broyles, R. W., Manga, P., Binder, D. A., Angus, D. E., and Charette, A. "The Use of Physician Services under a National Health Insurance Scheme: An Examination of the Canada Health Survey." *Medical Care* 21 (Nov. 1983): 1037–54.

Calabresi, G., and Bobbitt, P. *Tragic Choices*. New York: W. W. Norton, 1978.

Enterline, P. E., Salter, V., McDonald, A. D., and McDonald, J. C. "The Distribution of Medical Services before and after 'Free' Medical Care—The Quebec Experience." *New England Journal of Medicine* 289 (May 31, 1973): 1152–55.

Fuchs, V. R., and Hahn, J. S. "How Does Canada Do It? A Comparison of Expenditures for Physicians' Services in the United States and Canada." *New England Journal of Medicine* 323 (Sept. 27, 1990): 884–90.

Health and Welfare Canada and Statistics Canada. *The Health of Canadians: Report of the Canada Health Survey*. Ottawa: Ministry of Supply and Services, 1981.

Heckman, J. J. "Sample Selection Bias as a Specification Error." *Econometrica* 47 (Jan. 1979): 153–61.

Le Grand, J. "The Distribution of Public Expenditure: The Case of Health Care." *Economica* 45 (1978): 125–42.

Lewin-Epstein, N. "Determinants of Regular Source of Health Care in Black, Mexican, Puerto Rican, and Non-Hispanic White Populations." *Medical Care* 29 (June 1991): 543–57.

Maddala, G. S. *Limited Dependent and Qualitative Variables in Econometrics*. Cambridge: Cambridge University Press, 1983.

Manga, P., Broyles, R. W., and Angus, D. E. "The Determinants of Hospital Utilization under a Universal Public Insurance Program in Canada." *Medical Care* 25 (July 1987): 658–70.

Monheit, A. C., Hagan, M. M., Berk, M. L., and Wilensky, G. R. "Unemployment, Health Insurance and Medical Care Utilization." A special report prepared for the National Center for Health Services Research, U.S. Department of Health and Human Services. Washington, D.C.: Government Printing Office, 1983

Puffer, F. "Access to Primary Health Care: A Comparison of the U.S. and the U.K." *Journal of Social Policy* 15 (1986): 293–313.

Shannon, G. W., and Dever, G. E. A. *Health Care Delivery: Spatial Aspects*. New York: McGraw-Hill, 1974.

Taylor, M. G. *Insuring National Health Care: The Canadian Experience*. Chapel Hill: University of North Carolina Press, 1990.

U.S. Department of Health Education and Welfare. Public Health Service. *Health United States 1979*. Washington, D.C.: Government Printing Office, 1980.

Walker, M. "Canadian Health Care Is a Model for Disaster." *Wall Street Journal,* October 18, 1991.

Woolhandler, S., and Himmelstein, D. U. "The Deteriorating Administrative Efficiency of the U.S. Health Care System." *New England Journal of Medicine* 324 (May 2, 1991): 1253–58.

CHAPTER 6

Is Canadian-Style Government Health Insurance the Answer for the United States' Health Care Cost and Access Woes?

Edward Neuschler

Canada's government-operated health care financing system has received extensive attention in the United States over the past two years, both in the popular press and in the health policy community. This interest is fueled by the continuing escalation of U.S. health care costs, by growing concern over the millions of Americans who do not have health care coverage, and by the well-publicized observation that the Canadian system affords universal coverage while consuming a smaller percentage of total economic output than the U.S. system.[1] A number of advocacy groups and labor unions are actively promoting national health insurance schemes based on the Canadian model, and bills to establish publicly operated health insurance plans have been introduced in the U.S. Congress and in several state legislatures.[2]

This article is a shortened version of *Canadian Health Care: The Implications of Public Health Insurance, by Edward Neuschler, published as a Research Bulletin* by the Health Insurance Association of America in June 1990. Where more recent data and research were readily available, they have been incorporated.

1. See, for example, R. G. Evans et al., "Controlling Health Expenditures: The Canadian Reality," *New England Journal of Medicine (NEJM)* 320, no. 9 (March 2, 1989): 571–77.

2. See, for example, D. U. Himmelstein, S. Woolhandler, and the Writing Committee of the Working Group on Program Design, "A National Health Program for the United States," *NEJM* 320, no. 2 (January 12, 1989): 102–8. As of early May 1991, proposals to establish single, government-run public health insurance systems had been introduced in the 102d Congress by Reps. Marty Russo (H.R. 1300), Mary Rose Oakar (H.R. 8), and Pete Stark (H.R. 650). Sens. James Jeffords, Robert Kerrey, and Paul Wellstone and Rep. Bernie Sanders were also known to be drafting universal public health insurance proposals. Rep. John Dingell has again introduced the national health insurance proposal he has introduced in every Congress since he was first elected to the House of Representatives (H.R. 16). None of the proposals is given any chance of passage in this Congress.

In 1990 Canadian-style proposals were considered in the Ohio (H.B. 425) and Washington (H.B. 2252) legislatures. A 1989 Governor's Task Force in Michigan narrowly rejected such a proposal. See Peter Luke, "State Universal Health Insurance Rejected," *Ann Arbor News, Sep-*

When described at the simplest level—government pays most of the cost of health care for everyone out of taxes and sets all fees charged by doctors and hospitals; people can choose their own doctors and hospitals—the Canadian system can stimulate a favorable public response. In a 1988 public opinion survey of Americans, Canadians, and Britons, 61 percent of the Americans surveyed, when presented with this description, said they preferred the Canadian system.[3] A separate survey commissioned in 1989 by the Health Insurance Association of America (HIAA) found a smaller percentage of Americans (45 percent) preferred the Canadian system over the American when presented with the same description.[4] When asked why they liked the Canadian approach, these Americans said they were attracted by Canada's universal coverage, free choice of provider, and government control of provider rates. But, upon further questioning, it became clear that other aspects of the Canadian system were less attractive to them. Even those who said they preferred the Canadian system felt strongly that waiting many months to obtain elective surgery, as now seems common in Canada, would be unacceptable. They also said that they did not like Canada's prohibition against purchasing private insurance for benefits covered by the public plan and were inclined to be less supportive if substantially higher taxes would be needed to fund the system.

Because of the high level of public interest, the Health Insurance Association of America undertook an in-depth study of the Canadian health care system and its potential implications for the United States.[5] In addition to providing basic descriptive information on the Canadian system for the association's members and others, the study's main goals were to examine the contention that Canada has done a better job of controlling health care costs than the United States and to explore the potential fiscal impact on the public sector in the United States if the Canadian model of health care financing were to be adopted in the United States.

This chapter presents the major findings of the HIAA study. It begins with a very brief summary of the current structure of health care financing and delivery in Canada. The health care cost-containment records of the United States and Canada are then compared, and current access problems in the Canadian system are discussed. After reporting HIAA's estimate of the tax

tember 15, 1989, A1. In 1991 Canadian-style public health insurance proposals were introduced in a dozen or so state legislatures but rarely received serious consideration.

3. Robert J. Blendon, "Three Systems: A Comparative Survey," *Health Management Quarterly* 11, no. 1 (1989): 2–10.

4. Cindy Jajich-Toth and Burns W. Roper, "Americans' Views on Health Care," *Health Affairs* 9, no. 4 (Winter 1990): 149–57. See especially 154–55 and exhibit 4. In both the Blendon and HIAA studies, 37 percent of Americans said they preferred the U.S. health care system over the Canadian system. There were many more "undecided" respondents in the HIAA study.

5. Edward Neuschler, *Canadian Health Care: The Implications of Public Health Insurance* (Washington, D.C.: Health Insurance Association of America, June 1990).

cost of implementing a government-run health insurance entitlement program in the United States, the chapter ends with a discussion of political and cultural factors that cast doubt on the feasibility and advisability of adopting public insurance based on the Canadian model in the United States.

A Thumbnail Sketch of the Canadian System

Since 1971 the ten Canadian provinces have operated public health insurance plans that cover hospital and physician care for all residents of the province, plus some additional services depending on the province.[6] Private insurance for government-covered services is effectively prohibited.[7] There are no exclusions or dollar limits on medically necessary care, and there is no cost to the patient at point of service,[8] although two provinces charge small premiums.[9] (These premiums represent only a minor portion of expenses, and care cannot be denied for failure to pay the premium.) Financing is provided largely from general revenue, with the Canadian federal government contributing a declining percentage (about 38 percent in 1987)[10] of provincial health expenditures as a capitation grant. Growth in the federal contribution is linked

6. A brief history of the development of public health insurance in Canada and more details on its current structure are presented in Neuschler, *Canadian Health Care,* chapter 1. For a more detailed historical and political discussion, see either of two works by Malcolm G. Taylor: *Health Insurance and Canadian Public Policy: The Seven Decisions that Created the Canadian Health Insurance System and Their Outcomes,* 2d ed. (Kingston, Ont.: McGill-Queen's University Press, 1987); or "The Canadian Health Care System, 1974–1984," in *Medicare at Maturity: Achievements, Lessons and Challenges,* ed. Robert G. Evans and Greg L. Stoddart (Calgary, Alb.: University of Calgary Press, 1986), 3–39.

7. In some provinces there is a legal prohibition against selling such insurance. In others the provincial plan is the primary insurer, and supplemental insurance may exist provided that the resident does not receive duplicate reimbursement. See Canadian Life and Health Insurance Association, "Across Canada at a Glance," *Quarterly Review* 4, no. 2 (1988). John Iglehart notes that Canada is alone among industrialized nations in not looking toward private funding to relieve pressure on tax-financed programs: "What is unique to Canada is the virtual absence of private-sector involvement in health insurance and the unwillingness of policy makers to encourage the development of such alternatives, which could ease the financial pressure on the provincial health plans." See J. K. Iglehart, "Health Policy Report: Canada's Health Care System Faces Its Problems," *NEJM* 322, no. 8 (February 22, 1990): 562.

8. A few charges are still permitted. Patients pay out of pocket for noncovered physician services such as employment physicals. Hospital patients in chronic care are required to pay a room-and-board charge equivalent to what they would pay if they were in a nursing home.

9. Ontario recently eliminated its health insurance premium, effective January 1, 1990; a payroll tax was substituted. The two provinces now charging premiums are Alberta and British Columbia. See American Hospital Association, Office of Public Policy Analysis, "The Canadian Option: Background Information on Health Care in Canada and the United States," a special briefing for members, February 12, 1990, 7–8.

10. Author's calculation from Health and Welfare Canada, *National Health Expenditures in Canada, 1975–1987* (Ottawa: Minister of Supply and Services Canada, 1990), table 69. The 1987 figure is provisional.

to the growth rate of the overall economy, but continuing budget deficits have led the federal government to restrict the growth of its contribution in recent years.[11] Last year's federal budget froze the federal contribution for the following two fiscal years (April 1990 to March 1992) at the fiscal 1989–90 per capita rate.[12] The provinces are at risk for any cost increases.

Patients have free choice of doctor and hospital. Physicians are paid on a fee-for-service basis and must accept the provincial plan's payment as payment in full; no balance billing of patients is permitted (a result of the 1984 Canada Health Act). Fee schedules are negotiated periodically between each provincial health plan and the provincial medical association, an increasingly contentious process. There are no government-imposed prior authorization requirements or utilization review process.

Individual hospitals negotiate their budgets with the provincial plan on a total budget basis (not per patient). In most provinces there is no allowance for depreciation; capital improvements must be approved separately and are often funded by combinations of philanthropic, municipal, and provincial monies. In those cases in which capital improvements are funded by private philanthropy, the associated operating costs are still part of the total budget and must be approved by the province.

Canada's bed-to-population ratio is considerably higher than America's, as are overall hospital use and average length of stay. The physician-to-population ratio (210 per 100,000) is essentially the same as in the United States (212 per 100,000), although a significantly higher proportion of U.S. physicians are specialists. Unlike in the United States, there is very little physician ownership of major pieces of medical equipment, and all major surgery or high-technology diagnostic tests are done in hospitals. A few entrepreneurial physicians have opened private ambulatory surgery centers, largely for cataract surgery, that operate outside the public insurance system.

Although budgeted community health centers (CHCs) and limited capitation arrangements do exist in some places, alternative delivery systems that accept full financial risk for all the health care needs of their members, such as American health maintenance organizations (HMOs), do not yet exist in Canada.[13]

---

11. Beginning in 1986, two percentage points were subtracted from the average three-year nominal growth in GNP to determine the escalator. A third percentage point was subtracted from the escalator for the 1989–90 fiscal year (J. Bruce Davis [director, Program Administration, Health Insurance Directorate, Department of National Health and Welfare, Government of Canada] personal communication with author).

12. "The Budget Tabled in the House of Commons by the Honorable Michael H. Wilson, Minister of Finance, February 20, 1990." The budget document promises that, beginning in 1992–93, the growth of the total transfer to the provinces will not fall below the rate of inflation. See also "Canada Presents Austerity Budget," *New York Times,* February 21, 1990.

13. For a more detailed discussion of provider payment methods, delivery system structure, and utilization rates, see Neuschler, *Canadian Health Care,* chapters 2 and 3.

Canada's Cost-Containment and Access Records

References to the success of the Canadian health care system have become increasingly frequent in the American press. If we measure access by health insurance coverage and health care cost by percentage of gross national product, Canada is doing well. All Canadians have health insurance coverage, and Canada spends a smaller percentage of its total economic output on health care than the United States does. But if cost containment is measured by rates of increase in health care spending and access by prompt availability of needed services, the picture is less clear. An analysis of trends suggests that: (1) Canada has done no better than the United States in taming health care cost escalation; and (2) Canada may be starting to have problems with access to needed services, particularly when expensive, high-technology care is required.

This section examines the evidence on cost containment and reviews the ongoing debate in Canada over access to care.[14]

Health Care Cost Containment

International comparisons of health care expenditures must be adjusted in some way to account for differences in size among national economies. There are two ways to do this. One is to express health care expenditure as a percent of total economic output—gross national product (GNP) or gross domestic product (GDP).[15] The other is to express expenditure in per capita terms.

---

14. Quality of care is obviously the other major consideration, but the science of measuring quality is in its infancy. We are just beginning to learn how we might compare outcomes of care across hospitals. Collecting the volumes of data that would be necessary for a reasonably valid cross-national comparison of medical outcomes is a task that no one yet has attempted. Even if data were available, it would be difficult to prove that any observed differences in outcomes were due to differences in financing mechanisms. The gross health status measures that are available— primarily infant mortality and life expectancy at birth—favor Canada. (For a comparison of the United States with Canada and several European countries, see American Medical Association, Center for Health Policy Research, "Chartbook of Cross-National Health Care Comparisons: Demographics, Expenditures, Utilization and Resources," December 1989.) These measures are so influenced by factors other than the quality of medical care, however, that they can shed little light on that issue.

15. GDP measures the total value of production originating within the geographic boundaries of the country, regardless of whether the factors of production are owned by residents or nonresidents. GNP measures income received by resident factors of production regardless of where the production takes place. GNP is used here to measure total economic output because the United States traditionally has kept its national accounts in this form, and it is therefore familiar to American readers. Using GDP as the basis, as is usually done for international comparisons, would change the apparent differences between the United States and Canada only slightly. In Canada GDP exceeds GNP by about three percentage points. In the United States the reverse is true: GNP exceeds GDP by about one percentage point.

Comparisons between Canadian and U.S. health care expenditures often use the former method. On this measure Canada has been more successful than the United States in containing costs: health care expenditures as a proportion of GNP have not grown as fast in Canada as they have in the United States. Canada spent a slightly higher percentage of GNP on health than the United States in the 1960s but fell below the U.S. level in 1969 and has stayed there. The most recent available figures show Canada spending 8.9 percent of GNP on health care (1989, estimated) and the United States spending 11.6 percent (1989).[16] As will be demonstrated, however, when health care costs per capita are compared, the two countries have very similar growth patterns. Thus, it can be argued, the difference in the proportion of GNP going to health care is due not to differences in how the two countries finance and deliver health care but, instead, to differences in overall economic growth rates: The Canadian economy grew significantly faster than the U.S. economy over the past two decades.

The HIAA study examined the growth rate of per capita health spending[17] in Canada and the United States from 1967 through 1987 (the most recent twenty-year period for which final health spending totals are available for both countries). Figure 1 plots per capita health care spending in the United States and in Canada during that period, in the currency of each country and in the nominal dollars of each year (i.e., not adjusted for inflation). Canadian spending (Can$1,869 per capita in 1987; $1,520 after conversion to U.S. dollars)[18] is lower than U.S. spending ($2,019 per capita in 1987) in absolute

---

16. Personal communication from the Health Information Division, Health and Welfare Canada, May 2, 1991; Helen C. Lazenby and Suzanne W. Letsch, "National Health Expenditures, 1989," *Health Care Financing Review* 12, no. 2 (Winter 1990): 1–26.

17. Per capita health spending is defined here as total national health expenditures divided by total population (including armed forces). U.S. figures cited in this section differ slightly from those originally published in Neuschler, *Canadian Health Care,* chapter 4, because a more recent revision of the U.S. national health expenditure estimates (Lazenby and Letsch, "National Health Expenditures") has been used.

18. The conversion to U.S. dollars was made using the OECD's purchasing power parity currency conversion factor for 1987: Can$1.23 = U.S.$1.00. The OECD defines purchasing power parity (PPP) as "rates of currency conversion that equalize the purchasing power of different currencies. This means that a given sum of money, when converted into different currencies at the PPP rates, will buy the same basket of goods and services in all countries. Thus, PPPs are the rates of currency conversion which eliminate differences in price levels between countries." See *National Income and Expenditure Accounts,* vol. 1 (Paris: Organization for Economic Cooperation and Development). The Canadian per capita health spending figure given here is slightly higher than the figure ($1,483) reported in other recently published work (see n. 25) because more recent revised estimates of total Canadian health spending and population were obtained from Health and Welfare Canada. The U.S. per capita health spending figure given here is higher than the figure ($1,955 in 1987) published by the Office of National Cost Estimates, U.S. Health Care Financing Administration (HCFA) (Lazenby and Letsch, "National Health Expenditures"), because population figures from the U.S. Census Bureau were used rather than the higher Social Security Administration population estimates used by HCFA. The U.S. per

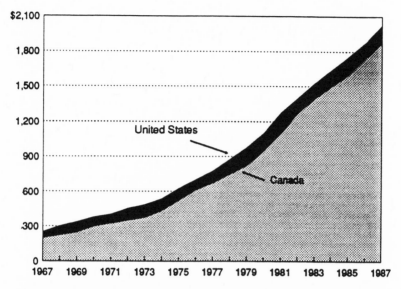

Fig. 1. Total health care spending per capita in nominal dollars, national currencies. Because currencies differ, the absolute difference in per capita spending is larger in each year than shown here. Twenty-year average annual growth rates—United States, 10.8 percent; Canada, 11.5 percent.

terms, but the similarity of the growth trend is striking. During the twenty-year period Canada's health care spending per capita grew at an average annual rate[19] of 11.5 percent, compared to a U.S. rate of 10.8 percent.

Because general inflation was greater in Canada than in the United States during this period, however, comparing growth in nominal dollars does not accurately measure the increase in real economic resources devoted to health care. To gain a more accurate picture of differences in the resources going to health care in the two countries, figure 2 displays health spending per capita in constant 1981 dollars.[20] To remove any distortion in the comparison due to the

---

capita figure is lower than the one shown by Schieber and Poullier (n. 25) because a new revision of the U.S. national health expenditure totals was used.

19. Throughout this article "average annual rates" are calculated as annual compound growth rates (ACGR), rather than as the average of the observed yearly growth rates. The ACGR is the single annual growth rate that, if it had been the actual rate for each year during the period in question, would have produced the same total growth over the entire period.

20. The conversion to constant 1981 dollars was made by dividing health care spending by the GNP implicit price deflator for the United States and by the GDP implicit price deflator for Canada, both indexed such that 1981 = 1.0. The price deflators were obtained from: Statistics Canada, *National Income and Expenditure Accounts: Annual Estimates, 1926–1986* (Ottawa: Minister of Supply and Services Canada, 1989), table 7; Statistics Canada, *National Income and Expenditure Accounts: Annual Estimates, 1977–1988* (Ottawa: Minister of Supply and Services

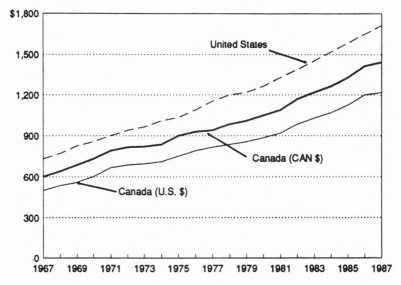

Fig. 2. Total health care spending per capita in constant 1981 dollars. Actual health care spending converted to 1981 dollars using GNP price deflator. Twenty-year average annual growth rates—United States, 4.42 percent; Canada, 4.58 percent.

varying relative value of the two currencies, Canadian expenditures are shown in both 1981 Canadian dollars and 1981 U.S. dollars.[21] The similarity in growth patterns remains striking whichever measure is used. In fact, on an inflation-adjusted basis the average growth rate over the twenty-year period is slightly lower in the United States: 4.42 percent per year compared to 4.58 percent per year in Canada. In figure 3 each country's real health spending per capita is displayed as the ratio of spending in that year to spending in 1967, so that the graph represents the cumulative growth of real per capita spending over the twenty-year period. With the visual distortion caused by the difference in base-year spending thus removed, the almost precise coincidence of the trend lines is absolutely clear.

Canada, 1989), table 7; and U.S. Department of Commerce, Bureau of Economic Analysis, *Survey of Current Business,* 69, no. 9 (Washington, D.C.: U.S. Government Printing Office, September 1989), table 3, 57. (The U.S. series, which sets 1982 = 1.0, was rebased to 1981 = 1.0 by dividing the deflator for all years by the deflator for 1981.)

21. The conversion to U.S. dollars was made using the OECD's purchasing power parity for 1981: Can$1.18 = U.S.$1.00. Robert Evans suggested this two-step approach to comparing growth rates between countries (first convert to constant dollars within each country, then convert currencies using the PPP for the "constant dollar" year). See R. G. Evans, "Perspectives: Canada's Split Vision: Interpreting Cross-Border Differences in Health Spending," *Health Affairs* 7, no. 5 (Winter 1988): 17–24.

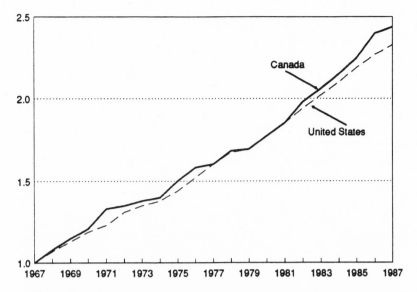

Fig. 3. Cumulative increase since 1967 in real health care spending per capita. Ratio of health spending in each year to health spending in 1967, adjusted for general inflation by GNP deflator.

But does the similarity of long-term trends mask some significant change during the 1967 to 1987 period? In particular, did Canada's growth rate slow after universal public health insurance was implemented fully, as some analysts have argued?[22] To examine this question, figure 4 presents average annual growth rates in U.S. and Canadian health care spending per capita over successive five-year periods, beginning in 1967. As shown, health care costs grew more rapidly in Canada than in the United States between 1967 and 1972. Canada's provinces implemented universal public medical insurance between 1968 and 1971,[23] so Canada's somewhat more rapid escalation of costs in this period may be due to increased demand for services from newly insured individuals. After full implementation of public insurance the rate of increase slowed significantly in Canada. But, despite the 1972 expansion of U.S. Medicare to include disabled persons under age sixty-five, the U.S. growth rate fell as well, suggesting that the advent of the public insurance system in Canada was not the only factor affecting health care costs at that time. Since 1977 real health spending per capita has grown a bit more slowly in the United States than in Canada. The average growth rate during 1977 to

---

22. Evans et al., "Controlling Health Expenditures."
23. Saskatchewan pioneered in 1962, but no other province adopted a universal public program until 1968.

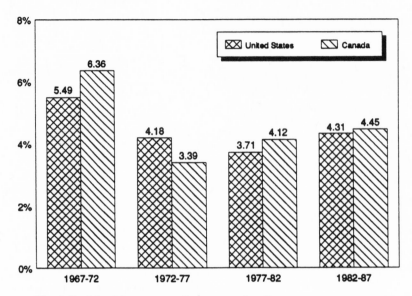

Fig. 4. Real health care spending per capita: five-year average annual growth rates by percentage increase. Growth in health care spending in excess of general inflation as measured by GNP deflator.

1987 was 4.28 percent per year in Canada and 4.01 percent in the United States.[24]

A final way of looking at the growth rate issue is displayed in figure 5, which plots per capita health spending in Canada as a percentage of per capita U.S. spending (in constant 1981 U.S. dollars) from 1967 through 1987. As can be seen, the percentage fluctuated in a very narrow range over the period. Canada was spending about 75 percent of what the United States spends per capita on health care before full implementation of universal public health insurance and has continued to do so since. The factors leading to different levels of health care spending in the two countries, therefore, must be more basic than the difference in health care financing arrangements.

The analysis presented here is consistent with recently published work of a pair of international experts. Writing in the fall 1989 *Health Affairs,* Schieber and Poullier compared growth rates of health care spending per capita

24. The Office of National Cost Estimates, U.S. Health Care Financing Administration, recently completed a thorough revision of the U.S. national health expenditure series from 1960 onward. The revision lowered the 1987 U.S. health spending total significantly—to about $7.8 billion below the originally published figure. If the originally published figures for 1977 and 1987 are used, the U.S. average annual growth rate for the ten-year period becomes 4.31 percent, almost indistinguishable from the Canadian figure.

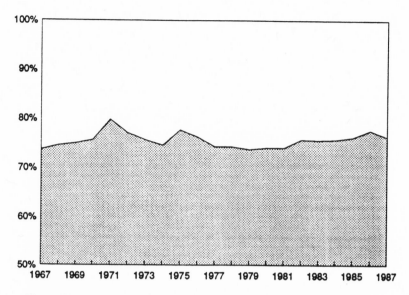

Fig. 5. Canadian health care spending per capita as a percentage of U.S. spending per capita. Comparison made in constant 1981 dollars using OECD purchasing power parity exchange rates (Can$1.18 = U.S.$1.00).

between the United States and Canada (along with five other large democracies), using price indices specific to medical care.[25] In this way they were able to divide overall growth in health care spending for 1960 to 1970, 1970 to 1980, and 1980 to 1987 into real growth in consumption of health care resources and medical price inflation in excess of general price inflation. In each period excess medical price inflation and growth in real consumption of health care resources per capita were very similar in the two countries (see table 1).

If per capita health spending is growing as fast in Canada as in the United States, why does health spending continue to consume a smaller proportion of total Canadian economic output than of U.S. output? A major reason appears to be that Canada's economic output per capita has grown faster than ours, particularly from 1967 through 1976. In 1967 Canada and the United States spent virtually identical proportions of GNP on health care (6.33 percent in the United States, 6.38 percent in Canada). Two years later the Canadian figure had fallen slightly below the U.S. figure; the gap widened noticeably after 1971 (see fig. 6).

25. G. J. Schieber and J. P. Poullier, "[Data Watch] International Health Care Expenditure Trends: 1987," *Health Affairs* 8, no. 3 (Fall 1989): 169–81. This article was published before the latest revisions of U.S. and Canadian national health expenditure data became available. Therefore, the article underestimates Canadian spending and overestimates U.S. spending.

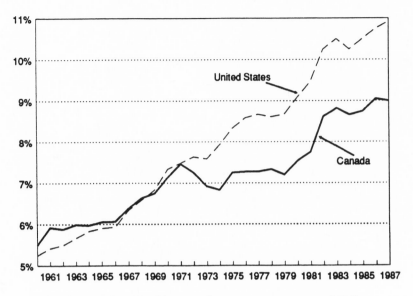

Fig. 6. Total national health expenditures as a percentage of GNP

TABLE 1. Annual Growth Rates of Health Care Spending, 1960–87

	1960–70	1970–80	1980–87	1960–87
	Nominal Health Spending per Capita			
United States	8.1%	11.5%	9.4%	10.2%
Canada	9.3	12.5	9.9	10.7
	Real[a] Expenditures per Capita			
United States	4.6%	3.9%	1.7%	3.9%
Canada	7.0	3.8	1.5	3.5
	Excess Medical-Specific Inflation			
United States	−0.9%	0.0%	3.0%	1.1%
Canada	−1.0	0.0	2.9	1.2

Source: George J. Schieber and Jean-Pierre Poullier, "[DataWatch] International Health Care Expenditure Trends: 1987," *Health Affairs* 8, no. 3 (Fall 1989): 174, exhibit 5.

Note: All entries are annual compound growth rates.

aIn this article we have used the term *real health spending* to denote comparisons made in constant (i.e., GNP-deflated) dollars. Schieber and Poullier had available to them price indices specific to the health care sector in each country. They were therefore able to separate increases in health spending into three components: general inflation (not shown), medical (price) inflation in excess of general inflation, and real growth in the consumption of health care resources. The entry "Real Expenditures per Capita" in this table reflects the last of the three components.

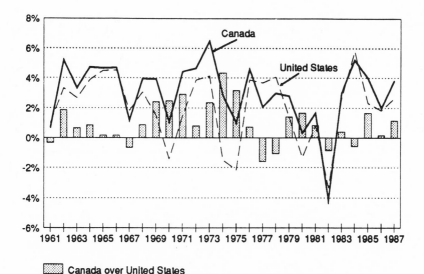

Canada over United States

Fig. 7. Annual growth in real GNP per capita by percentage increase over previous year. Lines show actual percentage growth in each country. Bar shows difference in growth rates.

Because universal insurance was implemented in Canada between 1968 and 1971, some analysts have attributed Canada's slower increase in health spending as a percentage of total economic output after 1971 to improved cost controls made possible by a universal government-financed system.[26] But an alternative explanation is possible, one more consistent with our observation that Canada's provincial health plans have not been more effective than the pluralistic U.S. health system in controlling per capita health spending. As figure 7 shows, beginning in 1968 Canada's economy grew faster than the U.S. economy (on a per capita basis) for a sustained period of nine years. In six of those years, the difference in growth rates was more than two percentage points per year. Over the entire twenty-year period (1967 to 1987), Canadian real GNP per capita grew 74 percent; U.S. real GNP per capita grew only 38 percent.[27] Given very similar growth rates of per capita health spending, the country that expands economic output more rapidly will spend a smaller proportion of that output on health care.

---

26. Evans et al., "Controlling Health Expenditures."

27. Author's calculation based on GNP figures from Statistics Canada, *National Income and Expenditures,* tables 4 and 7; and U.S. Department of Commerce, *Survey of Current Business,* table 2, 55, and appropriate population series.

TABLE 2.   Health Care Headlines in the Canadian Press

"Sick to Death: Caught between Rising Costs and More Restraints, Hospitals are Cutting Services."
MacLean's (Canada's national news magazine), February 13, 1989 (cover story)

"Soaring health costs a provincial headache."
Ottawa Citizen, May 29, 1989

"Bed closings blasted: 91 left on backlog for urgent surgery."
Winnipeg Free Press, July 5, 1989

"CO$T OF LIVING: Clogged heart programs are just a symptom of a system needing adjustment."
London Free Press, Ontario, June 10, 1989

"Ontario's Health Care Is in Critical Condition."
London Free Press, May 27, 1989

"Health system ill in Quebec, says founder."
Ottawa Citizen, January 25, 1990

"Need surgery, medical tests? Go to the end of the line."
Globe and Mail, Toronto, May 28, 1988

"Budget limit on MDs' services urged by major Ontario report."
Globe and Mail, May 24, 1989

"N.S. Royal Commission recommends controls on doctors."
Evening Telegram, St. John's, Newfoundland, December 9, 1989

"HSC staff denounce deplorable conditions in emergency ward."
Winnipeg Free Press, November 24, 1989

Access

Until recently, Canadians viewed their health care system as the best in the world. They perceived that every Canadian had access to necessary care with no financial barriers and that the most advanced procedures and technology were available to all. Many Canadians probably still hold that view. "Medicare," as Canadians call their health care program, remains the most popular government social program; Canadian politicians, federal or provincial, attack it only at their peril.

At the same time, there is growing evidence of access problems in the Canadian health care system, at least for high-technology specialty care, and growing concern over the continuing escalation of costs. The debate is raging in the popular press, as the headlines in table 2 suggest, making it clear that the Canadian health care system indeed suffers access problems and waiting lists at least for certain kinds of care in some parts of the country. Specific complaints about lack of access include the following:

Long waits for certain surgical and diagnostic procedures. Examples cited include not only surgeries such as coronary artery bypass grafts, hip replacements and lens extraction (cataract surgery), but also preventive tests such as mammograms. Deaths have been reported among patients on waiting lists for heart surgery.

In an effort to cut costs, most provincial governments have clamped down on hospital budgets at a time when many nurses are quitting their jobs to protest poor pay and working conditions. The result has been lengthening waiting lists and a toll of deaths among patients who cannot survive long enough to receive the surgery they need. In Manitoba, six heart patients died last year before they reached the operating room at Winnipeg's Health Sciences Centre. In Toronto—where an estimated 1,000 people are facing waits of as long as a year for bypass operations at three hospitals—two people have died since December. Last month, long waiting lists forced the city's highly regarded Hospital for Sick Children to send home 40 children who need heart surgery. (*MacLean's,* February 13, 1989, 32)

St. Clare's [Hospital, Newfoundland] four-month wait for a first-time mammogram makes it almost impossible to do preventive breast cancer screening; the hospital can handle only women who need an immediate diagnosis. (*Globe and Mail* [Toronto], May 28, 1988)

Temporary closure of hospital beds to remain within budget, even though the beds are needed for patients on waiting lists.

New Brunswick's hospitals, which were forced to take about 300 hospital beds out of service after Premier Frank McKenna's Liberal government tightened hospital budgets, are among the most seriously affected. At Moncton Hospital, some patients are kept in hallways and even in closets, while a total of 2,300 people were on waiting lists for surgery last month. . . . The situation in parts of the Prairies is equally alarming. (*MacLean's,* February 13, 1989, 33)

Overcrowded emergency rooms and inability to admit patients in need of emergency care, due to overcrowding.

Stella Lacroix's death started as a suicide. But most people here [Toronto] think it ended as something else. Moments after she swallowed a quart of cleaning fluid, she changed her mind and raced to the nearest emergency room. The hospital wasn't equipped to perform the surgery she needed to stop internal bleeding, so her doctor began a frantic search for an available bed elsewhere in the Toronto area. "She was turned away from 14 hospitals," the doctor . . . said after his three-hour search had failed. "There was no space anywhere and she just bled to death. This woman needed immediate care and we couldn't get it for her." (*Washington Post,* December 18, 1989, 1)

Nor has the debate been restricted to the press. The scholarly community has raised concerns,[28] and several provinces have established special commissions to make recommendations about the future of health care.[29]

Rigorous quantitative analysis of these problems has been notably lacking.[30] But the Fraser Institute of Vancouver, in cooperation with the British Columbia Medical Association, has surveyed a sample of physicians in the province to determine how long their patients have to wait for certain surgical procedures.[31] Responding ophthalmologists reported 882 patients had been

---

28. See, for example, Michael Rachlis, M.D., and Carol Kushner, *Second Opinion: What's Wrong with Canada's Health Care System and How to Fix It* (Toronto: Harper and Collins, 1989), 45.

29. Examples include:

The Ontario Premier's Council on Health Strategy reported early in 1989, calling for a cap on annual payments to physicians (Derek Ferguson, "Cap Urged on Fees Paid to Doctors," *Toronto Star,* May 23, 1989);

New Brunswick's Commission on Selected Health Care Programs produced "sixty-four wide-ranging recommendations on how the government could control the cost of medical care" (Robert Jones, "Supply of Doctors Must Be Checked, New Brunswick Task Force Reports," *Globe and Mail* [Toronto], August 25, 1989);

"After more than two years of research and public hearings, Nova Scotia's Royal Commission on Health Care released its report [in December 1989]" (Beverley Ware, "The Key to Controlling Health Costs," *Daily News* [Halifax], December 24, 1989);

A report from the Premier's Commission on Future Health Care for Albertans was submitted in late December 1989 and was to be made public in February 1990 (Karen Sherlock, "Health-Care Task Force Hands in Its Report," *Edmonton Journal,* December 30, 1989); and

British Columbia recently has established a "$2-million royal commission . . . to consider the dramatic restructuring of British Columbia's health services into independent, regional comprehensive health organizations" (Deborah Wilson, "B.C. Commission to Study Health-Care Alternatives," *Globe and Mail* [Toronto], February 23, 1990).

30. A recent exception is a study of hospital use by elderly patients with cardiovascular disease. See Geoffrey M. Anderson, M.D., Ph.D., Joseph P. Newhouse, Ph.D., and Leslie L. Roos, Ph.D., "Hospital Care for Elderly Patients with Diseases of the Circulatory System," *NEJM* 321, no. 21 (November 23, 1989): 1443–48. Comparing national data from the U.S. Medicare program with provincial data from Ontario and Manitoba, the researchers found very similar discharge rates for nonsurgical treatment of elderly patients with cardiovascular disease (defined as patients with diagnoses in Major Diagnostic Category 5—diseases and disorders of the circulatory system) in both 1981 and 1985. Discharge rates for *surgical* treatment of cardiovascular problems, however, increased significantly from 1981 to 1985 in both countries: by 10 percent in Canada and by 64 percent in the United States, raising the U.S. rate from 81 percent to 121 percent of the Canadian rate. In 1985 the most significant difference between the two countries was the discharge rate for coronary bypass surgery: the U.S. rate was 2.3 times the Canadian rate. This result may explain the prominence of bypass surgery in Canadian press reports about waiting lists. The researchers, however, were unable to assess the appropriateness or relative benefit of surgical interventions in either country.

31. Steven Globerman with Lorna Hoye, "Waiting Your Turn: Hospital Waiting Lists in Canada," *Fraser Forum* (May 1990): S-38.

waiting an average of 18.2 weeks for cataract removal. General surgeons reported 68 patients waiting for hernia repair, with an average wait of 24.6 weeks, and 39 patients waiting for cholecystectomies, with an average wait of 31.7 weeks. Cardiologists had 313 patients waiting for coronary artery bypass grafts, with an average wait of 23.7 weeks.[32]

More research of this kind will be required before reliable conclusions can be drawn about the prevalence of long waiting lists, whether they apply to many treatments or only a few, and how they affect the eventual outcome of care. Similarly, currently available data and research are insufficient to permit comparison of Canada's problems with similar problems, at least for some populations, in the United States.[33]

On the other hand, despite the lack of definitive research, the problem of waiting lists is real enough in Canada that at least two provincial health plans have felt it necessary to permit patients to seek care in the United States for certain conditions. Coronary bypass surgery and lithotripsy have been identified as areas in which Canada has significantly fewer resources available than the United States.[34] To reduce a waiting list of seven hundred patients needing cardiac surgery, the British Columbia Health Association contracted with at least two Seattle hospitals for up to fifty coronary bypass surgeries each (until a new cardiac service opened in Vancouver).[35]

In Ontario a volunteer organization called "Heartbeat Windsor" has arranged for several Detroit hospitals to provide cardiac surgery to Canadian patients and accept the Ontario Health Insurance Plan rate as payment in full. In its first seven months of existence the organization arranged 150 opera-

---

32. The questionnaire was sent to half (seventy-three) of the ophthalmologists in the province; nineteen responded. One third (eighty-three) of the general surgeons were surveyed; ten responded. All (twenty-seven) of the cardiologists were surveyed; five responded. The number of patients waiting is the raw total reported by those physicians who responded, not an attempt to project a figure for the entire province.

33. For example, overcrowding and resultant problems in providing needed emergency care have been reported in many U.S. cities. Critics of the American health care system discount the relevance of Canadian media reports about waiting lists and delays in treatment. For example, David West, director of a consumer organization called Washington Fair Share, has been quoted as follows: "Much of the opposition to this plan [to establish Canadian-style public health insurance in the state of Washington] is in the form of anecdotes various people have heard about the Canadian system. What these stories ignore is the fact that someone not getting treatment is front-page news in Canada while the horror stories of being uninsured in America happen all the time" (Alicia Priest, "Dose of B.C. Touted as Cure," *Vancouver Sun,* January 31, 1990).

34. Dale A. Rublee, "Medical Technology in Canada, Germany, and the United States," *Health Affairs* 8, no. 3 (Fall 1989): 178–81.

35. Washington State Hospital Association, *Weekly Report* 15, no. 8 (February 23, 1989); Howard Kim, "Canada Tabs Wash. Hospital," *Modern Healthcare,* March 26, 1990; and "[For the Record] Second Seattle Hospital Gets Canadian Contract," *Modern Healthcare,* April 2, 1990, 13.

tions.[36] Alberta's health plan also has said it will pay if Albertans wish to travel to Detroit to avoid waiting for heart surgery.[37] With only one lithotripter in all of Ontario (a second one is scheduled), half of the lithotripsy patients at Buffalo General Hospital in nearby New York are Canadians.[38] (Extracorporeal shock wave lithotripsy breaks up kidney stones without surgery, greatly shortening hospital stays.)

Reasons for the apparent access problems are a matter of considerable debate within Canada. Providers argue that the health care system simply is underfunded, that government is too concerned about costs and not enough about access and quality. Provincial health ministries counter that providers (especially physicians) are not using resources efficiently and are milking the system. They note that Canada spends more on health care than almost every other developed country in the world. (In per capita terms only the United States is higher; as a proportion of GDP, only the United States and Sweden rank higher, and Sweden ranks very close to Canada.)[39]

Providers disclaim responsibility for excess utilization.[40] They (and some other observers) blame consumers for any overutilization that might exist—noting that, because there are no out-of-pocket charges to the patient at the time of service, consumers have no financial incentive to avoid seeking care that may be medically unnecessary or only marginally beneficial.[41] Any such tendency is reinforced by the fact that, because consumers never see a bill or a premium invoice,[42] they have no real sense of how much the system costs.

Nevertheless, Canadians continue to believe strongly in the right to "free" health care. As one Ontario resident put it in a letter to the editor of the

36. Carol Goodwin, "U.S. 'Miracle Workers' Take Pay Cuts to Help Canadians," *Kitchener-Waterloo Record*, Ontario, February 15, 1990.

37. Karen Sherlock, "Detroit Offers Short Wait for Heart Surgery. Provincial Insurance Covers Bill," *Edmonton Journal,* January 6, 1990.

38. Information for the first five months of 1989 (American Hospital Association, "The Canadian Option," 16). A U.S. physician at a treatment center associated with Buffalo General also reports that 40 to 45 percent of his patients are Canadians (Suzanne Morrison, "Lack of Lithotripter Sends Health Cash to U.S. Patient," *Hamilton Spectator,* Ontario, December 21, 1989).

39. Schieber and Poullier, "[DataWatch]."

40. See, for example, remarks by the Ontario Medical Association's director of professional affairs, David Peacey, quoted in St. Catherine's *Standard,* Ontario, April 21, 1989.

41. See, for example, remarks by the chief of emergency medicine at a Toronto hospital and by the president of the Quebec Corporation of Physicians in *MacLean's,* February 13, 1989, 35.

42. As noted, only Alberta and British Columbia charge premiums, and these premiums never cover more than a minor portion of total costs. In Alberta the premiums are often paid by employers. British Columbia does bill all residents directly. See American Hospital Association, "The Canadian Option," 8.

Windsor Star (July 12, 1989): "The people of Windsor and of Ontario have a right to expect that their medical system will provide them with the best of care at no cost." The prevalence of this view was borne out by the unanimous parliamentary approval of the 1984 Canada Health Act, which outlawed extra billing by physicians and user fees (copayments), in the face of strong opposition from organized medicine and provincial governments. But the public's insistence on free care, coupled with continually rising health care costs, has led, in the view of some observers, to a system that emphasizes the provision of routine medical services for the large majority of the population at the "expense" of the minority with specialized needs. As one analyst from a conservative Canadian policy research institute has noted, "A growing number of operations are triaged because resources are used to continue first-dollar coverage for sniffles and splinters."[43]

Others have pointed out that the planning and resource allocation system does not work very well. The provincial role has been characterized as simply limiting the amount of resources available, relying on physicians and hospitals to allocate them in an efficient manner (without any procedures for putting available resources to better use).[44] In this view the people allocating the resources have a vested economic interest in those resources, which may not make for an efficient allocation of resources from a public perspective. Some have proposed privatization of diagnostic and outpatient surgical facilities as a possible remedy for these problems.[45]

As the debate progresses, the political popularity of free care motivates the government to avoid any proposals that appear to cut back on benefits or shift costs to the consumer. Government proposals usually seek to shift more of the risk of excess utilization to the providers. For example, the governments of Ontario and Quebec are promoting alternatives (called comprehensive health organizations [CHOs in Ontario and OSIs in Quebec]) that would be more similar to American HMOs than anything now on the Canadian scene.[46] The Ontario "Premier's Council on Health Strategy" in 1989 recom-

---

43. Michael A. Walker, "Neighborly Advice on Health Care," *Wall Street Journal,* June 8, 1988, 24.

44. The House Wednesday Group, "Public Health in the Provinces: Canadian National Health Insurance Strategy" (Washington, D.C.: Congress of the United States, September 22, 1989), 5. The paper cites Robert Evans as the source of this observation. See R. G. Evans, "The Welfare Economics of Public Health Insurance: Theory and Canadian Practice," in *Social Insurance,* ed. Lars Soderstrom (New York: North Holland, 1983), 83.

45. The House Wednesday Group, "Public Health in the Provinces," 19. The paper cites the *Ottawa Citizen* ("Canada's Costly Health Care System: A Suitable Case for Privatization?" February 15, 1986, A1).

46. Derek Nelson, "Latest Health-Care Remedy May Not Work Either," *Examiner,* Peterborough, Ont., April 16, 1989. "Quebec Sets Detailed Plans to Become First Province to Use

mended an overall annual cap on total reimbursement to physicians,[47] and several provinces now take past utilization increases into account when negotiating physician fees.[48]

Government critics, largely members of the provider community, want to shift more of the system's costs to the consumer at the point of service by introducing coinsurance and/or reducing covered services. This serves a dual purpose in their view: It discourages unnecessary utilization, and it brings more money into the system. Conventional wisdom in Canada suggests that, given the long-standing political dynamics, such a change seems very unlikely. But some surprising voices are beginning to be heard on this side of the debate. Early last year a committee of Quebec's National Assembly was startled when Claude Castonguay, considered the father of Quebec's Medicare system, recommended the establishment of privately run health care centers to compete with publicly run hospitals and a voucher system to encourage competition among providers.[49]

The Canadian resource allocation process and the debate over access issues are highly political. Since three quarters of the entire health care bill in Canada is allocated through government budgets, the health care sector has to compete against other priorities in the political arena. Thus, creating a sense of imminent crisis helps the health care industry argue for additional resources or fend off deeper cuts. Not surprisingly, physicians respond to every proposal for tighter fee controls with strong rhetoric about the damage to access and quality that will result. Hospitals struggling with fixed budgets may find it advantageous to release information on their waiting lists or close a few beds to dramatize their situation. Media reports become part of the political infighting and are, therefore, all the more difficult to evaluate.

The overall picture appears to be of a general struggle over how to adapt an enormously popular public entitlement that has fallen on hard economic times. As with many American Great Society programs, Canadian national health insurance was established during a period of vigorous economic growth. Financing the program for its first decade was relatively painless, but this is no longer true. Today Canada has access problems that hurt some patients, at least by diminishing potential quality of life for a period of several months or more. But it is impossible to quantify the extent of those problems

HMOs," *Medical Post,* Toronto, March 21, 1989. *OSI* is the acronym for "integrated health-care organization" in French.

47. *Toronto Star,* May 23, 1989.

48. J. Lomas et al., "Paying Physicians in Canada: Minding Our Ps and Qs," *Health Affairs* 8, no. 1 (Spring 1989): 80–102.

49. William Johnson, "Health Care Needs Competition?" *Windsor Star,* February 8, 1990. Castonguay was the Quebec minister responsible for health care from 1970 to 1973 after heading a four-year royal commission on health care in the 1960s.

or to compare them in any meaningful sense with the problems in other health care systems.

Estimating the Cost of Public Health Insurance in the United States

Canadians are more supportive generally of government-run social programs than are Americans. Excluding defense, Canadian governments (all levels combined) spend 18 percent more per capita than governments (all levels) in the United States. Nondefense public sector expenditures represent a 30 percent larger share of total economic output in Canada than in the United States (36.7 percent of GNP in Canada, 28.3 percent of GNP in the United States). The overall tax burden is also higher in Canada, although the magnitude of the difference is not as great, both because Canadian defense expenditures are lower than U.S. expenditures and because their combined government deficit is almost 50 percent higher (as a percentage of GNP, 1987 figures).[50]

Significant tax increases clearly would be needed to implement Canadian-style public health insurance in the United States. If implemented exactly as now structured in Canada, public health insurance in the United States would require an estimated $244 billion to $252 billion increase in public outlays (in 1991 dollars). Most of this amount would represent a shift from private to public financing, rather than entirely new spending. Thus, implementing universal government-provided health insurance would more than double current Medicare/Medicaid outlays (a 127 percent increase). If funded solely at the federal level, it would require a 46 percent increase in income tax receipts or a 59 percent increase in current FICA (Social Security and Medicare) payroll tax rates (from the current 15.3 percent to over 24 percent). If paid for solely at the state level, implementing such a system would require an increase in total state tax receipts of more than 70 percent.[51] In fact, if the fiscal burden of paying for health care were to be distributed exactly as it now is in Canada, almost the entire responsibility for new public funding would fall on the states. The U.S. federal government already pays for the same proportion of total health spending as does the Canadian federal

---

50. Author's calculations based on Statistics Canada, *National Income and Expenditures* (1989), tables 44 and 45; and U.S. Department of Commerce, Bureau of Economic Analysis, *Survey of Current Business* 69, no. 7 (July 1989): tables 3.1 and 3.2. The figures given here are on a National Income and Products Accounts (NIPA) basis, which may differ from presentations based on government budgets. In particular, investment income and interest earned by government are not counted in government receipts; instead, they are netted against expenditures.

51. For a more detailed comparison of the U.S. and Canadian public sectors and a discussion of how this tax increase estimate was derived, see Neuschler, *Canadian Health Care*, chapter 5.

government (29.1 percent in the United States and 29.6 percent in Canada in 1987).[52]

The Wider Social Context

The record shows that public health insurance run by government has not enabled Canadians to escape rising health care costs or the access problems that seem inevitably to attend efforts to control costs. Even so, the Canadian system covers all Canadians, is enormously popular with the people it serves, and has a number of supporters in the United States. This final section stands back from cost and access comparisons to examine other differences between Canada and the United States that make it unlikely that the United States could adopt successfully such a system or live comfortably with it if it were adopted.

Public Attitudes toward Government

Culturally, Americans and Canadians hold very different attitudes about the appropriate size and place of government. Canadians support government health and social welfare programs generally and typically believe that government can effectively and equitably manage major programs for the common good. Americans always have been suspicious of government control and skeptical of government's ability to operate programs effectively and seem to be increasingly so. They dislike taxes intensely—to the point of having enacted tax limitation initiatives by popular referenda in several states, initiatives that are unknown in Canada. It seems unlikely that Americans would tolerate the substantial increases in both taxes and government responsibility that would be an inevitable part of public health insurance based on the Canadian model.

Form of Government

Canada's parliamentary system of government, at both the federal and provincial levels, has strong party discipline and a policy-making process that integrates the executive and legislative branches. This is in sharp contrast to the United States. Even so, the current Canadian financing system was not imposed overnight; rather, it grew incrementally over a period of forty or more years, with many difficult political decision points along the way. It is unlikely that the American system of checks and balances would allow a major change

---

52. Lazenby and Letsch, "National Health Expenditures," table 10; Health and Welfare Canada, *National Health Expenditures in Canada, 1975–1987*, table 80.

such as universal public health insurance without a substantial shift in political attitudes and values.

It is also doubtful that the program would be financially stable if adopted. For example, some federal legislators have garnered special dispensations for hospitals in their districts under the U.S. Medicare program.[53] If the government program averaged 95 to 99 percent of a hospital's revenue, rather than the current 40 percent or so represented by Medicare, the incentive for providers to use political pressure to undercut cost-containment policies would be commensurately greater.

Roles of Different Levels of Government

The Canadian division of responsibility and authority in health care financing reflects a balance of power between federal and provincial governments that differs significantly from the federal/state relationship in the United States. The provinces have much more autonomy than the states. They have much larger budgets per capita and a more pervasive role in the lives of their citizens, and they operate with considerably fewer federal legislative and regulatory constraints.

In Canada administration of public health insurance is left to the provinces. Except for several very general conditions that provinces must meet to qualify for federal funding, federal administrative duties are limited to distributing the "block grant" funds and tracking the overall performance of the system. This is in sharp contrast to Medicaid, the U.S. health financing program for the poor, under which states are subject to an enormous number of federal requirements, both legislative and administrative, many of them quite picayune. States continually battle federal threats to withhold or deny matching funds for violation of one or another administrative requirement.

The relatively greater federal control and regulation of state participation in federal/state programs in the United States have broad implications for designing a publicly operated health insurance system. The strong provincial role in Canada overall assured that the public health insurance system would

---

53. The most obvious examples pertain to the prospective payment system for hospitals under Medicare. Under this system, begun in 1983, payments to hospitals moved over a period of several years from rates based on individual hospitals' past experience to rates based on overall national experience. In 1986 Congress enacted a one-year "pause" in this phased transition. Hospitals in several states would have benefited from a faster transition to national rates, but Congress exempted hospitals in only one state from the delay, allowing them the benefit of national rates immediately. A senator from that state played a key role at that time in the Senate Finance Committee, which has purview over Medicare. Other examples pertain to the classification of hospitals as "urban" or "rural" under the prospective payment system. Rural hospitals are paid less. The payment differential has led to congressionally directed changes in the classification rules usually benefiting one or a few hospitals in an individual member's district.

be administered at a level of government close enough to the people to be responsive to geographic differences in circumstances. Although the Canadian system is highly regulated, regulators are closer to the affected population and have at most hundreds rather than thousands of hospitals to deal with, as has the Medicare program in the United States. Furthermore, Canadian provinces are very small; six have fewer people than Nevada, the tenth smallest state. Only Ontario and Quebec have large populations by U.S. standards, but even the largest (Ontario) has only one third the population of California and only 204 general hospitals, compared to 474 in California.[54]

A satisfactory administrative solution for government-run health insurance would be difficult to devise in the United States. Because health care is a local product, approaches that work (for both cost control and access) in local areas probably cannot be devised at the federal level. Persuading fifty states to adopt universal public insurance would be virtually impossible. It was difficult enough in Canada twenty years ago, with only ten provinces and a much simpler health care system. Convincing the federal government to fund individual programs devised by the states would be just as difficult.

Freedom of Choice

From the American point of view a major defect of the Canadian health care system is the lack of choice not among specific doctors and hospitals but, rather, of overall delivery system and extent of coverage. Americans like choices, in health care as in other areas, and the current health insurance system allows a significant range of choice. If an employment-based group chooses to reduce its current outlays for insurance premiums and protect itself only against very major medical bills, for example, it can buy lower-cost insurance. Those who prefer comprehensive, first-dollar coverage can buy it at a higher cost. Those who want comprehensive coverage and are willing to make other concessions—longer waits for routine appointments, for example, or limitations on when they can see a specialist—can obtain this by enrolling at medium cost in an HMO.

These kinds of choices are not available to Canadian citizens. All must belong to the same system and accept its deficiencies as well as its benefits, unless they choose to be restricted to the very few private hospitals and physicians or seek care outside the country. Thus, if the government seeks to control costs by restricting the availability of hospital beds or new equipment, citizens needing care must either wait for service or pay privately to go outside the system.

---

54. There are 204 public general hospitals in Ontario, according to the *Canadian Hospital Directory 1988*, table 1, 202. California has 474 community hospitals, according to the 1987 edition of the American Hospital Association's *Hospital Statistics,* table 5C, 48. Both figures would be larger if specialty and long-term hospitals were included.

The Role of Innovation

Attempts to control costs in the Canadian system are based on the monopoly market power that provincial governments have as sole payer for all hospital and physician care. The system is thus characterized by very tight, administered budgets, particularly for hospitals, which are the focal point of the health care system even more than they are in the United States. Because anything new represents an additional cost, such a system discourages innovation, perpetuates existing inefficiencies, and leads to creeping obsolescence and service rationing. The much lower availability in Canada of cost-effective technologies such as lithotripsy testifies to this reality, as does the failure of provincial governments—at least until very recently—to support the development of freestanding ambulatory surgery facilities.

One strength of the American health care system is its ability to adapt quickly to changing health care needs and to develop and bring rapidly on-line new and better ways of treating illness. Such responsiveness clearly is not possible when all major resource allocation decisions are made by a government, particularly a government concerned primarily with cost control.

The Benefits of a Free-Market Neighbor

The Canadian health care system benefits from the presence of a free-market health care system right next door in two ways. First, Canadians need not spend large sums developing new medical technology; they can wait for the United States to develop it and reap the benefits when it is ready.

Second, the United States also relieves pressures that would otherwise build for expansion of the Canadian system and additional spending. For example, with few exceptions (e.g., cataract surgery), it is almost impossible for individuals to shorten their waiting periods for surgery within Canada because there are virtually no private hospitals, but Canadians who are willing and able to pay privately to obtain care sooner can come to U.S. hospitals and clinics. In a few recent instances in which long waiting lists had developed, particularly for heart surgery and lithotripsy, Canadian provinces even agreed to pay for surgery in U.S. hospitals to reduce the backlog. The provinces had no other short-term alternative for reducing surgical waiting lists. If the United States were to adopt the Canadian system, the safety valve would no longer exist for Canadians, nor would there be one for Americans.

Conclusion

Clearly, the United States must work to guarantee access to health care for all Americans. Equally clearly, we must do a better job of containing health care cost increases while maintaining quality of care. But public insurance based on the Canadian model does not seem to be an approach that would work well in the United States.

First, Canada has not solved the problem of escalating costs. Canada spends a smaller percentage of GNP on health care than the United States primarily because its economy grew faster than the U.S. economy over the past twenty years. Per capita health care costs are growing just as fast in Canada as in the United States, and access problems are emerging. Second, although all Canadians have health insurance coverage, universal coverage has led to a substantially larger public sector, a substantially higher tax burden, and a rigid, less innovative system. Finally, the Canadian system removes choice of financing and delivery systems from the consumer. Consumers must accept the system as it is; they cannot choose the degree or type of coverage.

There are substantial advantages to approaching health care reform in the United States by building on the strengths of the existing employer-based private system. The private market provides a direct incentive to respond to client needs, to develop and continually refine innovative health financing structures that will meet demands for quality health care at an affordable price. The private market is not subject to the procedural requirements and decision-making rigidity that are an inevitable part of government and that are exacerbated the more removed the level of government from the people who use the services. (The sheer size of the U.S. population compared to Canada's makes the latter a significant factor.) For example, legal requirements make it impossible, for all practical purposes, for government to develop effective managed care systems based on selection of efficient physicians and hospitals, as private insurers are aggressively beginning to do.

The U.S. private market is responding to the growing demand for cost containment and quality assurance and is moving aggressively to implement and improve managed care systems that will meet this dual need. Private insurers also recognize the need for universal availability of health care coverage and have developed specific proposals to make coverage available to a broad spectrum of Americans who currently are without it.

It would be a mistake to let the yearning for the chimera of a simple solution to complicated health care problems lead the United States to adopt public insurance based on the Canadian model and not apply the American talent for flexibility and innovation.

CHAPTER 7

Interpreting Canada: Models, Mind-sets, and Myths

Morris L. Barer and Robert G. Evans

When a man walks into your office, sits down in front of your desk, and tells you that he is Napoleon Bonaparte, do not get drawn into a discussion of cavalry tactics at the battle of Austerlitz.

—Robert Solow

The last three years have seen an extraordinary expansion in American interest in the Canadian health care system. This stands in sharp contrast to the lack of interest during the previous thirteen years. The question posed in the 1975 title *National Health Insurance: Can We Learn from Canada?*[1] was at that time answered in the negative. A few lonely souls continued to look, and point, across the border;[2] a few more became curious in the mid-1980s,[3] but it was only with the publication of the draft report of the National Leadership Commission on Health Care in January 1989[4] that the thermostat was really turned up. By February 1992 even George Bush had gotten into the act.

The pages of the journal *Health Affairs* are a barometer of this increasing American interest. No fewer than nine contributions focusing in whole or in part on Canada have appeared in the last five issues (since 1992).[5] Like the

---

1. S. Andreopoulos, ed., *National Health Insurance: Can We Learn from Canada?* (New York: Wiley, 1975).

2. See, for example, J. Feder, J. Holahan, and T. Marmor, *National Health Insurance: Conflicting Goals and Policy Choices* (Washington, D.C.: Urban Institute Press, 1980).

3. J. K. Iglehart, "Health Policy Report: Canada's Health Care System (Three Parts)," *New England Journal of Medicine* 315 (1986): 202–8, 778–84, 1608–10; D. U. Himmelstein and S. Woolhandler, "Cost without Benefit: Administrative Waste in U.S. Health Care," *New England Journal of Medicine* 314 (1986): 441–45.

4. *For the Health of a Nation: A Shared Responsibility,* Draft Report of the National Leadership Commission on Health Care Reform (Henry Simmons, chairman) (Washington, D.C., 1989).

5. M. V. Pauly, P. Danzon, P. Feldstein, and J. Hoff, "A Plan for 'Responsible National Health Insurance,'" *Health Affairs* 10 (Spring 1991): 5–25; J. Krasny and I. R. Ferrier, "A Closer

147

wider public debate that they mirror, these contributions range from genuine attempts to understand and inform to thinly veiled propaganda in support of readily identifiable American interests—what Marmor calls "misleading glances across the border."[6]

To appreciate the nature of the American debate one must understand its sources. Why this sudden explosion of interest? Our interpretation of the process is as follows: First, the U.S. system is uniquely unsatisfactory and is continuing to deteriorate, in objective, easily observable terms. The broad outlines of this situation are well known to the readers of *Health Affairs*— increasing numbers of un- and underinsured, uncontrollable cost escalation, failure of the "competitive" strategies of the 1980s, increasing third-party intrusion into the practice of medicine, growing documentation of excessive and inappropriate medical care, and rapid growth of the already large "overhead" costs of an unproductive health bureaucracy in the private sector. To quote Alain Enthoven, after summarizing these basic facts, "It would be, quite frankly, ridiculous . . . to suggest that we have achieved a satisfactory system that our European friends would be wise to emulate."[7]

Second, "you cannot fool all of the people all of the time," and Americans are becoming increasingly aware of their predicament. Their satisfaction with their system was the lowest among ten OECD countries in a recent Harris poll.[8] After an analysis of a wide range of polling data, Blendon and Edwards recently concluded that "citizens of this country have decided that fundamental change in our health care system is needed."[9] More significant for the debate over Canada, however, is the fact that a substantial majority of Ameri-

Look at Health Care in Canada," *Health Affairs* 10 (Summer 1991): 152–58; D. R. Waldo and S. T. Sonnefeld, "U.S./Canadian Health Spending: Methods and Assumptions," *Health Affairs* 10 (Summer 1991): 159–64; C. D. Naylor, "A Different View of Queues in Ontario," *Health Affairs* 10 (Fall 1991): 110–28; M. L. Barer, W. P. Welch, and L. Antioch, "Canadian/U.S. Health Care: Reflections on the HIAA's Analysis," *Health Affairs* 10 (Fall 1991): 229–36; E. Neuschler, "Debating the Canadian System: A Response from the Author," *Health Affairs* 10 (Fall 1991): 237–39; V. R. Fuchs, "National Health Insurance Revisited," *Health Affairs* 10 (Winter 1991): 7–17; P. Danzon, "Hidden Overhead Costs: Is Canada's System Really Less Expensive?" *Health Affairs* 11 (Spring 1992): 21–43; J. F. Sheils, G. Y. Young, and R. J. Rubin, "O Canada: Do We Expect Too Much from Its Health System?" *Health Affairs* 11 (Spring 1992): 7–20.

6. T. R. Marmor, "Misleading Notions," *Health Management Quarterly* 13 (4th qtr., 1991): 18–24.

7. A. C. Enthoven, "What Can Europeans Learn from Americans?" *Health Care Financing Review*, Annual Supplement (1989): 49–63.

8. R. J. Blendon, R. Leitman, I. Morrison, and K. Donelan, "Satisfaction with Health Systems in Ten Nations," *Health Affairs* 9 (Summer 1990): 185–92.

9. R. Blendon and J. Edwards, "Conclusion and Forecast for the Future," in Blendon and Edwards, eds., *System in Crisis: The Case for Health Care Reform* (New York: Faulkner and Gray, 1991), 269.

cans have repeatedly indicated that they would favor a national health insurance plan financed through taxation.[10]

Third, the traditional alliance between private insurers and physicians is fraying and threatening to crumble. The ever-increasing pressure to contain costs, although as yet wholly unsuccessful, is bearing more and more heavily on physicians. They find themselves increasingly harassed and their clinical judgment questioned and constrained, by their traditional friends, as insurers are forced to shift from underwriting to "managed care." Physicians also notice that a rapidly increasing share of health care costs is going not to themselves or even to clinical care but, rather, to the administrators of the payment process. The widely noted calculation that the excessive overhead cost of private insurance in the United States is large enough to pay for all the care of the uninsured implicitly suggests the possibility of transferring tens of billions of dollars of income from administrators to clinicians. Suddenly, a public system—preferably with little or no decrease in total expenditures, just a transfer from "unproductive" to "productive" activities and people—seems quite interesting.

Thus, we find physicians in the forefront of those calculating the costs of private insurance and even suggesting—seriously and with plausible arguments—the outright abolition of the private insurance industry.[11] The American Medical Association (AMA) is holding firm, for the moment, but the American College of Physicians has broken ranks and called for a national plan.

The extent of support for national health insurance is finally forcing the issue onto a reluctant political agenda. As Taylor and Reinhardt recently pointed out, Americans may not, in fact, be as different from citizens of other developed societies in their basic values as the opponents of national health insurance have routinely claimed.[12] They conclude that the reasons why the United States is the only such country without some form of universal coverage has more to do with the peculiarities of its political structure than with the

---

10. "Opinion polls indicate that support for a national health plan is at a 40 year high point, and more than 10 national and state-wide surveys conducted since 1989 indicate that between 60 and 72 percent of Americans are in favour of such a plan" (R. Blendon and K. Donelan, "The Public and the Future of the U.S. Health Care System Reform," in Blendon and Edwards, *System in Crisis,* 173–75).

11. T. S. Bodenheimer, "Should We Abolish the Private Health Insurance Industry?" *International Journal of Health Services* 20, no. 2 (1990): 199–220; Bodenheimer, "Payment Mechanisms under a National Health Program," *Medical Care Review* 46, no. 1 (1989): 3–43; S. Woolhandler and D. U. Himmelstein, "The Deteriorating Administrative Efficiency of the U.S. Health Care System," *New England Journal of Medicine* 324, no. 18 (1991): 1253–58.

12. H. Taylor and U. E. Reinhardt, "Does the System Fit?" *Health Management Quarterly* 13 (3d qtr., 1991): 2–10.

values of its citizens. But even that structure seems finally to be bending under the weight of public concern.[13] Harris Wofford's Senate victory in Pennsylvania suggested that the Republicans were vulnerable on this issue, and George Bush came out swinging.

Yet, as Blendon and Edwards point out, while most of the American public seems convinced that the status quo is no longer tenable, "they are immobilized by their disagreement over the form such changes should take. Until some middle ground is reached, our health care system is likely to follow along its current trajectory." A similar conclusion is reached by Fuchs.[14] It follows that defenders of and beneficiaries from the status quo— with or without minor tinkering—need not waste their time trying to defend the indefensible. They need only concentrate their attention on attacking each serious alternative while generating nonserious proposals to cloud the issue. Since Canada is at present a leading alternative, Canada must be attacked and discredited.

The reasons for this spirited response are quite transparent: The American health care system is acknowledged by all parties to be by far the most expensive in the world, and every dollar of that expense is a dollar of someone's income. A more efficient system that dispensed, for example, with the many tens of billions of dollars spent on a private insurance bureaucracy would destroy tens of billions of dollars of sales and incomes. A system that controlled the escalation of physicians' fees and reduced the volume of ineffective and inappropriate procedures would in the same motion reduce the incomes of providers and the market opportunities of drug and equipment manufacturers and marketers. The one is not merely a consequence of the other; cost control and income control are different labels for the same act.

Furthermore, these threatened incomes are highly concentrated. They have their proponents in the AMA, the HIAA, and the PMA, among others. While their members are vastly outnumbered by the millions of Americans desirous of fundamental reform (and national health insurance), the latter are relatively unorganized and have had (at least until recently) no effective lobby and no means of raising the funds necessary for such activity. It is a classic case of diffuse benefits and concentrated losses, and there is the very real possibility that the "outcome" may be dictated not by the merits of the argument but, instead, by the depth of the purse, in the same way that one might "win" a legal case by exhausting the resources of one's opponent.

---

13. M. Kramer, "The U.S. Voters' Latest Ailment: Health Care," *Time,* November 11, 1991, 54; "Health, the Lose-Lose Issue," *Economist,* November 16, 1991, 27–28, 31; M. Walker, "Poor State of Health," *Guardian Weekly,* February 16, 1992, 8.

14. R. Blendon and J. Edwards, "Conclusion and Forecast for the Future," in Blendon and Edwards, *System in Crisis,* 269; V. R. Fuchs, "National Health Insurance Revisited," *Health Affairs* 10 (Winter 1991): 7–17.

Who, then, has an interest in responding to these concentrated interests, presently focusing their efforts on discrediting the Canadian system? To a limited extent Canadians do, if only to try to set the record straight. But there are ten times as many Americans as Canadians. So, even if there were equal interests in the American quandary on both sides of the border, sources of Canadian response would be swamped. But the interests are not equal: Canadians have no stake in "selling the Canadian system" to the Americans.[15] There are no royalties to be earned by Canadian physicians, analysts, or governments if the United States should adopt a national health insurance plan. (The Americans would be free riders.) So the powerful economic motives behind the attacks on Canada have no defensive counterpart.

Furthermore, we have problems of our own. The American newspaper headlines discovering that the Canadian health care system is not perfect do not come as a complete surprise to Canadians. Indeed, some of those who might otherwise provide a more balanced view for American audiences are heavily involved in efforts to understand and improve their own system. Fortunately, one of the by-products of the explosion in American interest in Canadian health care has been a rapid growth of serious comparative scholarship among the American research community, in part responding to a heightened interest among American research-granting agencies.

A number of useful studies have been done, and more are in progress.[16] Of particular importance, these studies are increasingly focusing on differ-

---

15. In fact, if one were to take at face value the claims of some critics of the Canadian system, Canada would have much to lose were the American system to end up looking like that of its neighbor to the north. In particular, Canadians are accused of "free-riding" on American research and development (Danzon, "Hidden Overhead Costs: Is Canada's System Really Less Expensive?" *Health Affairs* 11 [Spring 1992]) and of being able to take advantage of the ready access to services and facilities in "short supply" in their own country. More substantially, and pointed out by a number of American business leaders, the excess costs of the American system place them at a competitive disadvantage in international trade. Canada is one of their competitors.

16. See, for example, L. L. Roos, E. S. Fisher, S. M. Sharp, J. P. Newhouse, G. Anderson, and T. A. Bubolz, "Postsurgical Mortality in Manitoba and New England," *Journal of the American Medical Association* 263 (1990): 2453–58; V. R. Fuchs and J. S. Hahn, "How Does Canada Do It? A Comparison of Expenditures for Physicians' Services in the United States and Canada," *New England Journal of Medicine* 323, no. 13 (1990): 884–90; A. Katz and M. Schwendiman, *Paying the Price: Health Care Spending by Businesses in British Columbia and Washington State,* rep. 2 of series, Health Policy Analysis Program, School of Public Health (Seattle: University of Washington, 1990); G. M. Anderson, J. P. Newhouse, and L. L. Roos, "Hospital Care for Elderly Patients with Diseases of the Circulatory System: A Comparison of Hospital Use in the United States and Canada," *New England Journal of Medicine* 321, no. 21 (1988): 1443–48. In addition, a number of cross-border comparative projects are currently underway, examining inter alia: trends in access to cardiac procedures by age and income and the appropriateness of the care received; administrative and other components of hospital costs; prenatal care and birth outcomes; and use and outcomes of long-term care by elderly patients. Most are funded by American foundations and involve collaborative Canadian/American research teams.

ences in the health outcomes achieved in the two systems. This is a basic question to be addressed in any health care system, whether or not it is being compared with another, and it has been evaded for far too long in the policy debates in every country. But this emerging evidence has not, and cannot, carry much weight in the current American political debate, because that debate has little or nothing to do with cross-border learning. It is about the defense of political and economic interests. And they are able and motivated to support a thousand points of darkness for every candle lit by the serious research community. The gross misrepresentation of the findings of Roos et al. on postsurgical mortality in the recent Bush health strategy document is a leading example.[17]

Like medical care itself, comparative information on different health care systems is difficult for the public to judge. And, while the incentives to produce distortion and nonsense are high, the costs to doing so are low. Furthermore, its producers adopt a variety of strategies to convey an aura of "scientific" legitimacy to their messages. In this they are following a trail long ago blazed by marketers of pharmaceuticals, who have become masters of the art of presenting advertising information as if it were scientific communications.[18]

Correspondingly, there will continue to be an oversupply of nonsense. It would be futile, particularly for Canadians, to try to deal with all of it in detail. But there is a deeper problem than the sheer imbalance of resources and incentives—a problem that has been clearly identified and dissected by Culyer. As we perceive them, many American commentaries on "the Canadian experience" are in fact discussions of an imaginary "Canada" that resembles only in name the "reality" in which we live and that we perceive. They bring with them images of what, on a priori grounds, "must be" to substitute for what we believe "is." At the same time they compare this "Canada of the (American) mind" with an American system as it is, or more often as they allege it might be, which again seems to us to bear little relation to *our* perception of the American reality.

"The stage is set, not merely for an unfruitful dialogue, but for a dialogue of the deaf." In what follows we will try to identify the ways in which the major discrepancies between this "Canada of the mind" and the reality that we and most other Canadians perceive are rooted in "fundamental differences in perception and observation . . . of how many of the key actors in any health

---

17. *The President's Comprehensive Health Reform Program* (chap. 6), Washington, D.C., February 1992. This is but one of many gross distortions of the Canadian experience in a proposal that "nobody expects . . . to pass Congress, not even Bush" (M. Bromberg, director of the Federation of American Health Systems, quoted in Walker, "Poor State of Health").

18. An observation made most recently in "Pushing Drugs to Doctors" (*Consumer Reports*, February 1992, 87–94), but having a long history.

care system operate, what their aspirations are, and how constrained they are in achieving them."[19]

Recent contributions to *Health Affairs* provide a number of examples of such "fundamental differences." For example, Krasny and Ferrier state that "it is unnecessary to prove that a market environment that provides abundant and varied resources . . . is inherently better than one that does not."[20] Indeed not. If one first *defines* hypothetical A as better than B, no subsequent proof is necessary. But, if one is claiming that one form of organization *in the real world* is or could be superior to another, some further evidence is called for.

Krasny is in a cleft stick. Either the present American circumstances represent a "close enough" approximation to the "market environment" he has in mind, or they do not. If they do, his claim fails monumentally on empirical grounds; if not, then the "environment" he finds so self-evidently superior exists only in his own mind, a hypothesized—and none too clearly spelled out—utopia or dreamworld. Marx used to have one of those.

Nor is Krasny alone. "Diverse consumer preferences are better satisfied . . . [by] . . . markets that offer choices among [insurance] plans . . . than if all must accept a uniform public plan" and, further, "rationing through waiting is likely to lead to a less efficient use of the scarce facilities than rationing through price and information-based systems. . . . It is highly likely that the limited number of beds and capital equipment [in Canada] are not being used to yield the maximum value to patients."[21]

When one considers that *no* health care system in the modern world is organized on market lines and that the closest approximation thereto, in the United States, is a uniquely unsatisfactory outlier in the judgment of its own citizens as well as everyone else, it is not hard to see why advocates of the market prefer to rest their arguments on the (unspecified) characteristics of systems existing only in their own minds. The imagination becomes the source not only of the possible but also of the inevitable.

Attempts to create a more efficient "market-based" system satisfactory to the American public have been tried for more than a decade and so far have clearly failed. Their advocates presumably feel that the failure is one of application, not of possibility, and that continued effort along these lines is justified. But their grounds for this conclusion seem only to be that they are able to imagine a hypothetical system that they believe would be superior to

---

19. A. J. Culyer, "The NHS and the Market: Images and Realities," in G. McLachlan and A. Maynard, eds., *The Public/Private Mix for Health* (London: Nuffield Provincial Hospitals Trust, 1982), 23–55.

20. J. Krasny and I. R. Ferrier "U.S./Canadian Comparison: The Authors Respond," *Health Affairs* 10, no. 2 (1991): 164–65.

21. P. Danzon, "Hidden Overhead Costs: Is Canada's System Really Less Expensive?" *Health Affairs* 11 (Spring 1992): 21–43.

any presently in existence. (So can we—so what?): "the relevant comparison for the national health insurance debate in the U.S. is between a public monopoly system and a *well-designed but practical competitive private insurance system* [our emphasis]."[22] Again, faith triumphs over experience, imagination over reality. (One of Aesop's fables described the consequences of comparing real with imaginary circumstances.)

On the other side of the border the system that Canadians overwhelmingly supported when it was introduced, and still do support, was based on an *explicit* rejection of the multiple–private insurer model. The observation that the original universal, community-rated system run by voluntary nonprofit organizations was inevitably sliding into a private, market-based insurance system was a powerful stimulus to the introduction of a universal, public program. There is *no* public support for reversing this decision. Canadians had a choice and still do.[23] A large majority of Americans say that they, too, would prefer a national health insurance system—but they do not have that choice, and Danzon, for one, does not think they should.[24]

Culyer refers to "fundamental differences in perception and observation" of the behavior and aspirations of, and the constraints faced by, key actors in any health care system. Such fundamental differences appear to have undermined a serious effort by Sheils et al. to inform the American debate. Their central conclusion is that the administrative savings resulting from moving to a single-payer system in the United States will initially be swamped by a massive "utilization response." We believe this prediction to be erroneous or at least unfounded. It is a straightforward consequence of the analysts' underlying *model* of the utilization process, and its validity stands or falls with that set of hypotheses. No such massive utilization response occurred in Canada with the introduction of universal, first-dollar coverage.[25]

There is *strong* evidence of a *cumulative* increase in utilization, relative

---

22. See P. Danzon, "Hidden Overhead Costs: Is Canada's System Really Less Expensive?" *Health Affairs* 11 (Spring 1992): 21–43. The model was laid out in an earlier contribution to this journal by M. Pauly, P. Danzon, P. Feldstein, and J. Hoff, "A Plan for Responsible National Health Insurance," *Health Affairs* 10, no.1 (Spring 1991): 1–25. Such a private-sector alternative might include "compulsory, income-related premiums" (M. V. Pauly, presentation to Metropolitan Life Insurance Co., July 1991)—which to the uninitiated sound very much like taxes. But they have the important distinction that they are collected by *private* insurers, not by any politically accountable body.

23. Royal Commission on Health Services, *Report* by the Hall Commission, no. 1 (Ottawa: Queen's Printer for Canada, 1964): chap. 18.

24. She is not alone. As Blendon and Donelan point out, the *one* survey that reports less than half of Americans polled as favoring a Canadian-style system was structured such that "the public [was] not given choices between a universal plan and the current system, or between alternative types of plans" (R. J. Blendon and K. Donelan, "Interpreting Public Opinion Surveys," *Health Affairs* 10, no. 2 (Summer 1991): 166–69). The survey was commissioned by the HIAA.

25. P. E. Enterline et al., "Effects of Free Medical Care on Medical Practice—The Quebec Experience," *New England Journal of Medicine* 288 (1973): 1152–55; M. L. Barer and R. G.

to that in the United States, in response to the constraints on fee escalation that resulted from bargaining with provincial governments.[26] This differential, observed by Fuchs and Hahn in 1990, has emerged over roughly twenty years of tension between provincial governments trying to hold down fees and a rapidly growing supply of physicians trying to maintain their incomes. It is interpreted by Sheils et al., anachronistically, as evidence of a utilization response at the beginning of the period to "free care for all."

The well-established behavioral link between fee controls and utilization response,[27] which is excluded from the theoretical framework employed by Sheils et al., invalidates their claim that one can "separate the potential cost savings due to health expenditure budgeting from the cost implications of Canada's unique administrative model." The utilization response is a direct consequence of the administrative process that has been applied to fees. It did not show up at the introduction of the plans, where it is predicted by their model, because it arises not from the behavior of *patients* but, rather, from that of *providers*.

That said, one should still be concerned about the potential for a "utilization response" to any national plan, arising from its effects on provider behavior. The United States of the early 1990s is very different from the Canada of 1967. A system that is awash with human and physical capacity and technical possibilities and chafing under utilization constraints that, while ineffective in aggregate, are still onerous and offensive, might very well respond to the extension of coverage with a significant increase in recommended diagnostic and therapeutic interventions.[28] After all, one of the most common arguments for a universal system is to provide "needed" care for those left out at present.

Thus, any program will have to have quite flexible, and enforceable, controls on who can be paid, for doing what, in what settings, and at what

---

Evans, "Riding North on a South-Bound Horse? Expenditures, Prices, Utilization and Incomes in the Canadian Health Care System," in R. G. Evans and G. L. Stoddart, eds., *Medicare at Maturity: Achievements, Lessons and Challenges* (Calgary: University of Calgary Press, 1986), 53–163.

26. M. L. Barer, R. G. Evans, and R. J. Labelle, "Fee Controls as Cost Control: Tales from the Frozen North," *Milbank Quarterly* 66 (1988): 1–64; J. S. Hughes, "How Well Has Canada Contained the Costs of Doctoring?" *Journal of the American Medical Association* 265 (1991): 2347–51. The net effect, however, has been significantly less rapid escalation of medical care costs in Canada than in the United States. The fee controls *have not* been swamped by the utilization response.

27. J. Lomas, C. Fooks, T. Rice, and R. J. Labelle, "Paying Physicians in Canada: Minding Our Ps and Qs," *Health Affairs* 8, no. 1 (1989): 80–102; Barer, Evans, and Labelle, "Fee Controls as Cost Control," 1–64.

28. The scope for this is large. B. J. Hillman et al. ("Frequency and Costs of Diagnostic Imaging in Office Practice—A Comparison of Self-Referring and Radiologist-Referring Physicians," *New England Journal of Medicine* 323, no. 23 [1990]: 1604–8) found that diagnostic imaging for patients with similar clinical presentations was more than four times as frequent, and fees about 40 percent higher, among patients of physicians who owned their own diagnostic equipment. There were no differences in direct charges to the two groups of patients.

levels, to prevent runaway "creative billing." While these controls will not be identical to those that the Canadian provinces (or the Western European countries) have developed over the last quarter century, they will have to do the same job. But this is not news to those public agencies in the United States responsible for reimbursement. The Physician Payment Review Commission, for example, is fully conversant with this foreign experience and has had to develop similar policies.

The expansionary pressures that would come with a universal plan are simply scaled-up versions of the American present. The introduction of prospective payment for Part A of Medicare, but not for Part B, led to the rapid growth of ambulatory diagnostic services and costs and the proliferation of supporting "organizational innovations"—physician/hospital joint ventures —which further boosted use. During 1991 several legislative and regulatory changes have been introduced to limit these opportunities for "gaming the system."

But no one in Washington should imagine that there is some final regulatory structure that, once found, can be left to run itself. That *is* a fundamental error. Payment for health care, in every system, is an ongoing game—a contest—between payers and providers. Predicting its outcome, in terms of utilization response, is like predicting the outcome of a horse race or a football game. Mathematical models, with analogies in physics, are notoriously unreliable for this purpose, because they are rooted in "games against nature," in which there is no organized human intelligence on the other side of the table or field.

The payment game is a very tough one, too tough for most patients, which is why providers would always prefer to play against *them* rather than against institutional payers. American experience to date suggests that it is also too tough for private corporations: Despite the predictions of a decade ago, their efforts to control health care by acting as prudent purchasers for their employees seem to have failed and are being abandoned; the problem is being passed back to the employees.

A principal argument for universal public plans is, and has always been, that only concentrated public authority can balance the power of providers. A number of imaginative alternatives have been developed, by advocates of the private sector, and one cannot rule out absolutely the possibility that one of them might someday work. But none does now or ever has. There are, by contrast, a number of variants on the "universal, public" theme that—warts and all, and with plenty of creaking and groaning—have in fact managed to balance the interests of providers and represent, albeit imperfectly, the financial interests of their citizens.[29]

29. Indeed, Pauly's reference to "compulsory, income-related premiums" in an ideal private plan essentially concedes the point. Public authority is necessary to run an effective plan, but he would prefer to place it in private hands!

By far the largest component of the utilization response, assumed by Sheils et al., arises from the elimination of cost sharing in current American health insurance coverage. Their estimate is based on the results of the RAND health insurance experiment. But that experiment was specifically designed to measure *patient* responses to a variety of user charges, holding constant, by assumption, the behavior of providers. It cannot therefore be used to draw conclusions about the behavior of entire populations of patients *and providers*. To do so is an elementary, but fundamental, fallacy of composition. (These authors are not the first and will not be the last.)

It is well known that all countries in the OECD, excepting the United States, have in recent years achieved a significant measure of control over total health costs. In none are user charges of any sort a central, or even a significant, component of the control strategy. Only the United States, which already relies heavily on such charges, has failed to control costs. Moreover, as is perhaps less widely known in the United States, the principal advocates of such charges in other countries are *providers,* who explicitly argue the need for *increased* funding—higher costs—and see user charges as the most promising way to get it. This rather undercuts the view expressed by Sheils et al. that "much of [the] increase in utilization could be averted by imposing patient cost sharing." Like the defenders of Singapore, they have their guns pointed the wrong way. (Their behavioral *model* says the Japanese must attack from the sea.)

What they miss, lacking familiarity with cost-contained systems, is that to date effective cost control has been based on direct regulation of fees and budgets. User fees are a way for providers to get around fee or budget controls, by tapping other sources of finance, and both they and the opponents of user fees are quite clear on this fact. If the payer refuses to grant a fee increase as large as requested, get it from the patient. And, on the other side, the payer is much less likely to take the political heat required for cost control, if the increases can be passed on to, and blamed on, someone else—the patients.

The "reality" is that health care utilization is the outcome of a complex interplay among the perceptions, objectives, and constraints of providers and patients. Providers' perceptions and recommendations of "appropriate" care, in particular circumstances, are the primary factor influencing patient "demands," and these perceptions in turn are heavily dependent upon their own past practices and the present conventions and capacity in their professional communities. Prices, when they are present at all, have a minimal effect on overall use, although they may have more impact on *who* gets care and for what.

An important role, however, is played by changes in available capacity—personnel, equipment, institutions, and technology. If capacity is available, it is used, and, if not, not. Thus, a key component of utilization management is capacity management—as, indeed, many Americans now recognize.[30]

Within the constraints imposed by the levels of available capacity, the critical allocation decisions about who gets what are primarily made by providers, in the form of the advice that they give to patients and the referrals they make. Initial access to the system, at least in Canada, is de facto as well as de jure "free"; the "waiting lists," which play such a large part in American mythology about Canada, simply do not exist in primary care. Indeed, there is increasing concern about an excess supply of primary-care physicians in a number of areas. The subsequent referral process, for diagnostic work, specialist care, or hospital services, is under the control of physicians themselves, and they do the "rationing." In effect, physicians in Canada run an internal "utilization review and management" system, within the externally set constraints on capacity, and always have. It is primarily through this process, rather than through queues and time prices, that capacity and use are matched and priorities established. And it is a generously resourced process; were it not for the United States, Canada would be by a small margin the world's most expensive health care system. If *we,* Canadians, are "underfunding" our system, it follows that everyone else, with the notable exception of the United States, is even more out of step.

But, according to Danzon, capacity management "imposes hidden costs of moral hazard control on patients [through] excessive patient time costs that result from proliferation of multiple short visits in response to controls on physicians fees; forgone productivity and quality of life from delay or total nonavailability of surgical procedures; and loss of productivity . . . due to underemployment of some medical inputs." And these hidden costs, she alleges, are very large: "Rough estimates suggest that these hidden overhead costs of public insurers exceed the measured costs of private insurance. This is not surprising, since public insurers that are both monopolists and monopsonists have weaker incentives than private insurers to use strategies that minimize overhead borne by patients and providers."

Once again we are dealing with a comparison between observable, recorded data on the one hand and "estimates" based on a hypothetical model of behavior located in the mind of the analyst on the other. These "costs" have no reality independent of that model. Danzon does refer to observations by Enterline et al. on changes in patterns of practice in Quebec in the early 1970s. But the conversion of these changes in patterns of practice into "costs" requires very specific, and highly questionable, assumptions about the behav-

---

30. J. E. Wennberg, "Outcomes Research, Cost Containment, and the Fear of Health Care Rationing," *New England Journal of Medicine* 323 (1990): 1202–4; J. S. Hughes, "How Well Has Canada Contained the Costs of Doctoring?" *Journal of the American Medical Association* 265 (1991): 2347–51.

ior, aspirations, and constraints of the "key actors" in the system. Furthermore, it presumes that whatever patterns predated universal coverage were, in some sense, "right," or at least preferable to those that evolved subsequently. Preferable for whom, and on what standard?

The answer seems to be, preferable according to the ethical standard at the heart of the neoclassical economic model, for example, concordance with individuals' willingness and ability to pay for goods and services whose value they fully understand. "Of course co-payments and utilization review entail rationing. But this is efficient . . . [and r]ationing by co-payment entails no excess burden." Thus, there is no need to calculate any hidden costs to *Americans* who are deterred by copayments from seeking care that would improve their health. One must be exquisitely sensitive to the costs imposed on those allegedly denied services that they "should" get, because they are willing (able) to pay for them. But no costs—or none that matter—are incurred by those who "choose" not to pay. Whether or not either group needs care never enters the model.

Such an ethical position, once spelled out, may not be widely shared. It certainly cannot emerge as a conclusion from economic analysis. Rather, it is a prior philosophical position, expressed through a certain style of analysis that does not and logically cannot provide any independent support for such value judgments.

But there are some very significant empirical assumptions made as well. The "hidden costs" allegedly generated by the public systems in Canada are inferred from a "before and after" comparison in Canada and then extended without comment to apply to a comparison between Canada and the present United States. Does that mean that Canada before public insurance represented an "optimal" equilibrium, in the strong sense of the neoclassical economic framework, and the United States does so now? That seems absurd, given what we know about the institutions and patterns in both places then and now. But, if the baselines for comparison are not themselves competitive equilibrium states, then it is not possible to tell, a priori, whether the observed changes represent costs or benefits.[31]

---

31. This intuitively plausible notion turns out to have a rigorous theoretical basis. On this, see R. G. Lipsey and K. J. Lancaster, "The General Theory of Second Best," *Review of Economic Studies* 24 (1956–57): 11–32. At a very abstract level it is demonstrable that, if there is only *one* distortion preventing the attainment of a competitive market equilibrium, removal of that distortion will result in an improvement in efficiency and a *potential*—but not guaranteed—improvement in overall welfare. But, if there are *two or more* distortions, then removal of *one* of them is as likely to lead *farther away* from theoretically defined "efficiency." Thus, there is no basis whatever, even at a purely theoretical level, for any a priori claim of "efficiency" in real-life systems. The question is, as it has always been, an empirical one: How do different systems perform relative to standards that are themselves matters of public choice and cannot be derived a priori?

So Danzon moves the uprights: "The measure [of costs] here is *excess time costs*, over and above the efficient level required to receive medical care in a *well-designed competitive private insurance system*" (our emphasis). Once again we are comparing the analyst's imaginary ideal with the grubby realities of Canada. But it gets worse: By assumption the American *present* is closer to that ideal—indeed, for purposes of analysis, identical with it. Although "because of the tax subsidy and other distortions," the current U.S. system "is *unlikely* [our emphasis] to conform to this benchmark," "the tax subsidy applies to medical and insurance inputs but not to patient time." Therefore, "there is no reason to add an estimate of excess patient time costs to the estimate of overhead for the U.S. under the status quo."

Those "other distortions"—which include the influences of professional licensure, restrictions on entry and scope of practice, regulations and legal restraints in markets for drugs and institutional services, the pervasive problem in imperfect consumer-patient information—were obviously not important enough to keep track of. And once they have disappeared, from the model at least, then one can use the rhetoric of efficiency to legitimate the competitive ideal.

By assumption, the U.S. system of health care finance and delivery embodies no significant distortions, relative to "a well-designed competitive private insurance system," except for the tax subsidy. Well, that should be easy to fix with a few lines in the tax code. We have gone back twenty years, to Martin Feldstein's diagnosis in the early 1970s. What, then, *is* everyone complaining about?

This breathtaking dismissal of all the other distortions in the U.S. system, together with the imposition by assertion of an imaginary "ideal" system rooted in an ethical standard acceptable only to neoclassical economists, and embodying behavioral assumptions that have no empirical support, then permits Danzon to select differentially only those hidden patient costs that are alleged to arise in the single-payer system of care. There is no mention of the consumer costs incurred in the process of working through a mind-numbing array of "benefit" packages nor of the patient costs associated with attempting to establish eligibility and collect those benefits. Information is perfect, or at least costless, in this imaginary world, and contracts are transparent and self-enforcing, so what costs could there be?[32] Finally, and perhaps most important of all, are the costs to Americans, unmeasurable but not so hidden, of the

---

32. There is in fact a fall-back position. If one finds these assumptions a bit strong, the argument is that competition among private insurers will generate a level of information that is, if not perfect, at least the best that one can hope for. But this position has no more empirical content than the "perfect information" assumption, because, by definition, whatever level of information emerges from "the market" is optimal. There is no external standard.

uncertainty associated with the health and financial risks borne even by those with U.S.-style coverage.

Will your policy, if you have one, cover you when you become ill? For what proportion of what services? Will it continue to do so if you lose your job or develop a chronic condition? The threats of financial ruin and/or denial of care are on the horizon of increasing numbers of Americans, or so they report.[33] If one is concerned to take account of "hidden" patient costs, one might want to estimate these, although, of course, if one counts only costs borne by those willing and able to pay, then they do not count. In Canada, however, the Hall Commission specifically identified "freedom from fear" as a major benefit of the public plan.[34]

Danzon in fact gets the Canadian and American situations exactly reversed on this point, when she refers to the higher "social costs of risk" borne by some hypothetical unemployed Canadian patient "unable to find a doctor if public deficits have stalled reimbursement through public programs." It is in employment-based private systems that the unemployed lose coverage; in Canada coverage follows from residency. And it is only in a system of multiple payers that providers can withdraw their services from those covered by an insurer, such as Medicaid, not paying the "going rate" or paying too slowly. We have had our share of recessions: in the Canadian system the scenario she envisages does not arise. Disputes over payment are resolved between governments and provider associations, and patients are not involved. Again, perceptions and habits of thought have been substituted for the Canadian reality.

Canadians freely admit that *we* do not know how large such "hassle and anxiety costs" are for Americans, although we, like everyone else, have heard some hair-raising personal accounts. Furthermore, Canadians understand that most of the work of employee benefits managers in the United States consists of health insurance matters; these costs are also excluded both from the official statistics and from Danzon's account.

But the delivery of services is not Danzon's primary concern. Much more important, she contends, is the loss of efficiency, which occurs when "competitive" insurance markets are converted to single-payer systems. The very large overhead costs, both in the insurance industry itself and imposed upon both providers and consumers/patients, of a system of multiple private insurers, have corresponding (hidden) benefits that, when combined with the

---

33. E. Friedman, "Insurers under Fire," *Health Management Quarterly* 13, no. 3 (1991): 23–27.

34. Hall Commission, 740.

(hidden) costs for patients in a single-payer system, more than redress the balance.[35]

Several specific types of benefits are alleged, but there is a general claim made that, we believe, reflects a profound misunderstanding. "In the real world where obtaining information, negotiating and enforcing contracts is costly, [overhead expenditures of insurers] can serve a useful function." Indeed. No one ever doubted that; rational for-profit firms would not incur them otherwise. Such expenditures are essential for survival in a *private* marketplace.

The key question is whether the private objectives thus served are consistent with the expressed objectives of the community as a whole. If that community has decided, for ethical reasons that are *not* consistent with Danzon's model of the perfect market, that the whole community shall be covered and that the share of the costs borne by each individual shall not be proportional either to his or her risk status or to his or her actual experience of use, then the underwriting and claims administration activities of private firms, and the expenses that support them, are indeed pure waste. The private industry cannot "deliver the goods"—which was the conclusion that led the Hall Commission in Canada to recommend a public system—and so must devote its energies to convincing Americans that they should instead want whatever it *can* produce, at a large and growing cost.

This raises a more fundamental question. If, as even Danzon would concede, the private industry cannot deliver comprehensive coverage and must, by the laws of the market, exclude those with the most significant health problems, then why is it worth "propping up," and, in particular, why should anyone presume that there is a public obligation to do so? The public sector already pays about 40 percent of the total U.S. health bill now and an additional large amount through the tax subsidy, which Danzon suggests represents a significant market distortion. Could the private industry even survive without this public subsidy, and in what form?

But is not the counterevidence in hand, that American consumers "prefer" diversity? "There is little reason to believe that the complexity and diversity of coverages that emerge in competitive insurance markets entail excessive costs, *i.e.*, costs that exceed the offsetting benefits." After all, they continue to pay for those benefits, and consumption decisions are the best evidence of willingness to pay. They may *say* to pollsters that they do not like the system and would prefer another, but they keep on buying.

---

35. These excess administrative costs are becoming subject to the same fate as estimates of the numbers of uninsured in the United States John F. Sheils, Gary J. Young, and Robert J. Rubin, "O Canada: Do We Expect Too Much from Its Health System?" *Health Affairs* 11 (Spring 1992), 7–20, estimate them at $46 billion in 1991, Woolhandler and Himmelstein estimate $69 to $87 billion in 1987, which, allowing for four more years, is about double, and we fully expect soon to see figures on both sides of this range. But, whatever the source, the number is *big*.

Here the argument has become completely circular. Since the private system is the only game in town and consumers keep playing, the fact that they keep playing is alleged as evidence that any alternative would obviously be worse—"whatever is, is right." But a similar expression of preferences through the political system, as for example by support for an alternative, has no evidentiary value at all.[36]

Danzon also offers specific benefits from the competitive insurance process, with particular emphasis on the role of a private claims administration that "devises [more cost effective] ways to control moral hazard." To the extent that this refers only to the old story about user charges lowering overall use and costs, by encouraging patients to be more selective in their use of care, it merely repeats the error made by Sheils et al., and by every economist who ever drew a demand curve without thinking about it.

But her comments on the role of utilization review (and its presumed corollary utilization management—otherwise why bother?) are much more interesting. The emphasis on utilization review and management (UR&M) by third parties implies that individual patients, responding to price signals, cannot exercise effective control over health care costs, let alone distinguish and weed out the least necessary or effective services. We strongly agree. Moreover, although we emphasized above that UR&M by physicians goes on in the Canadian system, as indeed it does in the American system and everywhere else, we certainly would not claim that the results could not be improved. There are currently a number of initiatives underway in Canada to improve this process, through cooperation between providers and government payers.[37]

---

36. Of course, one might also point out that the neoclassical economic model "predicts" that the decentralized decisions of a diversity of private consumers and providers, of risk-bearing as of services, will lead to a more "efficient" outcome. But this usage of the word *efficiency* derives from theoretical welfare economics and has no normative significance. Quite apart from the very extensive and powerful assumptions required for the decentralized competitive markets to yield an efficient result—the absence, for example, of *all* of those "other distortions," which disappeared so neatly above—an efficient outcome once obtained will not in general be preferable to any number of "nonefficient" outcomes. It represents only a particular point (of which there are an infinite number possible) on the utility possibility frontier in N-dimensional transactor space, from which no one can be made better off without making someone else worse off. The ranking of these points, relative both to each other and to nonefficient alternative outcomes, arises out of the processes of choice of a whole society; it cannot logically be derived solely from individual preferences. The use of efficiency in this technical sense in the present context represents a trap for the economically unwary, because it sounds like something good. It isn't. To be more concrete the organization of the illicit drug trade through private markets, such that no transactor can be made better off without making another worse off, is efficient in this limited sense. But this is not commonly advanced as an argument against the U.S. Drug Enforcement Agency (DEA).

37. J. Lomas, "Promoting Clinical Policy Change: Using the Art to Promote the Science in Medicine," in T. F. Andersen and G. Mooney, eds., *The Challenges of Medical Practice Variations* (London: Macmillan, 1990).

Where we would part company is with the blanket assertion that UR&M will be more effectively carried on in a competitive, multipayer environment. We believe that this is not only empirically incorrect but that it is inconsistent with the theoretical framework underlying Danzon's analysis. UR&M focuses on the appropriateness and effectiveness of care—its relation to needs. It thus introduces a criterion for the question "What is to be done?" that bears no relation whatever to the "willingness to pay" standard implicit in her theoretical conceptualization of the process. Such a relation can of course be forced. But one must be prepared to assume that the individual consumers who are not well enough informed to distinguish the beneficial care from the rest—hence, the need for UR&M and also all those other distortions of the competitive marketplace that vanished so smoothly above—are nevertheless able to make informed choices among the UR&M programs offered by competitive private insurers and to compare them with their costs. Once *this* leap of faith is made, the rest is easy; whatever pattern of UR&M emerges from that market is efficient, by definition.

Danzon claims that the incentives are more powerful in this competitive environment; that is an empirical question. But her "evidence" is only that, relative to Canada and Western Europe, the United States is overrun with UR&M activity. In this it looks to Canadians a lot like most other health care technologies. This is a process measure and says nothing about the effectiveness of all that activity. To date no system can demonstrate outstanding success in this area—and utilization continues to climb. Furthermore, such activity is more overt in the United States, where it is marketed, than in other systems in which it is not.[38]

Danzon also recognizes that this is still "early days" for utilization review, for all of us, but this does not seem to qualify her confident assertion that the competitive process will lead to an optimal "long-run equilibrium" pattern of UR&M. Wennberg's contrary assessment, that the incentives for and ability of providers to stay one step ahead of this process will continue to overwhelm the forces of the marketplace, seems to us better informed and more realistic. It is also supported by the findings "in the field" of Jones and Jones and the conclusions of Blendon and Edwards.[39]

The key distinction, as Wennberg points out, is between UR&M as a way

38. One might note, however, that where UR&M systems are marketed for a profit, there *are* powerful incentives to make inflated claims for their effectiveness. In a politically and professionally managed system the incentives are in the other direction, to downplay the existence as well as the impact of such activity. For better or for worse—and that too is an empirical question—implicit control is preferred to explicit everywhere but in the United States.

39. J. E. Wennberg, "Outcomes Research, Cost Containment, and the Fear of Health Care Rationing," *New England Journal of Medicine* 323 (1990): 1202–4; S. B. Jones and J. M. Jones, *Where Does Marketplace Competition in Health Care Take Us? Impressions, Issues, and Un-*

to improve the effectiveness with which a *given* quantity of resources is used and UR&M as a mechanism to determine the *overall* volume of resources used. The former it may do; the latter, in all probability, it cannot. In any case it has not. We suspect that the long-run equilibrium referred to by Danzon would be a moving equilibrium, whose "optimality" is defined by the fact that it emerges from a competitive process involving private firms, allegedly responding to "the diversity of consumer preferences," rather than by any external standard such as achieving cost-effective care.

Single-payer systems, on the other hand, have demonstrated the ability to control overall costs, and, contrary to Danzon's assertion, this does not represent "non-information-based rationing." Actual evaluations of care patterns suggest that the utilization process may be at least as well informed as in the United States and quite possibly better.[40] The "probable additional costs due to displacement of more serious by more trivial medical treatments," which she suggests, appears to us to be the exact reverse of what actually goes on in Canada relative to the United States; it suggests quite an extraordinary pattern of behavior by the physicians who allocate the available capacity in Canada. By repeating the phrase "non-price, non-information-based," Danzon seems to imply that the two are the same, or at least to encourage the reader to think so. There is, in fact, no connection between them.

Thus, her claim that "rationing through waiting is likely to lead to a less efficient use of the scarce [hospital] facilities than rationing through price and information-based systems" presents a dichotomy that is doubly false. It is false because it presumes that access to care in Canada is determined through waiting in queues (first in, first out) rather than through the judgment of physicians, expressed through the recommendation and referral process. And it is false because it treats price and information as if they were identical. It would certainly be possible to improve the information base underlying present patterns of use in both Canada and the United States, and a number of people in both countries are working on this problem. Modifying the bases on which people are paid for their services may well form part of this process. But that has absolutely no logical connection with the pricing of services, or insurance coverage, to patients.

answered Questions from the NHPF Site Visit to Minneapolis–St. Paul (January 14–17, 1991) (Washington, D.C.: George Washington University Press, 1991); R. Blendon and J. Edwards, *System in Crisis,* 27.

40. C. M. Winslow, D. H. Solomon, M. R. Chassin, J. Kosecoff, N. J. Merrick, and R. H. Brook, "The Appropriateness of Carotid Endarterectomy," *New England Journal of Medicine* 318 (1988): 721–27; C. M. Winslow, J. B. Kosecoff, M. Chassin, D. E. Kanouse, and R. H. Brook, "The Appropriateness of Performing Coronary Artery Bypass Surgery," *Journal of the American Medical Association* 260 (1988): 505–9; N. P. Roos and L. L. Roos, "Small Area Variations, Practice Style, and Quality of Care," in R. P. Wenzel and R. E. Dixon, eds., *Assessing Quality of Care: The New Hospital Epidemiology* (Baltimore, Md.: Williams and Wilkins, 1991).

But perhaps the most jarring of many discrepancies between Danzon's perceptions and ours is in her characterization of the role and benefits of the private underwriting and claims administration process. A somewhat different perspective is offered by Friedman, who notes that the fiduciary responsibility of the private insurer (which the market also enforces) is to the shareholders. Responsibility to the policyholder is secondary, to the general public nonexistent.[41] She refers to underwriting practices, which "seem to many to be ruthless," and which have replaced "reasonably equitable" ones. We infer that these changes are not a reflection of the declining humanity of insurers but, rather, a response to increasingly competitive market conditions—precisely Danzon's *solution* to remaining "imperfections." "Many conditions can trigger limitations and denials." Coverage is not only difficult to obtain but also easy to lose—creating "insurance hostages" tied to jobs. (This problem may be resolved if employers increasingly "go bare" and drop their coverage entirely.) Moreover, "the administrative cost issue is one of extreme vulnerability for private insurers."[42]

Friedman's is not, of course, the last word on this subject—and certainly not the first—but she seems to put compactly the growing concerns of Americans, which are simply dismissed in Danzon's account, where exclusions and limitations, experience rating, and administrative overhead, when "properly" perceived, are not problems but benefits. Compliance costs, misunderstandings and misinterpretations of horrendously complex policies, and the difficulties of making private insurers live up to their obligations are too unimportant even to discuss. After all, what do we have but anecdotes? Like Pangloss, Danzon assures us that this is the best of all possible worlds, or at least can be made so by a "well-designed but practical competitive private insurance system." For her the alternatives that the citizens of other countries find not only tolerable but relatively satisfactory have in fact large hidden costs of which they are apparently unaware.

In the end we would emphasize that the American debate is not about Canada (we are living one of those debates, but this is not it). It is about American problems and will have American responses, if not solutions. External observers may take comfort from Churchill's optimism that one can always count on the Americans to do the right thing, after having exhausted all the possible alternatives. But the history of American health policy suggests cycles, not convergence. And the predilection for misrepresentation and mud slinging, most recently displayed by George Bush in his comments on Canada in general and British Columbia in particular, has been encouraged by its recent successes in the United States. Our reading of the situation, and one

41. E. Friedman, "Insurers under Fire," *Health Management Quarterly* 13, no. 3 (3d qtr., 1991): 23–27.
42. Friedman, "Insurers under Fire," 24–25.

shared by many American observers, is that, on this issue, Churchill got it wrong.

But this difficult process of comparing alternatives will continue to be hampered by the creation of disinformation from "experts," because there are too many players and not enough umpires. "It is hard to distinguish [image from reality] since on the one hand our images condition what we see (and what we look for) and hence in part determine our realities, while on the other hand the realities we have experienced can limit the alternative images that we might invent about 'how things might be' in a reality yet to come."[43] This is particularly true when the issues are inherently very complex and charged with personal values and when the different alternatives represent very different distributions of gains and losses.

So work out your salvation with diligence, and good luck.

---

43. A. J. Culyer, "The NHS and the Market: Images and Realities," in McLachlan and Maynard, *The Public/Private Mix for Health*, 23–55.

CHAPTER 8

Health Care: What Can the United States and Canada Learn from Each Other?

David W. Conklin

The Average Citizen Prefers the Canadian System

Many books and articles compare the overall costs and benefits of the U.S. and Canadian health care systems. From the perspective of the average citizen it is clear that the benefits of the Canadian system are preferable, while its costs are much less. A 1989 poll by Louis Harris and Associates asked Americans, Canadians, and Britons an identical set of questions about their health care systems.

> Americans were found to be the most dissatisfied, with 89 percent saying their health care system needed "fundamental change or complete re-building." . . . Americans apparently are so frustrated and discouraged with their existing health care arrangements that 61 percent say they would favor a system like that in place in Canada, according to the survey. . . . Only 3 percent of Canadians and 12 percent of the Britons said they would prefer the U.S. system. (*Globe and Mail*, 1989)

A May 1991 Angus Reid poll found that 86 percent of Canadians are pleased with their system, ranking it as "excellent" or "good." "Canadians love their medicare system, there's no doubt about that," said Reid (*London Free Press*, 1991).

In both Canada and the United States the bottom 20 percent of income earners receive less than 5 percent of the society's total income. In a free market for health care low-income earners could not buy much—certainly not in comparison with the top 20 percent of income earners, who receive more than 45 percent of the society's total income. Canada's system provides basic health care services to everyone, while in the United States thirty-five to thirty-seven million people lack health insurance. The Louis Harris poll suggested that, of these, about eighteen million people generally choose not to

169

seek medical care because of financial reasons. For these people the U.S. system is particularly unfortunate.

The Canadian system is preferred by the average citizen in spite of the fact that it is much less expensive, with a per capita cost less than 75 percent of the U.S. cost. If the Canadian system were to be funded to the same per capita level as the U.S. system, then the Canadian system could provide considerably greater benefits, making public support for the Canadian system even greater than it currently is. Criticisms of Canadian shortages, queues, and rationing are criticisms of the level of funding and the political funding decisions rather than of the health care system itself.

Why Has the United States Not Adopted the Canadian System?

The free enterprise philosophy—alive and well among many Americans—supports the right of each person to exchange goods and services in an open market without government interference. It advocates the establishment of prices through the process of individual decisions concerning market transactions. It supports the allocation of incomes on the basis of the market value of goods and services that are supplied in the marketplace. Each person's income should be determined by the wages that purchasers are prepared to pay for that person's work, the interest that borrowers are prepared to pay for that person's capital, and the rent that others are prepared to pay for the use of that person's land and buildings.

The Canadian health care system violates this free enterprise philosophy to a considerable degree. So too do Medicare, Medicaid, and other U.S. initiatives that provide societal help to disadvantaged groups. But there are major differences between helping certain disadvantaged groups and adopting the Canadian system. Some supporters of the current U.S. system reject the Canadian system because of the extent of its government regulation and its collective decision making. Some believe that each individual should be free to purchase more and better health care if he or she wishes. In particular, some of the relatively well-to-do may support the U.S. system because they want this right. The fact that the average citizen prefers the Canadian system may not be relevant for the well-to-do or the politicians who represent them. This explains the U.S. refusal to adopt the Canadian system even though the average citizen believes that it is better. While the Canadian system provides a potentially valuable lesson, political realities may prevent the United States from learning from this lesson. A recent survey conducted for the Metropolitan Life Insurance Company indicates the considerable opposition to government acting as manager and administrator. *Employee Benefits Digest* (May 1991) has noted the following survey findings:

While fundamental change is needed, all stakeholder groups but one believe that it should be incremental, not radical. Union leaders favor big step changes to the nation's health care system.

All groups agree that government involvement is needed to improve the health care system. However, by sizable majorities all groups except union leaders believe that government's role should be rule maker, setting the rules for the private sector, rather than manager and administrator.

A majority of respondents in all but one stakeholder group—unions— believe that our insurance system should continue to work through employment-based plans. Half of the union leaders agree with this point.

To most stakeholder groups a health system with just one uniform benefit plan for all is unacceptable. Nearly half of the union leaders, however, prefer this option.

It is true that when a society places its health care expenditure decisions in the hands of its government the government may not spend as much on health care as the average citizen wishes. It may be difficult for the government to ascertain the wishes of society. In particular, it may be difficult to know which specific services the society wants to expand. In the May 1991 Angus Reid poll Canadians indicated specific areas in which they felt that government should increase expenditures. For example, 77 percent supported more spending on senior citizen homes, and 74 percent wanted more money for high-technology equipment.

The Canadian Experience

The average Canadian can state unequivocally that the U.S. preference for greater reliance on the free enterprise market is wrong. Canadians believe fervently in the right of every resident to equal access to the best health care that the system can provide, subject to rationing of limited equipment and personnel. The Canadian philosophy extends to the important point that an individual should not be able to purchase a quantity or quality of health care that is greater than or superior to the health care available to everyone else. Nor should a provider of health care be able to negotiate a fee or a price in the market higher than the fee or the price established by the government. Consequently, providers of health care earn an income that is constrained by government decisions. Of course, the existence of the U.S. private system offers an escape valve for disgruntled Canadians who can purchase better health care or who can reduce their waiting time for treatment by going to the United States, and it offers an escape valve for disgruntled Canadian physicians who can emigrate to the United States. If the United States were to adopt the Canadian system and if this escape valve were to disappear, would the Canadian philosophy and political realities change?

The Canadian experience provides the lesson that with universal public insurance a government can impose remarkably effective ceilings on cost escalation. Because the government is the sole payer for hospital and physician services, it imposes cost ceilings by prohibiting supplementary private payments or extra billing. Each province also places limits on hospital budgets, physician fee schedules, and the number of new medical students and interns.

By imposing an annual budget on each hospital, Canada's provincial governments are able to constrain the total number of inpatient days and the overall extent of hospital services, and they are also able to constrain the provision of physician services that require hospital facilities. This has been particularly effective in limiting surgery and the use of new, expensive technologies. To adopt a new technology each hospital's administration must petition the provincial government. Hospitals compete for the right to acquire new equipment and must present a convincing argument to the provincial department of health. Nevertheless, hospitals have had considerable freedom in resource allocation within their budgets, thereby encouraging cost minimization.

The Health Care Debate in Part Concerns Income Distribution and Poverty

While all Canadians receive complete coverage without deductibles for physician and hospital services, Americans participate in a wide variety of insurance plans, many of which involve deductibles, ceilings, and other limitations. Since 1966 U.S. Medicare has provided certain health care benefits to the elderly (and, since 1974, to the disabled), but complete health care coverage is not offered under this program. Also since 1966 the Medicaid program has provided limited coverage for the poor, but each state has its own program with its own eligibility requirements and its own list of included services.

In a 1990 article Marmor and Marshaw emphasized the "frustrating experience with Medicare and Medicaid" for both patients and physicians: "A federal agency recently estimated that about one million Medicare enrollees a year find filing claims so complicated or time-consuming that they do not seek reimbursement, losing about $100 million in benefits to which they are entitled. In some states, many physicians say they will not treat Medicaid patients, or do not bother to seek reimbursement for treating them, because the meager payments do not even cover the administrative overhead" (1990, 21–22). This hodgepodge of insurance arrangements leaves many people with no coverage or with inadequate coverage, resulting in abrupt personal financial crises as a result of health care problems. Writing in 1975, Marmor clearly stated, "Canadians take for granted now that illness no longer is associated with fears of destitution" (243).

The Canadian system has been built in accordance with national standards. The national government provides a substantial portion of total health funding to each provincial government, but to receive federal funds the province must adhere to the following four conditions:

> The plans must be comprehensive; that is, they must cover all hospital and physician services that are medically necessary, with no exclusions or dollar limits.
>
> The plans must be universally available to all eligible residents on equal terms and conditions. If premium financing is used, premiums cannot differentiate among individuals according to risk. Low-income families may be exempted from premium payments. User charges are permitted, but only if they do not impede reasonable access to necessary care. In practice, few provincial plans impose user charges, and no plan has deductibles or coinsurance provisions.
>
> The plans must be portable among provinces. Thus, an Ontario resident on a trip to Alberta must be able to receive health care in Alberta and have it paid for by the Ontario program.
>
> Finally, the plans must be operated on a nonprofit basis and managed by a public agency accountable to the provincial government.

Gross measures of population health attest to the success of the Canadian health care system, although the Canadian experience may also be the result of other factors, such as those associated with lifestyle. In 1985 the average life expectancy at birth in Canada was 72.9 years for men and 79.8 years for women, compared to 71.0 and 78.3 years for men and women, respectively, in the United States. Canada's infant mortality rate in 1985 was 25 percent lower than the U.S. rate: 7.9 deaths occurred per 100,000 live births in the United States.

Within the United States such measures of public health vary enormously among regions, among races, and among different levels of income. The well-to-do in the United States can buy better health care than Canadians receive. For them, and for Canada's well-to-do, the U.S. system is better. To a major degree the debate about health care systems is a debate about income distribution and poverty.

Government Constraints on Physicians

As the sole payer for physician services, the Canadian provincial governments are able to negotiate fee schedules from a position of strength. Ontario's 1989 fee increases, for example, averaged 1.75 percent, imposed essentially by force after negotiation with the Ontario Medical Association failed. Since fee-for-service physician payment accommodates and perhaps even encourages the expansion of patient demands, cost controls have also taken the form of the regulation of physician supply. The stock of medical practitioners is affected by the policies and activities of hospital medical advisory committees, medical schools, provincial colleges of physicians and surgeons, provincial governments, and the federal government. As an additional constraint on the number of physicians, the provincial ministers of health reached agreement with the federal government in 1975 to curtail the immigration of physicians to Canada.

Considerable evidence indicates that a major portion of the Canadian constraint has been the reduction in real terms of physician incomes below the levels they would otherwise have attained. Consequently, the lower Canadian expenditures on health care do not necessarily represent the delivery of less health care, and the higher U.S. expenditures do not necessarily represent the delivery of more health care. Higher U.S. spending represents higher incomes for health care workers, and U.S. incomes may be seen as containing monopoly rents. In Canada government constraints may be seen as preventing the development of such monopoly rents.

The Right to Choose Physicians

In Canada individuals generally have freedom regarding the choice of physician. In the United States the growth of health maintenance organizations (HMOs) and other prepaid plans have restricted some patients' choices among health care providers, particularly if the patient is a member of an employer-sponsored plan with specified providers. Today approximately thirty-one million Americans are enrolled in about five thousand organizations, and in most HMOs the physicians are salaried rather than paid on a fee-for-service basis. Approximately 150,000 U.S. hospital beds now are under such programs. While Canada's federal and provincial governments are involved in many health care decisions, freedom of patient choice is a feature highly valued by the general public.

New Balances between Free Enterprise and Government Intervention

We have reached a stage at which broad comparisons of the system as a whole may not be helpful. It is extremely unlikely that Canadians will accept greater reliance on free enterprise, and it is problematic whether the United States will accept significantly greater government intervention in the basic system design. Some commentators are more optimistic about the U.S. position. Marmor and Marshaw, for example, have stated, "In short, although movement toward something like Canadian national health insurance may appear ideologically a large step, most of the pieces needed for a state insurance program are already in place, and interest-group politics might join with popular sentiment to permit such a move" (1990, 27).

In both countries we now recognize the seriousness of the difficulties that arise when a society chooses a two-tiered system. Within this system the tier for the well-to-do will receive a great deal more funding per patient simply because the patients will be eager to pay a higher price for better care. Many health care providers will prefer to work in the tier for the well-to-do and will be able to raise their prices as the free market permits. In the bottom tier countless scams can develop, as individuals find loopholes in government regulations. Government control will be continually frustrated. The costs of a two-tiered system can escalate far above those of a single-tiered system. Canada has rejected a two-tiered system, while the United States is paying a heavy price for its adherence to the free enterprise philosophy for one tier, together with its hodgepodge bottom tier for the poor, disabled, and elderly. For the United States experimentation with new balances between free enterprise and government intervention may involve modifications in the funding, administration, coverage, and standards for the bottom tier. Canadian experimentation will be motivated by a desire to constrain costs.

There are a series of health system issues in which cross-country comparisons and the evaluation of alternative models may be useful. Theory cannot provide us with accurate predictions concerning the implications of alternative models, and so in a sense both Canada and the United States are experimenting with particular components of the system. We have reached a stage at which the analysis of these experiments in particular components of the health system can provide insights and guidance. The remaining sections of this chapter will discuss eight issues that deserve attention from this perspective:

1. health maintenance organizations;
2. diagnostic-related groups (DRGs) and case management;
3. adoption of new technology;
4. ambulatory health care;
5. expansion of the responsibilities of nonphysician health care personnel and the growth of home care as an alternative to days spent in the hospital;
6. malpractice suits;
7. the elderly and demographic change; and
8. profit incentives and decentralized decision making.

Health Maintenance Organizations

Do HMOs represent a more efficient way of organizing and delivering health services? In the United States HMOs provide comprehensive medical care for a prepaid fee to patients who agree to use participating physicians and hospitals. HMOs place emphasis on early detection and prevention of disease rather than on the standard crisis-oriented medicine. A 1984 study conducted by the Rand Corporation found that the "hospital utilization among HMO members was 40 percent lower than among people with full insurance coverage without cost sharing": "Hospital utilization was 59 percent lower than that of the general population (GAO study)" (Friedland 1987, 16). Both studies concluded that the lower utilization was due to HMO controls and procedures and not to the age, sex, and health characteristics of the populations enrolled.

It is becoming increasingly clear that the Canadian health care system must introduce new financial incentives to contain costs for patient treatment when medically feasible. It must use more auxiliary medical personnel in physicians' offices and in hospitals, more outpatient surgical care, shorter hospital stays, less costly drugs, and a greater amount of services for preventative care and health education. Perhaps HMOs can provide these financial incentives. In Ontario, in particular, some politicians have suggested the introduction of HMOs.

Many in the health care field believe that HMOs in the United States have not been as successful as some have suggested. Critics point to a number of possible disadvantages of HMOs. In particular, HMOs may limit patient freedom in the choice of physicians and hospitals. Furthermore, patients may not receive the extensive tests and care that they would expect under Canada's current system. Perhaps Canadians should not be so ready to copy this aspect of the U.S. health care system.

Somewhat related to the HMO concept is the expansion of preferred provider organizations (PPO). A PPO is a defined and limited set of health care providers that contract with an employer or an insurer to provide a comprehensive set of services on a fee-for-service basis. The contract usually involves a negotiated, discounted set of fees. Usually subscribers are not locked into receiving care from a single provider, and they may choose to receive care outside the contracted set of providers. Subscribers face financial incentives, however, to use the preferred providers. These incentives may include lower deductibles and lower subscriber copayments.

Another important aspect of PPOs is the price competition that they may foster among providers.

PPOs have been a method used to increase price competition among providers. Hospitals have always been in competition with one another, but not on the basis of price. Given previous payment systems and patient incentives, hospitals have competed for physicians and patients on the basis of facilities and services, amenities and quality. With the emergence of PPOs, hospitals are now engaged in price competition. . . . By offering a discount to a PPO, a hospital can increase its volume and total revenues. (Feldstein 1988, 318–19)

A central issue in these types of arrangements is whether physicians are paid on a fee-for-service basis or on a prepaid capitation basis. Physician incentives will be quite different with these alternatives. It is the latter concept of prepaid capitation payments that is attractive to some Canadian politicians, who see it as a way both to constrain escalating costs and to encourage preventative medicine.

(For further discussion of HMOs, see Evans 1984, 113–236; Feldstein 1988, 305–46; Jonas 1986, 166–213; McArdle 1987, 1–128, 169–78; Rakich and Darr 1978, 1–146; and Schramm 1987, 3–48.)

DRGs and Case Management

In the United States reimbursement of hospitals by Medicare, Medicaid, and insurance companies has increasingly shifted to a prospective payment system (PPS) for diagnostic-related groups. Payment on the basis of a specified amount for each type of medical problem focuses on the need to keep costs to a minimum for each type of illness, or "product line" with the hospital. The hospital retains any savings if patient costs are below the standard, and the hospital is penalized if costs are above specified maximums.

Under the DRG system, however, hospitals may become more reluctant to purchase new technologies that add significantly to their operating costs. Furthermore, the quality of patient care may suffer. Jonas has suggested:

> Use of classification schemes as the basis for hospital repayment assumes that the classifications are clinically meaningful and "reasonably" homogeneous with respect to resource consumption. There is, however, mounting evidence that some of the DRG categories do not satisfy either requirement (Prospective Payment Assessment Commission). Perhaps the most common criticism of the DRG categories is that they include patients with different resource needs, since they often do not account adequately for differences in patient complexity or severity of illness (Horn et al.). Variation in severity within the DRG categories is cause for concern if patient complexity can be assessed before admission to the hospital since this can create an incentive to transfer more complex patients to other hospitals. (Carol M. McCarthy and Kenneth E. Thorpe, in Jonas 1986, 322)

Raffel has also noted that there are "skeptics who believe that the DRG system will be manipulated since it creates a new incentive for hospitals and the physicians on their staffs to admit more patients, particularly those where the rationale for admission is marginal but still defensible in terms of professional judgment. Such cases may prove to be less costly to the hospital and yet the hospital will collect the same amount from Medicare" (1984, 246). Should Canada adopt this kind of hospital reimbursement?

Apart from the issue of DRGs as the basis for hospital reimbursement is their use for the analysis of financial results. Hospital administrators may find it helpful to use a DRG approach in determining which types of treatment, or which physicians, are costing more than the accepted standards. The DRG methodology can isolate those cases in which excessive costs may deserve special examination.

(For further discussion of DRGs and case management, see Jonas 1986, 465–82; Russell 1979, 1–173; and Schramm 1987, 252–74.)

Adoption of New Technology

It appears that Canadian adoption of new technology lags significantly behind U.S. adoption, as table 1 indicates. An important question concerns the differences between the adoption criteria in Canada and those in the United States, together with the implications of these differences for the health system as a whole. To what degree and in what areas can Canadians learn from the U.S. practices? Does the more rapid adoption of new technology mean significantly better care in the United States? If so, is the better care worth the additional cost? How can a society best make these decisions? What are the implications for health care costs and for budgeting procedures of an alteration in the criteria for adopting new technology?

Almost all industrialized countries have experienced rapidly rising health care costs, which has led to rapid changes in policies toward medical technology. Until fairly recently, the major involvement of governments in medical technology was to promote a new technology's development and adoption actively, through such means as funding biomedical research and technology development or assuring payment for the technology under a national health plan. In recent years, however, governments have become more concerned with whether or not new technologies were being used efficiently. Without making a judgment about the efficacy of the technology, governments have intervened to encourage greater efficiency in the production and use of technology. With increasing concerns about the cost effectiveness of technology, governments also have begun to question and test the benefits of medical technologies. (H. David Banta, in Jonas 1986, 478)

(For further discussion, see Jonas 1986, 465–82; Russell 1979, 1–173; and Schramm 1987, 252–74.)

TABLE 1. Comparative Availability of Selected Medical Technologies

	Canada (1989)			United States (1987)		
	Number of Units	Persons per Unit (1,000)	Units/ Million Persons	Number of Units	Persons per Unit (1,000)	Units/ Million Persons
Open-heart surgery	32	813	1.23	793	307	3.26
Cardiac catheterization	39	667	1.50	1,234	198	5.06
Organ transplantation	28	929	1.08	319	764	1.31

Sources: Canada—Canadian Hospital Association, Ottawa; Canadian Association of Radiation Oncology, Vancouver, B.C.; University Hospital, London, Ont.; and Canadian Medical Association, Ottawa. United States—American Hospital Association, Division of Technology Assessment, Hospital Statistics (Chicago: AHA, 1989).

Ambulatory Health Care

It appears that in the United States the growth of outpatient services has created financial difficulties for some hospitals at the same time that it has created new financial opportunities for other hospitals and health care centers. Together with shorter hospital stays, the growth of outpatient services has meant that many U.S. hospitals have experienced a large number of empty beds, with a consequent decrease in revenue below the levels they would otherwise have attained. On the other hand, care of ambulatory patients can be a profitable activity. Ambulatory patients use the hospital's ancillary services, a high-margin area, but do not require room, board, and nursing, all of which have traditionally been low-margin areas. There has even been a significant increase of ambulatory surgery in the United States performed without the requirement of hospital admission. Ambulatory surgery centers totally independent of hospital facilities now perform minor surgery on an outpatient basis, creating a new type of competition for hospitals. New medical techniques can facilitate the expansion of ambulatory care. To what degree can Canadian hospitals and medical clinics learn from the new practices in the United States?

(For further discussion, see Jonas 1986, 125–65; and Schramm 1987, 3–48.)

Expansion of Responsibilities of Nonphysician Health Care Personnel and Growth of Home Care as an Alternative to Days Spent in the Hospital

Many commentators believe that nonphysician health care personnel can be given greater responsibility for particular, specialized jobs. In some situations nurses may receive training for certain activities that enables them to assume responsibilities traditionally performed by physicians. This concept of expanded nurse responsibility may be seen as intimately linked with the growth of ambulatory health care and the expanded need for home care related to ambulatory patients. It may also be seen as intimately linked with the growing number of the elderly who may be living in their own homes or in nonacute institutional facilities. It has been estimated that from 40 to 90 percent of primary-care physician visits could be delegated to nurse practitioners (NPs) (Lomas et al. 1985, 119). Achieving this will require increased use of group practice and other structural changes in the health system. The perception of an oversupply of physicians may have been one of the factors discouraging greater use of NPs. To what degree would it be feasible to expand the responsibilities of nonphysician health care personnel in Canada? How would this affect the future demand for physician services?

Home care services are rapidly becoming a preferred method of providing health care to a large segment of the population. By bringing health care services to people in their own homes, hospitalization can often be prevented and residential health care facility placement can be delayed or averted. Reduced government spending and the frenzy over health care costs have boosted the appeal of home care as a growth industry. Home health care is especially attractive to institutions that are attempting to make the DRG system profitable by sending patients home "quicker and sicker." In the United States the overall home care market is growing at about 20 percent per year.

Home care has been called the sleeping giant of the U.S. health care industry. While it is still in its infancy compared to hospitals and nursing homes, home care is rapidly expanding as a result of pressure from an aging population, skyrocketing Medicare and Medicaid expenditures, a hospital and provider industry experiencing increasing financial stress, and a business community searching for more cost-effective health care benefits for its employees. To what degree should home care be encouraged as a way of cost containment? How would such an expanded usage impact the finances and practices of physicians in hospitals?

(For further discussion, see Feldstein 1988, 406–36; Fottler et al. 1988, 1–178; Jonas 1986, 90–124, 237–62; Lomas et al. 1985, 1–26; and Schramm 1987, 145–84.)

Malpractice Suits

Since the first American "malpractice crisis" in the mid-1970s several American and Canadian surveys have recorded changes in practice patterns that respondent physicians ascribe to the threat of malpractice liability. In addition to increased record keeping and communication with patients and other health care professionals, a substantial percentage of respondents have attributed increased diagnostic testing and specific treatment procedures to the liability threat.

The tort system can affect the incidence of medical injuries in two ways: First, by forcing providers to bear the costs of all negligently caused injuries, it encourages them to prevent such injuries; second, by internalizing the costs of these injuries to providers, it encourages the substitution of low-risk procedures for high-risk procedures and the displacement of low-quality providers by high-quality providers.

Institutional quality assurance and risk management programs have accompanied the recent increases in hospital and physician insurance premiums, the growth of hospital self-insurance plans, and the expansion of hospital liability both in Canada and the United States. While these programs have also been stimulated by government regulation, their earlier emergence and more advanced form in the United States may in part reflect differences in the liability environment. Liability concerns may encourage physicians to move from a highly litigious region to an area with fewer and less severe claims and lower malpractice premiums. The consensus among recent physician surveys is that the current liability environment is likely to affect their diagnostic and treatment procedures.

Canadian health care workers may reduce their legal exposure by learning from U.S. quality assurance programs and treatment documentation. Canadian patients and their lawyers may understand the legal complexities of potential suits by learning from U.S. judicial proceedings. Canadian legislators may design a wiser set of laws by learning from the U.S. "malpractice crisis."

(For further discussion of malpractice suits, see Brooten and Chapman 1987, 1–224; and Danzon 1985, 1–227.)

The Elderly

In providing facilities for seniors, each Canadian province has cobbled together its own set of programs and funding provisions. The private sector has played an active role in care for the elderly with a variety of accommodation facilities. It is expected that the number of elderly in Canada will escalate rapidly, creating a situation in which management of this segment of the health care system will increase in importance. The variety of programs throughout Canada and the variety of accommodation facilities make this a particularly interesting research subject.

The increase in the proportion of the "old-old" is reflected in projected nursing home statistics. Of all nursing home residents in 1978, 35 percent were aged eighty-five or over, compared to a projected 52 percent in 2003 (Terrie T. Wetle and David A. Pearson, in Jonas 1986, 216). Increasingly, nursing homes will be taking care of older patients, who in turn will require higher levels of service. This trend is likely to be exacerbated by cost-containment efforts in acute-care hospitals, such as those in the DRG system. These cost-containment efforts are thought by some to result in the early discharge from hospitals of elderly patients who are much sicker and more dependent than those discharged in previous years.

Feldstein has remarked, in regard to the United States:

> For those aged able to afford long-term care, we are likely to observe an increasing private market ready to provide both community and institutional services. Private long-term care insurance is also likely to evolve for those aged with greater assets and incomes. To protect themselves against the problems of adverse selection and moral hazard, insurance companies will use deductibles, cost sharing, and/or indemnity policies. . . . Medicaid is likely to remain as the long-term care insurance for the low income aged. (1988, 588)

The Employee Benefit Research Institute has discussed several aspects of this forecast:

> Many consider the current system of financing long-term care inadequate because the financial burden can be very large relative to retirement income and accumulated wealth. At a cost of $2,100–$4,500 a month, the expense of receiving care in a nursing facility can exceed retirement income, wiping out a lifetime's savings.
>
> The problem, however, is that there is no obvious financing mechanism one can use to help meet long-term care costs in advance of the time they are incurred. Although a private insurance market exists for acute care not financed by Medicare, no comparable market for private long-term care insurance has been developed. A public mechanism—Medicaid—exists, but this is a means-tested program that was not intended to finance the long-term care costs of the elderly.
>
> Approaches could be purely public, like an extended Medicaid or Medicare program; purely private, by encouraging long-term care insurance; or a mixture. (McArdle 1987, 231)

(For further discussion, see Feldstein 1988, 559–92; Jonas 1986, 214–36; McArdle 1987, 221–38; and Schramm 1987, 185–251.)

Profit Incentives and Decentralized Decision Making

As part of the concern for cost containment, major issues involve the creative use of profit incentives and decentralized decisions. For example, the U.S. system of PPOs and DRGs may enable a not-for-profit hospital to retain the difference between its revenues and its costs, thereby enabling the hospital to have discretion over a larger portion of its expenditures. In the United States many hospitals are in fact owned and operated on a private, for-profit basis. Nonhospital ambulatory care centers may be privately owned, often by physicians whose income will include a profit component as well as a salary component. Even in Canada special institutional facilities for the elderly are often privately owned and are operated on a for-profit basis.

For Canadians there has traditionally been a feeling that everyone should have access to the same quality of health care. Introduction of private ownership and profit in particular components of the system may bring with it a greater differentiation in service, with the well-to-do being able to afford better care. Consequently, this subject raises difficult political questions for Canadians. In these choices concerning profit incentives and decentralized decisions for certain components of the system, experimentation will be necessary. Theory and ideological conviction may not provide adequate guidance. Only on the basis of actual results will a society be able to see the advantages and shortcomings of alternative administrative arrangements.

(For further discussion, see Evans 1984, 127–238; Feldstein 1988, 305–46; Jonas 1986, 483–503; McArdle 1987, 47–80; Schramm 1987, 105–144; and Siaface 1981, 1–208.)

Conclusion

It may not be realistic to talk about the United States learning from the Canadian experience and adopting the Canadian health care system. Adherence to the free enterprise philosophy, together with the political power of the well-to-do, may prevent this from happening. Consequently, cross-country comparisons of the health care system as a whole may not be helpful in public policy formulation, even though they may be interesting. Nevertheless, we have reached a stage at which both Canada and the United States are experimenting with individual components of their health care systems. It is here that comparisons—with individual analyses and evaluations—can be useful in the modification of public policy. An advantage of free enterprise is the opportunity it fosters for experimentation and innovation. It is because of this U.S. attribute that many new concepts are being developed in the United States. Ironically, even though Canada's system is cheaper and better, Canada may have much more to gain through these cross-country comparisons than the United States.

BIBLIOGRAPHY

Andreopoulos, Spyros, ed. *National Health Insurance: Can We Learn from Canada?* New York: John Wiley and Sons, 1975.

Brooten, Kenneth E., and Stu Chapman. *Malpractice: A Guide to Avoidance and Treatment*. Fla.: Grune and Stratton, 1987.

"Canada Rated Best in U.S. Poll on Health." *Globe and Mail,* February 14, 1989, 1, 10.

Danzon, Patricia M. *Medical Malpractice*. Cambridge: Harvard University Press, 1985.

Dington, Dean C., and Keith D. Moore. *Market-Driven Strategies in Health Care*. San Francisco: Jossey-Bass, 1987.

Evans, Robert G. *Strained Mercy: The Economics of Canadian Health Care*. Toronto: Butterworths, 1984.

Feldstein, Paul J. *Health Care Economics*. Albany, N.Y.: Delmar, 1988.

Fottler, Myron D., S. Robert Hernandez, and Charles L. Joiner, eds. *Strategic Management of Human Resources in Health Services Organizations*. New York: John Wiley and Sons, 1988.

"Health Care System OK with Canadians." *London Free Press*. May 11, 1991, A2.

Jonas, Steven, ed. *Health Care Delivery in the United States*. New York: Springer, 1986.

Lomas, Jonathan, Morris L. Barer, and Greg L. Stoddart. *Physician Manpower Planning: Lessons from the Macdonald Report*. Discussion Paper Series. Toronto: Ontario Economic Council, 1985.

Marmor, Theodore R. In *National Health Insurance: Can We Learn from Canada? See* Andreopoulos 1975.

Marmor, Theodore R., and Jerry L. Marshaw. "Canada's Health Insurance and Ours: The Real Lessons, the Big Choices." *American Prospect* 1, no. 3 (October 1990): 18.

McArdle, Frank B., ed. *The Changing Health Care Market*. Washington, D.C.: Employee Benefit Research Institute, 1987.

Raffel, Marshall W. *The U.S. Health System: Origins and Functions*. New York: Wiley Medical Publication, 1984.

Rakich, Jonathan S., and Kurt Darr, eds. *Hospital Organization and Management*. New York: SP Medical and Scientific Books, 1978.

Russell, Louise B. *Technology in Hospitals: Medical Advances and Their Diffusion*. Washington, D.C.: Brookings Institution, 1979.

Schramm, Carl J., ed. *Health Care and Its Costs: Can the U.S. Afford Adequate Health Care?* New York: W. W. Norton, 1987.

Siaface, Ekaterini. *Investor-Owned Hospitals and Their Role in the Changing U.S. Health Care System*. New York: F and S Press, 1981.

"Trade-offs and Choices: Health Policy Options for the 1990s." *Employee Benefits Digest* 28, no. 5 (May 1991): 5.

CHAPTER 9

Proposals for Health Care Reform

Bert Seidman

There is a remarkable degree of consensus on the facts describing health care in America and on the shortcomings of the current system. With so much concern about health care focused on its undesirable aspects, it is not surprising that more thought is being given to health care reform than ever before. Many of those engaged in formulating health care reform measures are paying greater attention than in the past to the experiences of other countries, particularly Canada. No one expects to adopt completely any foreign health care system, but Americans are increasingly aware of the differences between the U.S. system and those in other countries and are wondering if we can usefully adapt any of their features to improve our situation.

Consideration of health care reform is not limited to the national level. In fact, Hawaii and Massachusetts have already enacted universal programs, and other states are considering that route. In the 1970s and 1980s some states adopted hospital rate-setting programs, measures to expand coverage of the noninsured, or both.

On another level changes have been instituted that could have a bearing on national health care reform. Cost-containment measures have been adopted for Medicare, first affecting hospitals and later physicians' services, that some proponents of health care reform would incorporate in a national program to be extended to the entire health care sector.

Perhaps of greatest interest are the proposals that have been offered and those that are in process for an American national health care program. A few proposals have been worked out in detail, but only the general principles of others have been agreed on. A number of them have been introduced as congressional bills.

Foreign Experience

Health care systems in industrialized countries generally fall into two categories, with both providing universal and comprehensive benefits.

> A *national health service,* with tax-financed government ownership of facilities and with doctors as public employees or on a kind of retainer and paid a fixed amount for each patient (capitation). This is the U.K. model.
>
> A *social insurance program,* with contributions paid either as taxes or premiums by some combination of employers, employees, and general revenue and with providers in an independent status.

A principal difference in health care systems between the United States and most other countries is that the latter establish an annual national health care budget that sets a limitation on national health care expenditures. Another important difference is that other nations set uniform payment levels to providers prospectively in annual negotiations. Without a myriad of insurance organizations and no problems in determining coverage either of patients or services, the administrative costs of these health care systems are invariably lower than those of the United States.

In the United States there is very little interest in trying to establish a national health service (or "socialized medicine," as it is sometimes called) like the United Kingdom's. Even those who favor that approach acknowledge that it has little or no chance of being adopted in this country. Therefore, attention has been directed to the social insurance models in other countries, especially in Canada, but also in Germany and perhaps in others. Here brief mention will be made of the Canadian and German systems.

Perhaps because of our proximity to Canada, much attention in recent years has been directed to its health care system. Some in the United States have advocated that we actually adopt a "Canadian-type system," and some proposals for an American national health program are said to be modeled on the Canadian system. Canada's universal health care system, like the United States' more limited program, is called "Medicare." It was implemented in two stages—hospitalization in 1956 and physicians' services in 1966. It combines national and provincial public financing with administration of payments to hospitals and physicians at the provincial level. Depending on the province, payments by the covered population are in the form of either premiums or taxes and are not employment based.

It is important to point out that when Canadian Medicare got under way only about one third of Canadians had private health insurance. As the United States contemplates health care reform today, most Americans have health care coverage as an employment benefit. If the United States adopts the Canadian way of paying for health care, far more drastic changes will occur than Canada experienced in starting its system.

Other features of the Canadian system, however, are conceivably transferable across the border. Five basic principles underlie Canada's health care system: public administration, comprehensiveness, universal coverage, portability, and reasonable access. Minimum benefits applicable to all provinces are specified in the federal law. Expenditures are controlled through allocation of global budgets to hospitals and negotiation with physicians' organizations of fees and, in some provinces, volume of service. There is no participation of private insurers as either insurers or intermediaries. The ministry of health in each province funds the operating budgets of hospitals. Hospital capital investment is funded from various sources, the major one being the ministry; the investment must be approved by the ministry. Spending for physicians' services is restrained by fee schedules that the ministry negotiates with provincial medical associations. Because there is a centralized system with a single payer in each province, administrative costs are considerably lower than in the United States, as are total costs of the system. This is despite the fact that the Canadian system covers all Canadians, while the U.S. system fails to cover a significant number of Americans. Yet the record of health care in Canada's less costly system is at least as good as the United States' record.

The German system is also a social insurance system, and it is also universal and comprehensive. It is, however, quite different from Canada's system and in some ways more like that of the United States. Both financing and delivery of health care in Germany are pluralistic. Only a very small proportion of German health care spending is publicly funded. Most of it is provided and financed by over a thousand fiscally independent nonprofit sickness funds (we would call them health insurance funds), which are private but subject to requirements set forth in national legislation. An annual assembly, composed of all the major groups involved in health care, in what is called the Concerted Action on Health Care, establishes economic guidelines for the health care system, including the overall expenditure growth rate. Although the assembly does not have mandatory powers, it has influenced annual fee negotiations and has helped to restrain German health care cost inflation.

The United States is not the only country considering reforms in its health care system. A number of European countries are discussing various changes that might make their universal systems more effective, including elements that would enhance regulated competition in health care. These developments should be watched to see if any of them might be incorporated, with whatever modification is appropriate, in the health care reforms the United States undertakes.

While it is worthwhile to examine the experience of other countries as we in the United States contemplate health care reform, it is neither realistic nor appropriate for us to consider adopting the system of some other country, however successful it may be in the eyes of the citizens of the country. If the United States decides on major changes, we will inevitably develop our own system, which will be different from those of other countries. We have no tradition of simply copying other countries' social programs. We have unique traditions, customs, and government structure that will influence our decisions. Therefore, any changes we make will necessarily involve starting with what we have and deciding how much to change it and in what respects.

Health Care Reform in the States

Confronted with runaway health care costs and concerned that large numbers of their residents are unable to get needed care, some states are moving ahead to enact their own health care reforms without waiting for federal action. Hawaii and Massachusetts, as noted earlier, have enacted sweeping health care changes that aim at universal coverage. Other states are in various stages of considering similar legislation.

In 1974 Hawaii enacted a requirement that nearly all employers provide health care benefits, either fee-for-service or HMO, for their employees working at least twenty hours a week. Although dependent coverage is voluntary, the state health department has estimated that there is 95 percent coverage. To fill the remaining 5 percent gap, in 1990 Hawaii launched the State Health Insurance Program, with emphasis on preventative and primary care. In this program costs are shared between the state and individual on a sliding scale based on income.

The universal health insurance initiative in Massachusetts stems from its Health Security Act of 1988. All residents were to have access to affordable health care by 1993. Implementation of the 1988 legislation began with coverage through a state program for the unemployed and a requirement for full-time college and university students to purchase health insurance through their institution or a comparable plan. For coverage of workers and their families Massachusetts had a "play or pay" requirement scheduled to go into effect in 1993. At that time businesses with more than five employees will be required to pay a surcharge of 12 percent of each full-time employee's first $14,000 in wages into a health insurance trust fund up to a maximum of $1,680 per employee. Employers who provide at least the level of benefits the law requires can deduct the cost of such benefits from the surcharge. Employees of firms that do not provide coverage would be eligible on a sliding scale of payments in the state program. There is now some question whether the Massachusetts program will take effect. The governor is calling for repeal. Others would postpone until 1994 the requirement for employers to provide or pay for coverage.

Perhaps another ten states are in various stages of developing legislation aimed at establishing universal coverage. Oregon will probably institute mandatory employer benefits in 1994, which will require employers to provide employee and dependent coverage or pay a tax. A companion measure sets up a state program to provide coverage to low-income people not covered by employers or Medicaid. Other states in which legislation looking toward universal coverage has been introduced or proposed include Washington, California, Michigan, Missouri, Ohio, Oregon, Connecticut, Minnesota, and New York.

It is not clear how state action will affect the movement for national health care reform. Some argue that if a significant number of states enact universal coverage it will relieve pressure on the federal government for a national program. Others feel that if a few more states, particularly large states, adopt universal coverage, national action for universal coverage is more likely.

Medicare Features Applicable to Health Care Reform

Any national health care program will have to limit the hospital costs the program will pay for. Medicare Part A has a prospective system for paying hospitals for inpatient stays that is based on the average cost for several hundred medical conditions called "diagnostic-related groups" (DRGs). If the hospital can meet Medicare requirements at less than Medicare's DRG rate, it pockets the difference. If it exceeds the DRG rate, it has to absorb the additional amount. This puts pressure on hospitals to reduce their costs and particularly the length of stay of Medicare patients. In 1991 the Health Care Financing Administration, which administers Medicare, announced a similar system for hospital outpatient care. Some proponents of national health care reform would incorporate the DRG system of hospital cost regulation in their programs. Others favor the system of negotiating hospital budgets used in Canada. Still others favor hospital rate setting along the lines of state programs. In any case, the introduction of hospital cost regulation in Medicare has shown that some form of limitation of hospital costs in a national program is feasible and, on the whole, acceptable.

A number of new provisions aimed at reducing costs and enhancing quality of physician care under Medicare Part B are also suggested for inclusion in national health reform proposals. The most radical feature calls for annual "volume performance standards" for Part B services, the term used for what are really total national expenditure targets. Based on recommendations of the Physician Payment Review Commission and the secretary of Health and Human Services, each year Congress will set the percentage increase for Part B spending. If it is exceeded in one year, the excess will be reflected in lower fees paid to physicians in the following year. Advocates of various national health reform proposals have incorporated the concept in their programs and would extend it by establishing annual spending caps on all health care expenditures.

Medicare fees are to be paid according to a fee schedule based on the relative worth of physicians' services. The criteria used in working out the relative value scale on which the fee schedule will be based were developed through cooperative efforts of physicians' groups, health care experts, and the federal government. It is expected that in the future Medicare will be paying highly specialized physicians relatively less and those providing primary care and what has come to be called "cognitive" care relatively more. The fees will also determine the amount that doctors will be permitted to charge Medicare patients. Beginning in 1991 the charges may not be more than 25 percent over the fee schedule amount; in 1992, 20 percent; and thereafter 15 percent. Organizations of the elderly have long advocated a system of "mandatory assignment," which would permit doctors to charge only the Medicare-approved fee.

One other innovation in Part B is the development of physician practice patterns. These are guidelines for medical procedures and treatment that are being developed by groups of physicians based on what they consider to be the most appropriate medical care. It is hoped that, when these guidelines are fully developed, they will reduce unneeded care and, at the same time, improve the quality of care.

All the features that have been introduced in Medicare have a relevancy for national health care reform. Indeed, if the United States does establish a national health program, Medicare may well have paved the way by demonstrating the practicability and acceptance of features that would have to be incorporated in any viable national health program.

Proposals for National Programs

In recent years a number of proposals for national health programs have been advanced, and others are in various stages of development. Sensitive to the widespread lack of health care coverage, the advocates of each of these proposals maintain that their respective plans will expand access to care and, at least eventually, achieve universal coverage. They also assert that their plans will moderate health care cost inflation and improve the quality of care. Most of the proposals involve the following two approaches:

1. mandatory employer coverage combined with a public plan covering a significant proportion of the population, including some who are not low income or poor;
2. a single federal or federal-state program.

Some proposals involve neither, however, and they will be described first.

Limited Proposals

In February 1990 the Health Insurance Association of America (HIAA) announced its "Strategy for Containing Health Care Costs." Although HIAA's recommendations focused mainly on costs, they also included recommendations to expand coverage in various ways and to achieve quality improvement. Together these recommendations did not constitute a national health program, nor was this HIAA's intention. HIAA stressed the desirability of retaining a role for private insurance. There is no indication that if all of HIAA's recommendations were followed the result would be universal coverage. To achieve broader coverage, however, HIAA has recommended establishment of state risk pools financed by state general revenues or other broad-based financing. These funds would permit small employers, people with severe health problems, and other individuals to purchase private health insurance at lower rates than they could otherwise obtain. HIAA also recommends that Medicaid cover all people below the federal poverty level. It has a number of recommendations relating to cost containment but particularly stresses the greater use of managed care.

In fact, in its public statements HIAA has offered managed care as an alternative to a national health program. Others would incorporate expansion of managed care and some of the other HIAA recommendations in their broader national health reform proposals. Federal legislation has recently been introduced somewhat along the lines of HIAA's recommendations that would require, in one bill, employers with three to twenty-five employees and, in another, insurers selling to such firms to offer a basic health insurance package for voluntary purchase by employees. Although some twenty million employees and their dependents would be eligible to buy the insurance, undoubtedly far fewer would do so.

The Heritage Foundation has proposed a program that is explicitly intended to "give all Americans access to adequate health care services." The foundation defines such services as including only catastrophic health care and would require individuals, not employers, to purchase the insurance. Low-income workers would receive subsidies to help them buy the insurance. Medicaid would be continued for the poor, although states could provide narrower benefits than are now required. Medicare would also be continued, but mainly for catastrophic illness. A means-tested long-term care program would be established to be supplemented by private funds in various forms. Thus far, the Heritage program has received very little support. Most people would not be content with only catastrophic coverage. Moreover, most are reasonably satisfied with employment-based coverage and would not want to exchange it for a system based on individual insurance. In addition, it is hard to see how the Heritage proposal would not greatly add to already excessive health care administrative costs.

The Bush administration was opposed to both mandatory employer coverage and any new public program. Former secretary of Health and Human Services Louis W. Sullivan would not recommend to the president federally funded national health insurance because "the belief that putting an insurance card in every pocket will cure all our health care ills is false prophecy from those preaching easy solutions." Sullivan had pointed to problems such as poor diets, the spread of AIDS and substance abuse, the lack of health care facilities and health professionals especially in the inner cities, and the financial problems faced by some hospitals, all of which would not be automatically solved by national health insurance. Most proponents of universal health care programs would agree with him, but they would also maintain that assuring access to care for all Americans would mitigate such problems even if additional targeted action would still be required.

Comprehensive Proposals

A number of proposals have been advanced or are being developed that would require all employers to provide, or in some way pay for, health insurance for their employees. These are the play-or-pay plans. Because a majority of the uninsured are employees or their dependents, such a requirement would by itself constitute a long step toward guaranteeing universal access. But there would still be uninsured people not holding jobs. To insure most of the remaining who are not covered, advocates of mandating employer coverage recommend Medicaid expansion or some other public program.

Like the state programs in Hawaii, Massachusetts, and Oregon, most of the employer mandate proposals would require employers who do not wish to provide health insurance for their employees at a specific minimum level of coverage to purchase it from Medicaid, or another public program, or to pay into a public fund that would finance care for employees not covered by employer plans. Among the proposals that fit this pattern are those of the National Leadership Commission (now the National Leadership Coalition) on Health Care Reform, the United States Bipartisan Commission on Comprehensive Health Care (the Pepper Commission), and the AFL-CIO. The American Medical Association favors an employer mandate and broader Medicaid coverage, but it has not recommended the play-or-pay approach. In addition to their coverage provisions, most of these proposals also include measures aimed at cost containment and quality enhancement.

In June 1991 a number of Senate Democratic leaders in health care (Senate Majority Leader George J. Mitchell and Senators Edward M. Kennedy, Donald W. Riegle, Jr., and John D. Rockefeller IV) introduced a bill based on the play-or-pay approach. It would require employers to provide at least a specified health care package for their employees or to pay a payroll tax to finance coverage for their employees through a new public program. The public program would also cover the poor, replacing Medicaid, and other uninsured people.

All of these proposals are predicated on the continuance of private health insurance in an employment-based system, although most of them would assign a large supplementary role to a parallel public system serving certain individuals and groups. Another group of proposals would either exclude private insurers altogether or assign them only the intermediary administrative role they have in Medicare; that is, they would be administrative agents of a publicly funded program. Again, the proposals in this category are not all alike. Generally, however, they involve what is called a single payer (i.e., payer of providers), a state or federal governmental or quasigovernmental organization, with payments to that payer in the form of either premiums or taxes by employers, employees, and others. Health care for the poor would be subsidized, and those not employed would pay on some basis related to income.

Proposals along these lines have been offered by Representatives Fortney ("Pete") Stark and Marty Russo as well as other members of Congress, Physicians for a National Health Program, the Health Security Action Council, and the National Association of Social Workers. These proposals, like those based on the employer mandate approach, include various cost-containment and quality improvement features, emphasize expanding managed care, and are often referred to as "Canadian-type."

In February 1991 the AFL-CIO Executive Council in a unanimous statement called for expeditious enactment of federal legislation for national health care reform. While maintaining its traditional goal of a national social insurance program for universal access to health care, as an immediate measure it set forth a play-or-pay plan. The AFL-CIO urged that all employers, including the federal government, be required to contribute fairly toward the cost of care. Specifically, employers could meet the requirement either by providing health care benefits themselves or by paying into a fund that would provide health care benefits for their employees. The latter would be a "national social insurance program" that would include employees not covered by employer benefits, as well as the unemployed and others not in the labor force, and would incorporate Medicare and Medicaid. The AFL-CIO program also calls for:

> —a national cost-containment program that includes a cap on total health care expenditures, a capital budget, and all-payer uniform reimbursement of rates negotiated by a federal authority with hospitals, doctors, and other providers;

—a national commission of consumer, labor, management, government, and providers to administer the program;

—a core package of benefits with voluntary supplemental benefits;

—progressive and equitable financing;

—streamlined administration with involvement of intermediaries that, among other responsibilities, would have to guarantee that no one would be denied coverage;

—dropping the Medicare eligibility age from sixty-five to sixty;

—various measures to improve quality and encourage avoidance of unnecessary tests and procedures and, as a related matter, developing a better system for handling malpractice disputes; and

—developing a strategy for universal access to long-term care, including home health care.

President Lane Kirkland of the AFL-CIO has emphasized that his organization is "not committed to any rigid, single plan" and is prepared to negotiate the details of a plan that will garner the broadest possible support.

Issues in National Health Care Reform

Coverage

Concern about escalating health care costs is the engine driving health care reform. But deprivation of access to care and its devastating consequences for millions of Americans deeply trouble the consciences of more fortunate Americans. This is why access to health care has come to be widely recognized as a fundamental right. It is worthwhile, then, to consider what would and would not result in universal coverage.

Clearly, simply requiring employers to provide health insurance for their employees would not guarantee universal coverage; the nonemployed must also be assured of access to affordable health care. But there is a further question. Should the United States break the link between employment and the right to obtain health care, as other countries have done? Payments for health care could be required of employers and employees as well as others, but failure to discharge such financial obligations would not affect anyone's eligibility to obtain needed health care to the extent the national legislation provides. There might be other penalties for not paying health care taxes or premiums, but not denial of health care. Denial of health care as a penalty for failing to meet financial obligations affects dependents, especially children, who have no responsibility in the matter. Also especially affected are low-income people who might be unable to meet their financial obligations, even if these were reduced, but who are also most likely to need care.

Staging

Another issue is whether universal coverage should be achieved in stages or all at once. There are some who feel that, just as Medicare began with the elderly and then was extended to the severely disabled, the next group to be universally covered should be children. Indeed, recent expansion measures under Medicaid have aimed at complete coverage of poor children in the foreseeable future. But to extend universal coverage to all children while denying it to older family members would create both social and administrative difficulties. It seems very unlikely that legislation would be enacted requiring employers to provide coverage for their employees' children but not the employees themselves. Thus, the only way to guarantee access to health care for all children would be through a public plan. Once children, the elderly, the disabled, and the poor are covered under one or more public plans, it is likely that the next step would be to extend public coverage to employees too so that families would not be split between employer-based plans and the public plan or plans.

Other staging issues relate to how much time should be given to firms not now providing health insurance to their employees to purchase insurance or contribute to an alternative public plan. Also, particularly with respect to small firms, there is the question of whether they should receive a tax credit or subsidy when they begin to provide coverage or contribute to the public plan and, if so, for how long. The Pepper Commission plan would be staged in over a seven-year period, depending on the size of firm, with a subsidy for newly covered firms phased out over the same period.

Public versus Private

The issue is not really public versus private because approximately 30 percent of current health care spending is already public. Rather, the question is whether there should be a public plan in addition to Medicare and Medicaid (or subsuming Medicare, Medicaid, or both, as the AFL-CIO has proposed) that supplements private coverage or, alternatively, one that entirely replaces it, as a number of groups have recommended. The distinction between these two approaches may not be as sharp as it seems. Advocates of the play-or-pay approach would require employers to cover their employees. But they also recognize that some employers would choose to cover their employees under an alternative public plan.

On the other hand, it would be possible to have a program based mainly on a public plan but permitting employers meeting specified standards and requirements relating to access, cost, and quality to opt out of the public plan in favor of private coverage. Again, it is hard to predict how many employers would choose this route. But assuming the characteristics of the two alterna-tives, and they are not altogether improbable, a private-public plan might not be so different from a public-private plan. Both would involve a large propor-tion of the population under private coverage and a large proportion under public coverage. There might be other important differences, however, in-cluding the proportions that would be privately and publicly funded and the amount that would show up in the federal (or state in a federal-state program like Canada's) budget. Also, even the public plan does not have to be totally public. Along the lines of the AFL-CIO proposal that plan might follow the Medicare plan of using private insurance firms to administer the program. Their role might be similar to what they are already doing in employer-sponsored plans that are self-insured.

If the program includes a public plan, it is essential that such a plan not turn into the second-class plan that Medicaid has become. A unified reim-bursement system would discourage providers from either avoiding the public plan or providing second-rate service to its participants. Also, inclusion of large numbers of nonpoor people under the public plan would mean that it should not be stigmatized as a poor person's, or welfare, plan, as Medicaid has been. Nevertheless, strong efforts would have to be made to guarantee that the public plan provides affordable access, and not just eligibility, as well as high-quality standards.

Financing

Traditionally, benefit programs in the United States, both public and private, have been employment based. Whether they have been privately insured like health care and pensions or publicly financed like social security and unem-ployment compensation, they have been largely funded by employer and, in some programs, employee payments in the form of either premiums or payroll taxes. This has proved to be an acceptable way of financing these social protections, and, therefore, there is no reason for shifting to a program based on individual financing of either private insurance or public expenditures for health care. Sometimes the Canadian experience, which does involve individ-ual premiums or taxes, is cited, but the situation in the United States is now quite different from what Canada's was when it began its Medicare program. Retaining employment-based financing would tend to minimize disruption and dissatisfaction in the transition to national health care reform.

A second issue relating to financing is how the financial burden of the cost of health care should be spread. There are several aspects of this ques-tion, and all relate to the extent to which health care funding can be geared to what the various elements in society can afford. Of course, effective health care cost containment will lighten the total financial burden, but it will not eliminate the question of how it should be distributed.

The present system of financing health care is regressive in that small employers and their employees and individuals not only pay a higher percentage of income or payroll than large firms and their workers but are also likely to pay higher dollar amounts. At one time so-called community rating was widespread in the United States. Under community rating insurance rates are set on the same terms to all purchasers, regardless of factors such as preexisting conditions, claims experience, demographic characteristics, or the size of the firm. Community rating tends to hold down premium levels for higher-risk groups. The Pepper Commission and the AFL-CIO would require community rating. The National Leadership Commission on Health Care recommended a play-or-pay plan in which employers choosing to pay into a public fund would be liable for a percentage of payroll and employees for a percentage of wages. The commission's plan therefore would offer a progressive financing alternative to employers wanting to take advantage of it. If a program is adopted that includes private and public components, reasonably equitable financing can be achieved by requiring community rating in the private component and in the public component relating premiums to payroll or income.

A major point of contention between unions and employers has been the shifting of costs from employers to employees. This raises the question of cost sharing. Sometimes the issue is posed whether there should be "first-dollar coverage" or whether deductibles, copayments, or coinsurance and premium sharing should be permitted. Canadian law prohibits the imposition of payments on patients at the point of service. Canadians pay for their health care in taxes and premiums, not when they are sick and need care. They have first-dollar coverage guaranteed by law. But first-dollar coverage has almost disappeared in the United States. Except for HMO members and Medicaid participants, who generally pay very little or nothing in deductibles, copayments, or coinsurance, nearly everyone else is liable for cost-sharing payments. It is unlikely that cost sharing would be eliminated in national health care reform. Most of the proposals offered thus far permit cost sharing but with limits on the level of deductibles, coinsurance, or copayments and shared premiums. The proposals also set a maximum for total out-of-pocket costs to be paid by an individual or family.

The argument for cost sharing is not just that insured persons should pay for part of the cost of the care that they and their families receive but also that requiring them to pay part of the cost encourages consumers to seek and use health care more judiciously. One way of doing this is to place less onerous cost-sharing requirements on those who elect to obtain their care in managed care systems that are considered more cost effective. Those who look with disfavor on cost sharing believe that it is likely to discourage preventative care and early treatment, with care being given at a later stage, resulting in both more suffering and higher costs. Opponents also point to the fact that as few as 10 percent of patients, generally the sickest ones, incur perhaps as high as

75 percent of total medical care costs. Moreover, especially if these high users have chronic conditions, they are likely to have reduced incomes resulting from their inability to work. Some national health care reform proposals, such as that of the National Leadership Commission on Health Care, provide for income-related cost sharing. This might be a more equitable approach, but it is also likely to engender higher administrative costs.

It is unlikely that cost sharing will be eliminated in the United States in the foreseeable future. As proposals are developed for health care reform, however, it is important that whatever cost-sharing payments are included should not be so burdensome as to discourage or bar needed care. Unfortunately, it is not easy to determine at what level of cost sharing that will occur, because it depends very much on factors such as income, health condition, and physical access to care.

Cost Containment

It is most unlikely that any national health care reform program will be adopted unless strong cost-containment features are built into its structure. A consensus is beginning to develop on what these should be, although not all groups that have made, or are developing, proposals agree on all of them. Most are already being applied or are about to be applied in either public or private programs or both. Measures relating to cost are closely related to access and quality, and most observers of the health care scene agree that cost containment does not have to lessen access and quality and, in fact, is essential to enhancing them.

The following are some of the main elements of a cost-containment policy:

A *national budget for health care*. Countries like Canada and Germany have found that an annual national budget, which if exceeded in one year results in lower payments to providers in the following year, is perhaps the strongest available tool for achieving cost containment. The U.S. system has this tool now, but it is limited to physicians' services under Medicare Part B. While the National Leadership Commission on Health Care did not endorse the concept, it referred to it favorably. The AFL-CIO and other groups have recommended it outright. Inclusion of a cap on health care spending in national health care reform might be the best guarantee that expenditures will not be open-ended.

Comptroller General Charles A. Bowsher in testimony presented to the House Ways and Means Committee said that the United States "must move from incremental cost-cutting initiatives to reforms that encompass the entire

U.S. health care system." He then went on to recommend that "we should cap total expenditures for major categories of providers and services, including physicians, hospitals and new technology." He said that maximum health expenditures could be adjusted each year so that if spending for a particular category exceeded its target in one year it would be reduced the following year.

Negotiation of uniform payments to hospitals, doctors, and other providers to be used by all payers. This will require a decision about what systems are effective in determining payments to hospitals and how they should be established or negotiated. It will also require negotiation of fee schedules with the representatives of physicians. Further, it is important that the payment systems be flexible enough to be appropriate for and encourage participation in HMOs and other forms of managed care.

Controls on capital expenditures. The United States has the most advanced medical equipment in the world. Progress in medical technology should be encouraged. Nevertheless, we need to insure that our medical plant and equipment are used in the most effective manner. This calls for assessment of new technology and procedures similar to the assessment system we already have for new drugs as well as controls on the proliferation of medical equipment. This would guarantee that new technology and procedures are used in the most cost-effective manner, that unnecessary duplication is eliminated, and that quality is maintained.

Physician practice patterns. Because decisions of physicians largely determine the cost and quality of medical care, it is important that guidelines be developed to assist physicians in their practice. This will not only enhance the quality of their care, but it will also discourage unnecessary tests and procedures.

Malpractice reform that is fair to both patients and providers. There is probably less of a consensus on what ought to be done in this area than in any other affecting health care costs. But the experience of other countries with considerably lower malpractice insurance rates may help the United States to develop ways of dealing with this problem.

Quality

The great variation in the ways physicians practice medicine affects its cost and also reflects differences in quality of care. The underlying problem seems to be an inadequate scientific base for the decisions that doctors and other providers have to make every day. Therefore, the development of systems for measuring outcomes of care is essential to quality enhancement. This will require building a national data base on the cost and quality of care. It is encouraging that a number of national health care reform proposals stress the importance of incorporating a quality improvement initiative and allocating dedicated funds for that purpose. Some aspects of quality enhancement are inevitably technical and, therefore, must be left to physicians and others with the appropriate scientific knowledge. It is, however, important that consumers and payers are also involved both in encouraging the quality improvement efforts of the professionals and in utilizing their own experience with the health care system as one important indication of medical outcomes.

CHAPTER 10

How to Assess National Health Policy Proposals and Create the Single Best Plan

Paul W. Sperduto

The damning statistics are well known. In 1990 the United States spent over $660 billion on health care.[1] That represents about 12 percent of U.S. gross national product (GNP) or over $2,600 per year per person. From 1970 to 1988 health care costs increased at an average annual rate of 17 percent, whereas the consumer price index increased at an average annual rate of 11 percent.[2] At the present rate of growth health care costs will double in just six years and will represent 25 percent of U.S. GNP by the year 2000. Today the Department of Health and Human Services alone has a budget greater than the entire budgets of every other country except the former Soviet Union, Japan, and, of course, the United States. Clearly, the U.S. health budget is far greater than any other health budget in the world. But are Americans getting their money's worth? Hardly. There are between thirty-three and thirty-seven million Americans (one in seven) without health insurance[3] and many more who are underinsured.[4] The United States ranks seventeenth in the world in infant mortality and sixteenth in the world in life expectancy.[5] High costs and limited access are only the most glaring aspects of a deep-rooted set of systemic problems.

---

1. Bureau of Data Management and Strategy, *1990 HCFA Statistics* (Baltimore: Health Care Financing Administration, 1990); and S. W. Letsch et al., "National Health Expenditures, 1987," *Health Care Financing Review* 10 (1988): 109–29.

2. Bureau of Labor Statistics, Consumer Price Index, *Social Security Bulletin* 53, no. 57 (1990).

3. D. Chollet, *Uninsured in the United States: The Nonelderly Population without Health Insurance* (Washington, D.C.: Employee Benefit Research Institute, 1987).

4. P. J. Farley, *Who Are the Uninsured? National Health Care Expenditures Study* (Hyattsville, Md.: National Center for Health Services Research, 1984).

5. World Health Organization (WHO), *World Health Statistics Annual* (Geneva: WHO, 1986).

The Grading Criteria

Any successful reform proposal will need to address all aspects of the problem. There are seven major components to the crisis: access, cost, market failure, quality, malpractice, efficiency, and administrative burden. All of these are interrelated but require unique solutions and thus will be addressed separately.

Access

It is certainly a painful paradox that the United States spends so much money on health care and yet so many people get little or none at all. Any pretext that the current system fulfills the utilitarian principle of John Stuart Mill that social programs should be designed to achieve the greatest good for the greatest number is shattered by the statistics. While the uninsured cry out for care, 35 percent of all hospital beds on any given day are empty.[6] There will soon be a physician for every three hundred to three hundred fifty people, yet at a time of such resource excess health care is already being rationed. The insured receive care; the uninsured or underinsured do not—that is rationing. It affects not just the poor but also a growing portion of the American mainstream: the middle class, young families, children, and the elderly.

A quantitative grading scale for access is presented in table 1. An A grade corresponds to universal access, while B, C, D, and F grades correspond to ten million, twenty million, thirty million, and thirty-seven million Americans without insurance, respectively. The current system receives a grade of F.

Cost

Even the above statistics do not fully convey the magnitude of the cost of American health care. National health care expenditures in 1970 were $75 billion; by 1990, as noted, they had reached $660 billion. Contrary to popular belief, the major buildup during the Reagan administrations was in health spending and not in defense. The Medicare Trust Fund will soon be bankrupt, and Medicaid, designed to cover the poor, now covers less than half those in need.[7] American industry endures a competitive disadvantage compared to Japanese and European firms that are not so heavily burdened by health care costs. Chrysler pays Blue Cross/Blue Shield more for health insurance for its

---

6. Letsch et al., "National Health Expenditures."

7. National Leadership Commission on Health Care, *For the Health of a Nation: A Shared Responsibility* (Ann Arbor, Mich.: Health Administration Press, 1989).

TABLE 1. Grading Criteria for Each Element of the American Health Care Crisis

Element	A	B	C	D	F
Access (million uninsured)	0	1–10	11–20	21–30	>30
Cost (% of GNP)	8%	9%	10%	11%	12%
Market failure (number of causes eliminated)	4	3	2	1	0
Quality					
Adherence to quality assurance standards	100%	50%	No change	10% decrease	20% decrease
Infant mortality	50% decrease	25% decrease	No change	10% increase	20% increase
Malpractice (% of health dollars spent on defensive medicine)	0	5%	10%	15%	20%
Efficiency (% of treatments with c/b, c/e support)[a]	>80%	60–79%	40–59%	20–39%	<20%
Administration (% of health dollars spent on administrative costs)	<5%	6–10%	11–15%	16–20%	>20%

[a]c/b, c/e = cost-benefit, cost-effectiveness

employees and retirees than it pays to any other single supplier, including steel for its automobiles.[8]

A quantitative grading scale for cost is as follows. An A grade has been assigned to a health care system that costs less than or equal to 8 percent of GNP. Grades B, C, D, and F correspond to health care costs of 9, 10, 11, and 12 percent of GNP, respectively. The current system (about 12 percent of GNP) therefore receives a cost grade of F.

Market Failure

Perhaps the most important—and the most overlooked—component of the American health care crisis is the economic structure of the system itself. Access and cost are the symptoms, not the causes, of the problem. Where did these dramatic symptoms originate? The health care financing system of today can be traced back to the Great Depression and World War II, when the widespread inability to pay forced hospitals to seek insurance plans as a way

8. Walter B. Maher, director of Federal Relations, Chrysler Corporation, personal communication with author, 1991.

to guarantee a steady cash flow by spreading the financial risk more widely.[9] During the 1950s and 1960s there was rapid growth of the third-party payment system, in which transactions between physician and patient were paid for by either an insurance company or the government. Since the 1973 Health Maintenance Organization (HMO) Act[10] and the 1975 Supreme Court decision that medicine was not exempt from antitrust laws,[11] health care in the United States has been found increasingly in the marketplace. While there was some enthusiasm for regulation-based reform in the 1970s, most authorities agree that a competition-based reform is preferable.

Pure supply and demand market theory fails, however, with embarrassing inefficiency when applied to health care. Why? Evidence presented here will make clear that market failure is the single greatest cause of the current health care crisis. While many of the most prominent health policy thinkers acknowledge the market failure problem,[12] few of the proposals for national health policy reform make the elimination of market failure a priority. This is either oversight or the result of a belief that the market failure problems of a competitive plan are an inevitable but lesser evil than the problems of any noncompetitive, regulation-based, or "socialized" system. One thesis herein is that it is possible to create a competition-based system in which the causes of market failure are eliminated.

What is market failure? The essence of market failure in health care can be summarized in five points, four of which have clear-cut policy implications:[13]

1. Agency relationship
2. Moral hazard of third-party payment
3. Merit good argument
4. Redundant capital expenditure
5. Externality relationship

9. S. Butler and E. Haislmaier, *A National Health System for America, Critical Issues Series* (Washington, D.C.: Heritage Foundation, 1989).

10. Health Maintenance Organization Act, 1973, in *United States Code,* Annotated, title 42, sec. 300e (St. Paul, Minn.: West, 1982), 882–932.

11. Supreme Court Justice Marshall, Opinion of the Court, *Hospital Building Company v. Trustees of Rex Hospital,* 425 U.S. 738, in *United States Supreme Court Reports,* Lawyers ed.; 48 L. Ed. 2d 338, 46 SC+ 1848.

12. H. H. Hiatt, *America's Health in the Balance: Choice or Chance?* (New York: Harper and Row, 1987); A. Enthoven, "The U.S. Health Care Economy: From Guild to Market in Ten Years," *Health Policy* 7 (1987): 241–51; A. Enthoven and R. Kronick, "A Consumer-Choice Health Plan for the 1990s," *NEJM* 320 (1989): 29–37, 94–101; and J. A. Califano, *America's Health Care Revolution: Who Lives? Who Dies? Who Pays?* (New York: Random House, 1986).

13. M. Drummond et al., "Health Economics: An Introduction for Clinicians," *Annals of Internal Medicine* 107 (1987): 88–92.

The so-called agency relationship, or the black-box-of-knowledge phenomenon, is one in which the doctor acts as an agent for the patient. The patients do not have the knowledge to make sensible choices, therefore the doctors, to a large extent, control both the supply of and demand for health care.

Second, market theory fails in health care because of the so-called moral hazard of third-party payment. This simply means that consumers do not pay a price that reflects the true cost of the goods and services consumed. There is a tendency therefore to consume more care than they would otherwise. This phenomenon is common to all insurance markets.

The third cause of market failure in health care is the merit good argument. Health economists consider health to be a merit good, whereas alcohol and tobacco, for example, are considered demerit goods. People are encouraged to accumulate merit goods, that is, to be as healthy as possible. Patients are encouraged to consume more care than they actually need, falsely increasing the demand for care.

Fourth, the technology-laden health sector requires huge capital outlays for any competitor. That competitor is then burdened by a financial incentive to oversupply that expensive technology to pay for it. This not only encourages unethical application of that technology, but it also results in redundant capital expenditure and underutilized services for the system overall. Pure market theory would put that competitor out of business, but in the health sector, where demand can be created, high-technology, underutilized facilities limp along siphoning funds from a runaway system. For example, there are five institutions in North Carolina alone in which one can receive a heart transplant. This supply far exceeds the demand. Pure market theory has failed again.

The fifth cause of market failure does not have direct policy implications beyond the basic principles of public health and will not be considered in the grading system. This is the so-called externality relationship of certain types of health care, an awkward obstacle for a market system. This describes a type of care in which the benefit of a given intervention may not be limited to the person who actually receives the care. For example, a vaccine benefits not only the person who receives it but also the general population with whom that person comes in contact. In this setting the value to the consumer understates the total value of the care, and so it defies market definition.

While some components of market failure are responsible for greater waste (the agency relationship, the moral hazard of third-party payment, and capital redundancy) than others (the merit good argument and the externality relationship), a simple linear grading scale has been devised. An A grade will be given to the reform proposal that eliminates all four major causes of market failure. Grades B, C, D, and F correspond to eliminating three, two, one, and zero causes of market failure, respectively. The current system receives a grade of F on the market failure test.

Quality

The quality of health care is exceedingly difficult to quantify. The American health care system remains a paradox of excess and deprivation, high- and low-quality care.[14] The United States is the world's leader in most areas of medical technology and research, yet it ranks seventeenth and sixteenth in the world in infant mortality and life expectancy, respectively. Furthermore, there are increasing reports of erroneous or inappropriate care.[15] The National Academy of Science has reported that, because of serious flaws in much of the scientific literature, it is not possible to judge the effectiveness of U.S. technology or develop appropriate recommendations for its use.[16] In fact, much of the technology has been disseminated without adequate evaluation.

Because little research has been done comparing the outcomes of care using competing technologies, there is a growing outcry for quality assurance testing and research. The gaps in knowledge result in uncertainty among physicians. That uncertainty leads to major variations in clinical practices and major differences in resource expenditure, but no discernible differences in outcome. The delivery of too much or too little health care will be discussed below as a factor in the efficiency component of the crumbling system, but erroneous or inappropriate care is a matter of quality. A Pulitzer Prize-winning series in the *Wall Street Journal* reported error rates in Pap smear readings of 50 to 60 percent and high error rates in cholesterol testing as well.[17] The Center for Disease Control has estimated that there are ten thousand preventable deaths every year from nosocomial (hospital-acquired) infections because of inadequate quality control.[18] Leaders in the auto industry may be forced to suddenly recall a million vehicles for a leaky radiator hose; these same leaders are shouldering the huge health care costs of the current system and are beginning to demand a recall procedure, some kind of quality control, for health care. The Joint Commission on the Accreditation of Health-Care Organizations recently reported that a large proportion of institutions are not adhering to the rudimentary quality standards that already exist.[19]

Any quantitative scale for measuring the quality of health care will be imperfect. We will apply a twofold quality scale: (1) infant mortality; and (2)

---

14. Enthoven and Kronick, "A Consumer-Choice Health Plan."

15. National Leadership Commission, *For the Health of a Nation.*

16. National Academy of Science, Committee on the Conduct of Science, *On Being a Scientist* (Washington, D.C.: National Academy Press, 1989).

17. W. Bogdanich, "Medical Labs Trusted as Largely Error-Free Far from Infallible," *Wall Street Journal,* February 2, 1987, A1.

18. National Leadership Commission, *For the Health of a Nation.*

19. Joint Commission on the Accreditation of Health-Care Organizations, *Committed to Quality: An Introduction to the Joint Commission on Accreditation of Health-Care Organizations,* 4th ed. (Oakbrook Terrace, Ill., 1990).

the extent to which health care providers and institutions adhere to quality assurance standards as defined by the Specialty Boards and the Joint Commission on the Accreditation of Health-Care Organizations. To acknowledge the excellent care available in some settings the current system has been given a grade of C, despite overwhelming problems in infant mortality and quality assurance. Of the seven tests used in this study to assess health care, this test for quality is the only one that did not receive an F. Grade A will be given to the proposal that yields a 50 percent improvement in infant mortality and a 100 percent adherence to quality assurance standards as set forth by the relevant credentialing bodies. Grade B corresponds to a 25 percent improvement in infant mortality and a 50 percent adherence to quality assurance standards. Grade C corresponds to the current system. Grade D describes a 10 percent increase in infant mortality and/or a 10 percent decrease in adherence to quality assurance standards. Grade F will be given to any system that would yield a 20 percent increase in infant mortality and/or a 20 percent decrease in adherence to quality assurance standards.

Malpractice

One of the fastest-growing components of total U.S. health expenditures has been professional liability insurance. The average premiums for self-employed physicians have increased at an average annual rate of 21.9 percent.[20] In obstetrics and gynecology rates increased from $10,800 per year in 1982 to $29,300 in 1986.[21] The rising premiums are a result of increased malpractice claims and rising levels of jury awards. From 1981 to 1986 professional liability claims rose from 3.2 to 9.2 claims per 100 physicians. By 1986 more than one third of all physicians had been sued at least once in their careers. Between 1980 and 1987 the median jury award increased from $150,000 to $825,000.[22]

The causes of this explosion are multifaceted and may reflect social and legal trends to a greater extent than trends in health care. A variety of provocative solutions has been proposed, including tort law reform.[23] Any successful solution must eliminate "defensive medicine." Physicians feel obligated in the current medical-legal quagmire to order excessive tests, imaging scans, consultations, and hospitalizations, even when clinical judgment suggests that

20. American College of Physicians, "Access to Health Care," Position Paper, *Annals of Internal Medicine* 112 (1989): 9, 641–61.

21. Center for Health Policy Research of the American Medical Association, *Socioeconomic Characteristics of Medical Practice, 1987* (Chicago: Center for Health Policy Research, 1987).

22. O. H. Solon, Jury Verdict Research, Inc., "Current Award Trends," in *Socio-Economic Factbook for Surgery, 1989* (Chicago: American College of Surgeons, 1989), 72.

23. P. Danzon, *Medical Malpractice: Theory, Evidence and Public Policy* (Cambridge: Harvard University Press, 1985).

a minimum of significantly abnormal results are likely. Clinicians rich with experience are well familiar with the corollary of this observation, that is, a marginally indicated test routinely renders minimally abnormal results. The clinician then feels obligated, for medical-legal reasons, to send the patient on an odyssey of expensive and sometimes invasive tests that are clinically irrelevant. Defensive medicine and high technology have definitely threatened the art of medicine so essential to quality and efficient care. Conservative estimates suggest that defensive medicine accounts for over 20 percent of all health care costs, or more than $132 billion per year.

A quantitative scale of the malpractice problem should not focus on the number of claims, awards, lawyers, or premiums but, rather, on how the problem is manifested clinically; therefore, the percentage of health dollars spent on defensive medicine will be the indicator of malpractice. Although this is perhaps more difficult to estimate, it better reflects the magnitude of the problem in the system overall.

The current system receives a grade of F regarding malpractice. That designation will be applied to any system in which more than 20 percent of health care dollars is spent on defensive medicine. Grades A, B, C, and D are defined as delivery systems in which less than 5, 10, 15, and 20 percent of health care dollars is spent on defensive medicine, respectively.

Efficiency

The American health care system is riddled with faulty incentives. Although such incentives are not causes of market failure, as described, they seriously impair the efficiency of the system.

Fee-for-Service and Incentive for Over-Care

In the traditional fee-for-service system the physician's financial incentive is to provide as much care as possible: The more procedures done, the more money earned. This fosters the merit good argument for market failure. Non-medical literature is brimming with accusations of unnecessary surgery, endoscopy, and other procedures and tests. The danger of the fee-for-service system is over-care. For example, the United States has an epidemic of caesarean sections. Twenty-five percent of American babies are delivered surgically, the highest rate in the world. There is no evidence that mothers and babies benefit from these very high rates or that the U.S. outcomes are better than nations that do one fifth as many surgical deliveries. Our dismal infant mortality rate persists. The cause of this epidemic again illustrates the synergy of faulty incentives. Not only are obstetricians paid more for the caesarean section surgery and the fetal monitoring that accompanies it, but some feel that it also reduces the likelihood of costly malpractice claims.

Prepaid Plans and Incentive for Under-Care

Health maintenance organizations and other prospective payment plans accept an annual prepaid capitation fee for each enrollee in return for comprehensive health care services. In such a system the fewer procedures done, consults requested, or patient days in the hospital, the more money saved from the capitation payment pool. The physicians and the managers of the plan have a faulty financial incentive to provide less care. The danger here is under-care. Although these so-called managed care plans have obvious cost-cutting potential, physician autonomy in clinical decision making is often limited. This is unacceptable to much of the medical community. Managed care proponents, on the other hand, cite the continued growth of such plans as evidence that they are not only popular but also economically advantageous. Many physicians are attracted to managed care plans not because such plans are the way they want to practice medicine but because they are fed up with the administrative burdens of running the office and dealing with third-party payment paperwork. To a growing number of physicians managed care plans represent the lesser of two evils. The current system has crumbled to the point where physicians are accepting impingement upon their clinical autonomy in the managed care plans rather than the overwhelming administrative burdens of the traditional fee-for-service system.

Cost-Benefit and Cost-Effectiveness Analyses

Another major cause of inefficiency is the lack of adequate cost-benefit and cost-effectiveness research. While cost-benefit analyses compare the cost and benefit of a given intervention, cost-effectiveness analyses compare two or more competing interventions on a common scale so that decision makers can determine which one offers the greatest positive impact per society health dollar spent. While new studies are trickling into the literature, many major interventions continue to be widely applied without the support of a sound cost-effectiveness study. The most common and most expensive examples include the widespread overuse of coronary artery bypass grafting, angioplasty, and pacemakers and the massive misuse of antibiotics and laboratory testing.

The price tag for such inefficiencies is incalculable. Rather than estimating such a figure, for our quantitative scale we will apply the following grading criteria. The grade of A will be given to any system that would render cost-benefit, cost-effectiveness studies for more than 80 percent of all diagnostic and therapeutic interventions and technology. Grades B, C, D, and F correspond to programs that have cost-benefit and cost-effectiveness support for more than 60, 40, and 20 percent and less than 20 percent of all diagnostic and therapeutic interventions and technology, respectively. The current system receives an F by this criteria. Such research must be applied in pilot programs for each new intervention or technology before its widespread dissemination and application.

Administrative Bureaucracy and Related Costs

Administrative costs are among the fastest-growing components of health care costs. They include the costs of recording, billing, reviewing, processing, auditing, and justifying medical charges. Also included in these expenses are the costs of insurance marketing, the profits and reserves of private insurance carriers. Conservative estimates suggest that up to 24 percent of all health care costs are spent on administration.[24] On the other hand, public programs are relatively austere regarding administrative costs, largely because they do not need to attribute a specific charge to a specific person. Medicare and Medicaid in the United States currently average 2 percent administrative costs, and administrative costs in Canada's universal health insurance system average 11 percent of all health care spending.[25] Clearly, substantial savings could be obtained by reducing these costs. The current payment and reimbursement mechanisms in the United States necessitate large bureaucracies and enormous administrative expenses to guarantee that each syringe and service provided by institutions, physicians, and other providers is attributed to a specific patient.

With the gross national product approaching six trillion dollars, the savings generated could fully pay for a new universal access health plan in the United States. Each one percentage point reduction in the proportion of GNP now attributed to health care would yield savings of over sixty billion dollars per year.[26]

The grading system for administrative costs has been assigned as follows. The grade of A will be given to the system that spends less than 5 percent of all health dollars on administrative costs. Grades B, C, D, and F will be assigned to systems spending less than 10, 15, and 20 percent and more than 20 percent on administrative costs, respectively. Canada, at 11 percent for administrative expenses, would be given a C, whereas the United States again earns an F.

Grading the Proposals

There are six major constituents in the health policy arena: industry, labor, providers, consumers, the government, and the media. All will be involved in the evolving debate regarding national health policy reform. These six constit-

24. S. Woolhandler and D. U. Himmelstein, "The Deteriorating Administrative Efficiency of the U.S. Health Care System," *NEJM* 324 (1991): 1253–58.

25. Ibid.

26. American College of Physicians, "Access to Health Care."

uents, along with academia, have produced eleven major proposals for reform that can be compared to the traditional fee-for-service system and the current system. In addition to these thirteen approaches, there are the Bush administration proposal[27] and the proposal that emerges from this study based on the above analytical methods. Each of the fifteen proposals will be graded on the seven-point scale defined above and will be assigned a grade point average (see table 2). The rationale for the grades will be briefly discussed. The grades are, of course, predictions of the performance of these theoretical proposals, and thus some estimation and arbitrariness are inevitable. The author readily admits that a two-decimal point interpretation of these grades represents false accuracy. Such an interpretation is not intended. Instead, it is hoped that such a mechanism will allow useful comparison of multiple proposals on multiple criteria. From this base further progress toward consensus and reform can be achieved.

Proposal #1: No Change from the Current System

Although there is no consensus on how the current system should change, there is widespread consensus that something must be done. The current system received all F's except on the quality test, on which it received a C. The rationale for these grades is given above with the definitions of the grading criteria. To calculate the grade point average an A was given a numerical value of 4.0, and the grades B, C, D, and F were given numerical values of 3.0, 2.0, 1.0, and 0.0, respectively. The overall GPA of the current system would be 0.29 on a scale of 4.0.

Proposal #2: Traditional Fee-for-Service System

The traditional fee-for-service system had even fewer cost controls and no access guarantee whatsoever. Accordingly, it received the same grades as the current system, for an average of 0.29 on a scale of 4.0.

Proposal #3: Managed Care Plans

Prepaid plans have been increasingly popular since the HMO Act of 1973. Despite physician dissatisfaction with the pressure on their clinical autonomy, such plans are seen by many as an effective cost-containment strategy. But, if the system continues with piecemeal growth, without comprehensive application it will fail. While cost, access, and efficiency may improve somewhat in some managed care plans, quality may actually decline due to the incentive to

27. C. Horner, "The Bush Administration and Health Care," in *Is Tax Reform the Key to Health Reform*, ed. S. Butler, pub. #298 (Washington, D.C.: Heritage Foundation Conference, 1991), 8.

TABLE 2. Grading the Proposals

Proposal	Access	Cost	Market Failure	Quality	Malpractice	Efficiency	Administration	Overall GPA
Current	F	F	F	C	F	F	F	0.29
Fee/service	F	F	F	C	F	F	F	0.29
Managed care	D	C	F	D	F	D	F	1.00
Consumer choice	A	C	C	C	F	C	F	1.71
Kennedy	A	F	F	C	F	F	F	0.86
Pepper	A	D	F	C	D	D	F	1.29
Canada	A	B	B	C	C	C	A	2.86
M.D.'s National Health	A	B	B	C	C	C	A	2.86
HIAA	D	F	F	C	F	F	F	0.43
Heritage	C	C	D	C	F	C	F	1.29
AMA	A	C	F	B	A	B	F	2.43
ACP	A	B	B	B	A	B	A	3.43
National Leadership	A	C	F	B	B	B	F	2.14
Bush administration								
Seven tests	A	A	A	A	A	A	A	4.0

Note: Grading scale: A = 4.0, B = 3.0, C = 2.0, D = 1.0, F = 0.0

under-care. Market failure, malpractice, and administrative burden would be unchanged or worse than in the current system. The overall GPA therefore would be 1.00 on a 4.0 scale.

Proposal #4: Consumer Choice Health Plan

This system builds on the managed care concept.[28] The plan suggests that everyone not covered by Medicare, Medicaid, or other public program would be able to buy affordable coverage either through their employers or through a "public sponsor." In addition, these sponsors, such as the Health Care Financing Administration (HCFA) and large employers, would contract with competing health plans and manage a process of informed cost-conscious consumer choice that would reward providers who delivered high-quality care economically. In this system access would be universal, and costs and inefficiency would be reduced. The cost-conscious consumers would ameliorate the market failure problem, but the moral hazard of third-party payment would persist. Quality, malpractice, and administrative burden would not change significantly. The overall GPA for such a system would be 1.71 on a 4.0 scale.

Proposal #5: Minimum Health Benefits for All Workers

This proposal was sponsored by Senator Edward Kennedy and Representative Henry A. Waxman.[29] It mandates that employers provide basic health coverage to employees and their families. Self-employed and unemployed people would be covered by expanded public programs. Despite federal assistance for small businesses, such a plan would threaten small businesses and perhaps increase unemployment. The proposal is valuable in that it put universal health insurance on the national agenda, but it is not intended to be a comprehensive proposal for all that ails the health care system. Accordingly, because only access would be improved, the proposal scores poorly. The other six tests of a national health policy would score the same as in the current system. The overall GPA would be 0.86 on a 4.0 scale.

Proposal #6: Pepper Commission

The bipartisan Pepper Commission, chaired by Senator John D. Rockefeller, produced a plan that provides health insurance for all Americans by broaden-

---

28. Enthoven and Kronick, "A Consumer-Choice Health Plan."
29. Senator Edward Kennedy, U.S. Senate 1265, Minimum Health Benefits for All Workers Act, 1987.

ing the current job-based/public coverage system.[30] All employers would be required to either provide insurance for employees or contribute to a public plan. It also calls for government-sponsored long-term care, although it does not explain how the program would be funded. Without detailed policy proposals it also recommends malpractice reforms, mandatory cost sharing, and increased use of managed care plans. Senator Rockefeller is correct when he argues that, by simply providing universal access, cost shifting of uncompensated care would be eliminated.[31] While access would be universal, improvement in cost and efficiency would be modest. The malpractice problem would be mitigated by this plan, but it is shy on specific recommendations in this regard. The other criteria would remain unchanged. The overall GPA would be 1.29 out of 4.0.

Proposal #7: Canadian System

Since 1971 all of Canada's provinces have provided universal health insurance.[32] The federal and provincial governments each pay roughly half of the bill from tax revenues. The Canadian people have free choice of hospitals and doctors and pay virtually nothing at the time the care is provided. Private health insurance is also available, but private insurance companies are barred by law from offering services that compete with the basic but comprehensive provincial plans. Fee-for-service is the dominant form of payment to physicians, although some hospital doctors are paid a salary. All physicians are reimbursed according to a fixed fee schedule for services. These fees are negotiated between the provincial governments and the provincial medical associations.

While many look north for a panacea,[33] others criticize the Canadian system and argue that having one like it would not solve the American health care crisis.[34] The crux of the controversy regarding whether the Canadian system is desirable for the United States comes down to the elements of market failure. Economists know that, when prices are kept artificially low, consumer demand rises rapidly. Critics argue that the merit good argument of market failure in health care would encourage people to seek more care than they actually need because it is free at the point of dispersal. This would add a

---

30. Pepper Commission, *Call for Action: Pepper Commission Final Report* (Washington, D.C.: Government Printing Office, October 1990), print #101–14.

31. B. McCormick, "Cutting Costs Key to Expanding Care, Medical Leaders Told," *American Medical News*, March 4, 1991, 1.

32. J. K. Iglehart, "Canada's Health Care System," *NEJM* 315 (1986): 778–84.

33. D. U. Himmelstein and the Physicians for a National Health Program, "A National Health Program for the United States," *NEJM* 320 (1989): 102–8.

34. E. Neuschler, *Canadian Health Care: The Implications of Public Health Insurance* (Washington, D.C.: Health Insurance Association of America, June 1990), 9–18.

heavy burden to the already stressed system, and the only way to prevent spiraling costs would be for the government to lower prices artificially or limit access. Both of these policy implications are undesirable, if not unacceptable.

Proponents, on the other hand, argue that prices would not be kept artificially low, so the above argument would not apply. More important, it would eliminate the expensive moral hazard of third-party payment and eliminate capital outlay redundancy because a central body would dispense all funds and determine how much capital expenditure (such as hospitals and number of subspecialists) is needed for a given region. This would completely eliminate the two most important components of market failure in health care. Progress might also be expected regarding the agency relationship component of market failure because consumers, free of financial constraints, would seek the best care, not the care they could afford. This would encourage them to learn more about their physicians and alternative therapies. It is important to note that greater consumer knowledge is encouraged but not necessary (unlike some proposals that follow) for the successful functioning of this plan. In sum, three of the four causes of market failure would be improved or eliminated, and one cause (the agency relationship) might be exacerbated.

Reviewing the Canadian plan overall, access and administrative burden would be optimized. Market failure and overall cost would be nearly optimized. Quality would not change. Efficiency would improve because the central planning would eliminate redundant capital expenditures. The plan is still hampered by the lack of cost-benefit and cost-effectiveness analyses for specific diagnostic and therapeutic interventions. Malpractice in Canada results in roughly the same number of claims and size of awards as in the United States; however, the liability insurance premiums are much higher in the United States.[35] It is entirely unclear if the malpractice crisis would be improved by the mere adaptation of a Canadian-style system. This would result in an overall GPA of 2.86 on a 4.0 scale.

Proposal #8: Physicians for a National Health Program

This plan has been proposed by a Harvard-based group of over three thousand physicians who call for a Canada-style system. The arguments and grading rationale are identical to the Canadian system.

Proposal #9: Health Insurance Association of America

The Health Insurance Association of America is the trade union for the private insurance industry. HIAA proposes to expand the Medicaid program to cover

---

35. P. Coyte et al., "Medical Malpractice—The Canada Experience," *NEJM* 324 (1991): 89–93.

everyone below the poverty line.[36] Today only 40 percent of the poor are covered by Medicaid. HIAA also proposes changing the coverage for small businesses to limit premium increases. Finally, it recommends creating high-risk pools for those considered uninsurable by private health insurance companies in the present system. Legislation authorizing creation of such high-risk pools has been passed in twenty-three states. Bovbjerg and Koller have studied the performance and potential of the concept.[37] They conclude that about only 1 percent of the general population is uninsurable and that such a high-risk pool policy would be prohibitively expensive and contains no incentive for efficiency.

Piecemeal at best, this plan may be summarily dismissed as offering a marginal impact on only one (access) of the seven major tests of a national health policy proposal. Overall GPA would be 0.43 on a 4.0 scale.

Proposal #10: Heritage Foundation Plan

One of the most intellectually provocative proposals for a national health system comes from the Heritage Foundation, a conservative think tank in Washington, D.C.[38] In this plan consumers would buy health insurance directly from the insurance companies rather than through their employers. Consumers would receive a 20 to 30 percent tax credit for insurance for out-of-pocket medical expenses. An expanded Medicaid program would cover the long-term unemployed and the very poor.

Proponents argue that such a system maintains an individual's choice of provider, encourages competition in a market-based environment, and encourages consumers to be more cost conscious.[39] Other advantages include converting the often inequitable tax subsidies of the current system to more equitable tax credits. Greater efficiency should be achieved with this plan, which subsidizes the first, not the last, dollar spent on health care. This should reduce interference with market choices made by the consumer. In other words, the system not only acknowledges but also embraces the agency relationship component of market failure and attempts to reduce it by encouraging the consumer to become as knowledgeable as possible about available choices. This idea is positive but limited in scope. It is not realistic to expect consumers to understand and keep current with a field that requires seven to

36. C. Matthiessen, "Bordering on Collapse," *Modern Maturity*, October–November 1990, 30–85.

37. R. Bovbjerg and C. Koller, "State Health Insurance Pools: Current Performance, Future Prospects," *Inquiry* 23 (1986): 111–21.

38. Butler and Haislmaier, *A National Health System for America.*

39. S. Butler, ed., *Is Tax Reform the Key to Health Care Reform?* pub. #298 (Washington, D.C.: Heritage Foundation Conference, 1991).

fourteen years of specialized postcollege training. Ultimately, the agency relationship will persist.

Two other advantages are that the tax credit system is progressive (i.e., it provides more benefits to the people who need them more) and that it would offer a potential mechanism for budget control. Voters could decide to increase or decrease the health tax credit. If other concerns such as defense or education are given a higher priority in the voter's mind, he or she can vote to decrease the health tax credit. The current system is open-ended in that it has a built-in growth scale that is not subject to budget control every year.

The major disadvantage of the system is that it is a piecemeal, not a comprehensive, approach that is more likely to result in cost shifting than cost saving. Another problem, as discussed, is that the average citizen may not have the capacity or interest to become the educated consumer required by this plan. People outside of think tanks and ivory towers and, especially, the primary-care providers in the front lines of the health war will declare such a premise wholly unrealistic.

In summary, this proposal would improve access, but it would not be universal. Costs and inefficiency would decline somewhat. Quality would remain unchanged. The issues of administrative burden and malpractice would remain unchanged or deteriorate further. Regarding the important market failure test, the agency relationship might improve, but the other causes of market failure are not addressed. Overall GPA would be 1.29 out of 4.0.

Proposal #11: Health Access America

The American Medical Association (AMA) has produced a sixteen-point plan that would increase access through Medicaid and Medicare reform, employer-based coverage, and the creation of high-risk pools in all states for the otherwise uninsurable.[40] It would also expand long-term care coverage. Unlike many other proposals, the AMA plan focuses on professional liability reform, including a $250,000 limitation on recovery of noneconomic damages. Cost-cutting measures include changing the tax treatment of employee health care benefits, encouraging cost-conscious decisions by patients, and seeking innovation in insurance underwriting. It is significant that it also seeks to improve the quality and efficiency of care by emphasizing prevention and developing "professional practice parameters" or standards, based in part on cost-benefit and cost-effectiveness analyses. It also calls for expanded federal support for medical education, research, and the National Institutes of Health. Last, the AMA proposal calls for streamlining the administrative burden but does not offer specific recommendations in this regard.

---

40. American Medical Association, *Health Access America* (Chicago: February 1990).

In summary, the plan scored relatively well on the seven tests. Access would be universal. The malpractice solution is specific and far-reaching—the best of any proposal in this review. Quality and efficiency would improve based on the professional practice parameters and increased attention to cost-benefit, cost-effectiveness analyses. Costs would be moderately reduced. Although the AMA is most eager to relieve the administrative burden under which its members are suffering, it is unclear if significant improvement could evolve from this plan. Finally, and importantly, the AMA plan would not eliminate any of the causes of market failure in health care. This would limit the success of the otherwise sound efforts regarding cost and efficiency. Overall GPA would be 2.43 on a 4.0 scale.

Proposal #12: American College of Physicians

In addition to the American Medical Association, the other major body in organized medicine is the American College of Physicians (ACP), which represents the specialty of internal medicine and its subspecialties. The ACP has proposed a plan significantly different than the AMA proposal.[41] The ACP rejects mandated employer coverage, creation of high-risk pools for the otherwise uninsurable, the expansion of Medicaid eligibility, expanded charity care, and tax incentives to encourage individuals and employers to purchase private insurance. Instead, the ACP favors the establishment of a universal access program modeled on but not identical to the Canadian system. The malpractice problem would be reduced by recommendations similar to those in the AMA proposal, including tort law reform. Quality and efficiency would both improve based on extensive cost-benefit and cost-effectiveness analyses. The administrative burden would be streamlined, as in the Canadian system. The elements of market failure in health care would also be markedly reduced based on the same rationale presented above for the Canadian system. Overall GPA would be 3.43 on a 4.0 scale.

Proposal #13: National Leadership Coalition
for Health Care Reform

This coalition brings together some of the nation's largest corporations—including Marriott, Ford, AT&T, Kodak, and Lockheed as well as a number of the nation's largest labor unions—in an effort to unite industry and labor in a powerful lobby for a national health insurance program.[42] Their proposal

---

41. American College of Physicians, "Access to Health Care."

42. National Leadership Commission, *For the Health of a Nation;* and H. Simmons, "Reforming the Nation's Critically Ill Health Care System," speech given to the Committee on New American Realities, National Planning Association, San Francisco, October 16, 1990, and excerpted in *Looking Ahead* 12, no. 4 (March 1991): 1–7.

builds a public-private partnership and stresses four elements of reform: universal access to basic care; a quality improvement initiative based on well-defined standards and effectiveness analyses; malpractice reform; and a cost-containment strategy based on consumer education. Regarding access, the plan would allow continued reliance on employer-based care and private insurance; thus, the moral hazard component of market failure would plague this plan. The market failure and administrative burden components of this system would not be significantly changed from the current system. Quality and efficiency would improve, and the malpractice crisis would be ameliorated. Regarding cost, the approach of an educated consumer is reminiscent of the Heritage Foundation plan. Overall GPA would be 2.14 out of 4.0.

Proposal #14: Bush Administration

The past administration's proposal for health care reform remained suspended in political animation.[43] An essential and continually overlooked explanation for the lack of a feverish public outcry and the resulting political motivation for health care reform is the moral hazard of third-party payment. It has already been discussed as an important cause of market failure, but it also leads to political failure. The public is insulated from the true costs of health care and accordingly will never mount the mutiny needed to push politicians into action. For this reason, although the system continues to crumble, it will never achieve anything but a relatively low political priority.

Proposal #15: Seven Tests

Based on the seven tests defined above and the grades of proposals #1–13 summarized in table 2, it is possible to put together a proposal that combines the best aspects of the thirteen plans. The ACP proposal, with an overall GPA of 3.43, is the best of the plans, but it still has room for improvement. The remaining element of market failure in the ACP proposal is the merit good argument. Access to care that is free at the point of dispersal does encourage a falsely increased demand for care. While it is clearly important to encourage preventative health care, this false demand could be largely eliminated by a nominal charge at the time care is provided for those able to pay. Ten dollars per visit should be sufficient to block most of the insignificant complaints that plague the English National Health Service. Conversely, ten dollars is not so expensive as to cause access problems. Those unable to pay the fee could be identified on their national health card. This simple measure, when applied nationwide, would further reduce costs and inefficiency. The only remaining test that has not been optimized is quality. The ACP, the AMA, and the

---

43. Horner, "The Bush Administration and Health Care."

National Leadership Coalition for Health Care Reform proposals all received a grade of B with emphasis on adherence to quality assurance standards.

The other component of the quality grading criteria is infant mortality. A renewed effort in maternal education, drug awareness, nutrition, and perinatal care must become a priority. Significant improvement in quality assurance and infant mortality will require constant vigilance and may not be detectable for many years. Nonetheless, such improvement is necessary to develop an optimal national health program.

Conclusion

Political feasibility, of course, is of paramount importance. In an idealized vacuum the single best public policy could be created without regard for the political implications. This is clearly impossible. The political power of the major competing interest groups has for years dissuaded fundamental health care reform, as the system continues to crumble. This review shows, however, that every major constituency not only agrees that reform is now needed but has published a proposal for reform. The one conspicuous exception is proposal #14, which has not been published. Furthermore, there are general areas of consensus that are easily seen by comparing the columns in table 2. The feared political firestorm of opposition may be fading somewhat as the need for reform becomes increasingly clear.

What does the single best system look like, and how would it work? The country would be divided into regions of one million to three million people. All the health care needs of the people in each region would be organized by a regional health board, which would be a nonpartisan, nonprofit, nongovernmental body of representatives from the health professions as well as the business and civic communities. Patients would receive a national health card labeled with their name, social security number, and an asterisk denoting whether they could pay a fee of ten dollars per visit. Each patient would have the option, at defined intervals, to switch from one doctor to another or from one hospital to another within the region. All health care expenses, except the ten dollars per visit antimarket failure fee, would be covered by premiums paid to the regional board on an annual basis (capitation payments). The government would pay for the poor, elderly, and unemployed. For the employed a health tax would be paid directly to the regional health board.

All health care expenditures would be controlled by the regional board, eliminating costly duplication of capital outlays and services. If the board determined that the people of the region would be better served by converting a community hospital into a nursing home, the board would have the authority to implement that change. Each year the board would negotiate contracts with the hospitals, nursing homes, and all other health care institutions in the region and with representatives of physicians, nurses, social workers, and other providers. Physician reimbursement could be based on a simple capitation equation: the number of people for whom the physician provided care multiplied by the percent of the patient's total care provided by that physician. This product would then be multiplied by the negotiated specialty-specific factor.

It is important to note that the provider's income is based on the number of people for whom he or she provides care, not the number of procedures done. It is entirely possible that the competent, caring, hard-working provider would enjoy an increased income compared to the present system. True to U.S. capitalist roots, effort is rewarded. This is not socialized medicine, in which the physician gets a salary even if he or she does nothing but play golf. The reimbursement policy coupled with the regional board's control of health resources would intensify competition for patients and strengthen the correct-care incentive to provide quality, compassionate care while eliminating the faulty under- and over-care incentives in the current system. This should remove the wedge the current system has driven into the doctor-patient relationship and indirectly ameliorate the malpractice crisis. Some physicians might resent the competition, but, when they realize that they would be liberated from today's administrative burden, they will welcome the change. Practice styles (group, solo, or HMO) would remain the same, but each entity would have to negotiate with the regional health board.

The private insurance industry will certainly object, but it will be able to offer supplemental insurance policies as long as its members do not compete with the basic services of the regional health plans. Long-term care may be an important niche for the private insurance industry to develop, as the graying of America accelerates.

After all the analyses, economic theories, educated estimates, and frank guess-timates are in, a clear picture of the broad spectrum of constituents and proposals emerges. The seven-test methodology was selected because, although these are inevitably interrelated, each element requires a distinct solution. The solutions have been profiled. Of equal importance is the methodology used to derive the solutions because, rather than vested interests battling to out-shout one another, the seven-test mechanism clarifies the relative value of competing proposals in this complicated policy arena. This should facilitate consensus regarding, first, the means and, eventually, the ends of health policy reform.

Political leaders will continue to give this issue low priority because it will never generate the intensity of public outcry needed to threaten politicians into a "reform or lose the next election" dilemma. Indeed, despite the grave state of affairs, most of the leading members of Congress do not anticipate serious debate on the issue in the present Congress or in the foreseeable future.[44] As noted, the reason for this disregard is the structure of the current health system, specifically the moral hazard of third-party payment. The public is insulated from the true costs of the crisis. In addition to market failure, emphasized throughout this chapter, this aspect of the present system is also responsible for political failure. Because the people are insulated from the raging costs, the public outcry for reform is far less than proportional to the magnitude of the disaster at hand. Because of this market and political failure, health care policy is unique among all issues of public policy.

The Bush administration had perfected the art of consensus building as good politics. The involved constituents now realize the need for reform—an important first step. They should welcome an objective methodology by which to select that reform, the essential second step. The third and final step of implementation will be less political and less arduous and relatively easy to achieve. True, not political, leadership and a growing consensus could quickly conquer the political failure factor in this unique and complicated challenge to the American public policy process.

---

44. S. Rich, "Clashing Group Interests Make Health Care Overhaul Unlikely Soon," *Washington Post,* April 29, 1991, A5.

CHAPTER 11

Insuring National Health Care

Malcolm Taylor

The Continuing Agenda

Let us shift our perspective from what has been accomplished in the past to major problems and opportunities that will confront Canadians in the future. Five major areas have been selected: cost containment, the aging of the population, the impending surplus of physicians, the shifting emphasis from sickness care to "wellness," and the possibilities of introducing innovations in the health services delivery system. Obviously, this list is not exhaustive. Other problems include the rapid expansion of high technology, the increasing costs of malpractice litigation, the difficulties inherent in fee negotiations and hospital budget setting, and the unknown impact of the AIDS epidemic on health care resources.

Cost Containment

As in every other industrially advanced nation, in Canada containing costs within the health care system will remain the number one concern for the foreseeable future. Even though Canada has been one of the nations most successful in containing health care costs in the past two decades, nevertheless, health expenditures now account for up to one third of provincial budgets. Moreover, the pressures for increased spending appear inexorable: the aging of the population, the expanding physician supply, the disincentives for efficiency inherent in the fee-for-service method of paying physicians, lack of incentives for hospital efficiency, breakthroughs in medical technology, and the difficulties of introducing potential innovations in health care delivery because of the "uniform terms and conditions" requirements of the Canada Health Act.

Although our primary concerns are the two programs of hospital and medical care, it will be helpful to place those expenditures in the context of total public and private health spending. Table 1 presents data on total health

TABLE 1. Total of Canada's Health Expenditures, 1975, 1981, and 1987

Category	1975 Millions $	1975 % of Total	1975 % of GNP	1981 Constant $[b]	1981 Millions $[b]	1981 % of Total	1981 % of GNP	1981 % Increase 1981/1975	1987[a] Millions $	1987 % of Total	1987 % of GNP	1987 Constant $	1987 % Increase 1987/1981	1987 % Increase 1987/1975
Total expense	12,271.3	100.0	7.26	20,249.7	26,698.0	100.0	7.75	31.8	47,934.7	100.0	8.90	37,129.9	39.1	83.3
Personal health care	10,699.7	87.2	6.33	17,656.3	23,162.7	86.8	6.72	31.1	42,136.1	87.9	7.81	32,638.3	40.9	84.8
Institutional	6,730.7	54.8	5.98	11,106.7	14,383.6	53.9	4.17	29.5	24,347.2	51.2	4.60	19,014.1	32.2	71.2
Hospitals	5,443.0	44.4	5.22	8,981.4	10,983.0	41.1	3.19	22.3	18,808.0	39.2	3.52	14,569.2	32.6	62.2
Other institutions	1,194.0	9.7	.71	1,978.4	3,031.0	11.4	.88	53.2	4,945.6	10.3	.93	3,830.9	26.4	93.6
Home care	37.4	.3	.02	61.7	163.6	.7	.05	165.1	377.5	.8	.07	292.4	78.7	373.9
Ambulances	56.2	.5	.03	92.7	186.0	.7	.05	100.6	415.3	.9	.06	321.7	73.0	247.0
Professional services	2,655.5	21.6	1.57	4,382.0	5,806.0	21.7	1.68	14.2	10,933.3	22.8	2.05	8,468.9	45.9	93.2
Physicians	1,924.4	15.7	1.14	3,175.5	3,983.2	14.9	1.14	25.4	7,678.8	16.0	1.44	5,947.9	49.3	87.3
Dentists	596.6	4.9	.35	984.5	1,500.3	5.6	.44	52.4	2,609.6	5.4	.49	2,021.4	34.7	105.2
Chiropractors	66.5	.5	.04	109.8	173.2	.6	.05	57.7	336.7	.7	.07	276.3	59.5	151.6
Optometrists	34.3	.3	.02	54.6	72.4	.3	.02	32.6	141.8	.3	.05	109.8	51.6	101.0
Podiatrists	13.3	.1	.01	22.0	21.8	.1	.01	-.1	36.3	.1	.01	20.1	-.1	-.95
Private nurses	13.9	.1	.01	22.9	15.2	.1	.01	-50.6	26.0	.1	.00	20.1	32.2	40.6

Physiotherapists	5.1	.0	.00	8.5	38.4	.1	.01	351.7	82.8	.2	.02	64.1	66.9	687.0
Drugs and appliances	1,313.6	10.7	.78	2,167.4	2,973.1	11.1	.86	37.1	6,655.5	13.9	1.25	5,155.3	73.4	137.8
Prescribed	578.7	4.7	.34	954.9	1,307.1	4.9	.38	36.9	2,821.0	5.9	.55	2,105.8	61.1	120.5
Nonprescribed	532.5	4.2	.30	845.7	1,099.9	4.1	.32	30.0	2,731.1	5.7	.51	2,315.5	110.5	173.7
Eyeglasses	170.1	1.4	.10	280.7	431.0	1.6	.13	53.5	838.2	1.7	.16	649.2	50.6	131.2
Hearing aids	14.8	.1	.01	24.4	31.0	.1	.01	27.0	48.0	.1	.01	37.2	20.0	52.4
Other appliances	37.6	.3	.02	62.0	104.2	.4	.03	68.0	216.4	.5	.04	367.6	252.8	492.9
Other health expenses	1,571.6	12.8	.93	2,595.3	3,535.3	13.2	1.03	36.2	5,798.7	12.1	1.09	4,491.6	27.0	73.0
Prepayment admin.	209.6	1.7	.12	345.9	407.4	1.5	.12	17.7	578.3	1.2	.11	447.9	9.9	29.4
Public health	515.8	5.0	.31	851.3	1,117.3	4.2	.32	31.2	2,130.8	4.4	.40	1,650.5	47.7	93.8
Capital expense	412.4	4.2	.36	1,010.5	1,409.4	5.3	.41	39.4	2,132.4	4.4	.40	1,651.9	17.9	63.4
Health research	100.5	.8	.06	165.9	245.5	.9	.07	45.0	411.5	.9	.08	316.6	28.9	90.8
Miscellaneous	133.2	1.1	.08	210.9	355.6	1.3	.10	68.6	545.7	1.1	.10	422.7	18.8	100.4

Source: Health and Welfare Canada.

[a]Provisional.

[b]Deflated in accordance with the implicit deflator of the GNP (1981 = 100).

expenditures for the years, 1975, 1981, and 1987. Overall health expenditures increased from $12.7 billion in 1975 to $47.9 billion in 1987. The proportion allocated to hospitals declined from 44.4 percent in 1975 to 41.1 percent in 1981 and 39.2 percent in 1987. The proportion allocated to physicians' services declined from 15.7 percent in 1975 to 14.9 percent in 1981 but increased to 16.0 percent in 1987. Overhead administration costs of the prepayment system dropped from 1.7 percent of the total in 1975 to 1.5 percent in 1981 and to 1.2 percent in 1987, an extraordinarily low figure when compared with administrative overhead expenditures in the United States.

However, to make inter-year comparisons more meaningful, the fourth column under each year heading presents the expenditures in deflated dollars (1981 = 100). Even when expressed in constant dollars, the increases are dramatic, far exceeding the 10.5 percent increase in population over the 1975–1987 period.

Over the twelve years, total expenditures on health increased by 83.3 percent. Expenditures by hospitals increased by 62.3 percent, and for all other institutions 93.6 percent (mainly due to the rapid expansion of long-term care facilities). Expenditures on physicians' services increased by 93.2 percent, owing in part to a large increase in physician supply. Some increases were extraordinary: home care, 373.9 percent (undoubtedly contributing to the slower growth rate of hospital expenditures); ambulance services, 247 percent; and drugs and appliances 137.8 percent. (All provinces provide drug programs for seniors and most subsidize appliances for those on low incomes.)

The gap between Canada and the United States in the percentage of gross national product (GNP) allocated to the health system (8.6 and 10.6 percent, respectively, in 1986) is of special interest. R. G. Evans of the University of British Columbia has analyzed the contributing factors. He finds that with respect to hospitals it is the difference in "service intensity," i.e., the volume of more and more expensive technology. During the period 1971–82 the volume of servicing per capita received by Canadians from the hospital system rose by 0.6 percent per year, while in the United States it rose 3.7 percent annually. Over the eleven years the difference cumulated to 6.4 percent versus 48.8 percent. With respect to physicians the difference is accounted for almost entirely by the difference in fees, which, after extraordinary increases in 1969–71 (when Medicare was introduced in Canada), during the eleven years, 1972–82, actually declined relative to the general price level by 2 percent per year on average, while fees in the United States were outstripping inflation by 1.4 percent per year. This difference of 3.3 percent per year cumulated over the period as a whole to 39.8 percent.[1]

The main explanation for the lower costs in the hospital sector is that the

1. R. G. Evans, "Illusions of Necessity: Evading Responsibility for Choice in Health Care," *Journal of Health Politics, Policy and Law* 10, no. 3 (Fall 1985): 439–68. See also Alan Detsky et al., "The Effectiveness of a Regulatory Strategy in Containing Costs: The Ontario Experience, 1967–81," *New England Journal of Medicine* 309, no. 3: 151–59.

three major functions relating to the system are administered by one agency, the Ministry of Health. These functions are: (1) hospital planning, including the location, size, and equipment of hospitals and the programs they offer; (2) determining the annual percentage increase to be granted for hospitals' "global budgets"; and (3) making the payments. In the medical sector fee increases are negotiated between the medical association and the Health Ministry, with the Treasury officials much involved, and, in some provinces, recourse to binding arbitration.

Although it seems likely that the ability to control the acquisition of new technology on an orderly basis will continue, there is less reason to be optimistic about medical expenditures. The extraordinarily high incomes generated by the introduction of Medicare established a new norm for physicians' "target incomes." When annual fee increases following 1970 failed to keep pace with the rates of inflation, major confrontations between provincial governments and medical associations occurred, especially in 1981 and 1982, leading to unprecedented fee increases that in general have brought physicians' incomes approaching their high levels of 1969–70. But the pressures are building again, and, as Manitoba's recent experience suggests, even the mechanism of binding arbitration may not provide the necessary resolutions.

We thus have the seemingly irresistible force meeting the immovable object. But the confrontations of the past are something that neither the profession nor the public can tolerate. Perhaps changes in the delivery system, such as U.S.-style health maintenance organizations (HMOs), may make a greater contribution to profession and public alike.

The Changing Demographic Profile

Central to the future needs for and the costs of health services in all Western nations are the rates of growth of the total population and the demographic shift of the age groups within it, particularly, in Canada as elsewhere, in the rapid "graying" of the population—the increasing proportion of the elderly.

This phenomenon of a rapidly aging population has prompted a flood of reports by Statistics Canada, Health and Welfare Canada, government commissions and task forces, and individual academics. Most recently (1983–84), the Canadian Medical Association appointed and financed the Task Force on the Allocation of Health Resources, which commissioned Woods Gordon, a management consulting firm, to analyze the likely effects of an aging population on the health care system. Its report, *Investigation of the Impact of Demographic Change on the Health Care System in Canada,*[2] provides prob-

---

2. Canadian Medical Association, Task Force on the Allocation of Health Resources, *Investigation of the Impact of Demographic Change on the Health Care System in Canada* (Woods Gordon Report) (Ottawa: The Association, 1984).

ably the most extensive projections now available on the magnitude of the problems Canada confronts in providing essential services for the elderly.

The analysts dealt first with population projections. Their high, medium, and low projections are shown in table 2, indicating that Canada's population in 2021 is likely to range between 29.3 and 32.9 million persons. But the most striking data are the projections on the proportion of the elderly.

In the census of 1981 those sixty-five and over represented 9.7 percent of the total population. Even more significant for the health and social services systems, those eighty years and over totaled 451,000 (or 19 percent of those sixty-five and over), and that number is projected to double by 2021, constituting by then almost one quarter of the elderly. Those seventy-five and over now receive approximately three times as many days of hospital care as those aged sixty-five to seventy-four.

The analysts then calculated the effect of these projected changes on utilization in each of five health services areas, assuming that no changes are made in the status quo health services delivery system. Those projections are shown in table 3. They then calculated what these increases would mean in terms of increased resources on the assumption that current resources were in balance with demand in 1981 (table 4). These projections were then translated into dollar amounts based on 1981 average per diem operating costs and construction costs, expressed in 1981 dollars (table 5). Continuation of the present system would require a return to the high level of hospital bed construction characteristic of the high-flying 1960s. Almost one thousand 300-bed nursing homes would need to be built.

The task force concluded, "If we continue to put old people into institutions at the rate we do now, the costs will not only be prohibitive, we will perpetuate the callous practice of warehousing the elderly." The alternatives? "The thrust in the redirection of health care resources undeniably needs to be in the development of community resources to keep the elderly out of institu-

TABLE 2. Projected Canadian Population to 2021 and Proportion of the Population Aged Sixty-Five or Over

	Total Population 2021 (millions)[a]	Percentage Change 1981–2021	Annual Percentage Increase	Proportion 65 or Over[b]	
				2001	2021
High	32.9	35.2	0.76	12.8	17.5
Medium	31.3	28.6	0.63	13.0	18.2
Low	29.3	20.2	0.46	13.2	19.0

Source: Woods Gordon Report.

[a] 1981 = 24.3 million.

[b] 1981 = 9.7 percent.

tions for as long as possible, not only to reduce costs, but to enhance the quality of life." At the direction of the task force Woods Gordon then tested four scenarios on its projected model: (1) reduce institutionalization from the current level of 9.45 percent to 6.0 percent (the U.S. level) and provide the "released" patients with home care; (2) reduce mental health facilities utilization to the low level already achieved by Saskatchewan; (3) reduce average length of stay in general hospitals by one day for the nonelderly patients; and

TABLE 3. Projected Percentage Increases in Health Services Use, 1981 to 2021

Health Service Area	1981–2001		1981–2021	
	20 Years	Annual	40 Years	Annual
General hospitals	48.8	2.01	89.1	1.61
Long-term care	68.3	2.04	118.8	1.98
Mental health facilities	38.3	1.63	68.0	1.31
Physician services	27.2	1.21	45.0	0.93
Home care nursing visits	62.6	2.46	117.8	1.97

Source: Woods Gordon Report.

TABLE 4. Projected Percentage Increases in Health Service Demand because of Demographic Change

Health Service Area	Resource	1981–2001	1981–2021
General hospitals	Beds	44	84
Long-term facilities	Beds	63	110
Mental health facilities	Beds	11	35
Physician services	Physicians	28	47
Home care nursing visits	Nurses	64	121

Source: Woods Gordon Report.

TABLE 5. Projected Operating and Construction Cost Increases by 2021

Health Service Area	Annual Operating Costs ($ million)	Capital Construction Costs ($ million)
General hospitals	7,100	17,700
Long-term facilities	4,300	12,400
Mental health facilities	380	360
Physician services	1,900	—
Home care nursing visits	43	—
Total	13,723	30,460

Source: Woods Gordon Report.

TABLE 6.   Financial Savings of Three Scenarios (1981 dollars)

| | Savings from Status Quo Scenarios (by 2021) | |
Scenario[a]	Annual Operating Costs ($ million)	Capital Construction Costs ($ million)
1—Elderly	5,900	16,300
2—Mental health	225	360
3—Hospital use	630	370
Total	6,755	17,030

Source: Woods Gordon Report.
[a]In the fourth scenario 2,700 physicians are offset by 2,700 nurse practitioners.

(4) introduce nurse practitioners into the primary health care system to offset some of the future need for more physicians. (This last recommendation will be difficult to implement given the oversupply of general practitioners and adherence to the fee-for-service payment system.) Scenario 1 would reduce the need for the construction of 65,000 hospital beds and 150,000 long-term beds. Total financial savings are estimated in table 6. To achieve the goal of deinstitutionalization would require, over the period to 2021, a sevenfold expansion of home care services.

At a colloquium, "Aging with Limited Health Resources," sponsored by the Economic Council of Canada in Winnipeg, Manitoba, in May 1986, there were a number of outstanding contributions, two of which are especially relevant here. The first was by John Horne, a health economist at the University of Manitoba.[3] He made several adjustments to the Woods Gordon scenarios.

1. He calculated that Woods Gordon had overestimated the number of nursing home residents who could be transferred back to the community and raised the nursing home target from 6 percent to 7 percent.
2. He believed that Woods Gordon had overestimated the costs of long-term patients in hospitals and, therefore, the savings to be gained in transferring them to nursing homes.
3. He believed that a similar miscalculation had been made in estimating the savings in transferring patients from nursing homes to the community, since most would be discharged from less-intensive-care (and therefore less expensive) facilities.

3. John N. Horne, "Financial Savings from a More Radical Approach to Alternative Delivery Methods by the Year 2021," Colloquium on Aging with Limited Health Resources (Ottawa: Economic Council of Canada, 1986). Mimeographed.

4. Using data from Manitoba's ten-year program of home care, he similarly concluded that Woods Gordon had underestimated the costs of that type of service.

5. He pointed out that the Woods Gordon target of reducing average length of stay (ALOS) of the nonelderly had already been achieved in a number of provinces; indeed, if all provinces were to reduce the ALOS to those levels, the savings would be $340 million higher than the Woods Gordon estimate. He also believed that nationwide recourse to day surgery, short-stay obstetrics, early discharge programs, pre-admission testing, self-care units, and statistical discharge prompting systems could reduce hospital days of care by 30 percent.

6. Horne then added a fifth scenario, involving increasing the operational efficiency of hospitals. Horne supported the feasibility of savings through increased efficiency by reference to the extensive 1969 *Task Force Reports on the Cost of Health Services in Canada,* which had indicated potential savings of 10 to 30 percent by use of work study techniques and other recommended measures.[4] To be on the cautious side Horne estimated cost savings of 7 percent, which would total $680 million.

7. Scenario 6 involved eliminating some marginally effective medical services. As he said, "This scenario is added to the list in recognition of the growing literature indicating that some services are either ineffective or, more commonly, are used at rates in excess of those compatible with marginal effectiveness." He cited studies of surgical procedures in Manitoba, the frequency of well-baby examinations, and routine diagnostic technologies such as chest X rays, electrocardiography, and endoscopy. "The problem is the paucity of good evaluative studies that most bedevils provincial governments who are bound by their own health insurance statutes to pay for any service deemed medically necessary by a physician." He selected an arbitrary figure of 10 percent to illustrate how important it is to improve the quality of evaluative studies in this area. The projected financial benefit of scenario 6 is $450 million in 2021.

Horne summarized the potential savings in his revision of the Woods Gordon scenarios (table 7).

These various projections alert us to the magnitude of the shifting pat-

---

4. *Report of the Committee on the Costs of Health Services* (Ottawa: Health and Welfare Canada, 1969).

TABLE 7.   Financial Savings from Status Quo Projections of Annual Operating Costs in the Year 2021 (1981 dollars)

Scenario	Woods Gordon ($ million)	John Horne ($ million)
1—Elderly	5,900	2,300
2—Mental health	225	225
3—Hospital use	630	1,700
4—Nurse practitioners	—[a]	630
5—Hospital costs	—[b]	680
6—Medical care	—[b]	450
Total	6,755	5,985

Sources: Woods Gordon Report; John N. Horne, "Financial Savings from a More Radical Approach to Alternative Delivery Methods by the Year 2021," Colloquium on Aging with Limited Health Resources (Ottawa: Economic Council of Canada, 1986 [mimeo.]).

[a]Not calculated.
[b]Not scenarioed.

terns of health care demands that Canada can expect to encounter in the decades ahead, and the scenarios suggest policy choices that Canadians can make if the political will is there to make them.

The other significant contribution at the colloquium in Winnipeg was that of Noralou Roos and colleagues, reporting on their longitudinal studies of medical and hospital utilization by the aged in Manitoba.[5] Among their studies they have focused on the wide variation in surgical procedures and hospital admission rates across small areas and across physicians' practices. Their conclusions are constructive refinements of the nature and extent of the problems and add a new perspective:

It is not "the elderly" and it is not even "the very elderly" who are high users of health care services. The great majority of elderly individuals are healthy and infrequently hospitalized. Only a small segment of this population produces the statistics of concern to health care planners.

Hospital stays of elderly patients, particularly the very elderly, are much less likely to be resource intensive [i.e., expensive] than are the hospital stays of younger individuals. Elderly patients' hospital days are more likely to be spent in low-cost small hospitals, rather than in high technology teaching hospitals, and in lengthy stays [which include substantial amounts of custodial care] than are those of younger individuals.

5. N. P. Roos and B. H. Shapiro, "Aging with Limited Resources: What Should We Be Worried About?" in Colloquium on Aging with Limited Health Resources (Ottawa: Economic Council of Canada, 1986). Mimeographed.

Dying is a much more important factor than aging *per se* in the high usage of hospitals. For the elderly, as for the non-elderly, a dramatic increase in utilization occurs in a relatively short period before death [one year or less].

The elderly population's use of health care resources is strongly influenced by factors other than "need." *The availability of hospital beds, how physicians practice medicine, and the increase in physician supply over the next several decades will undoubtedly influence hospital consumption more than will the aging of society.* (Emphasis added).

The results of these and related studies on high hospital utilization and on the idiosyncratic patterns of physicians' practices, combined with the impending surplus of physicians, reinforce the case of the advocates of a rationalization of the health services delivery system, if the needs of Canada's aging population (indeed, of all Canadians) are to be met adequately and economically. Clearly, Woods Gordon's and Horne's scenarios point in the right directions. Their contributions and those of a host of related studies have illuminated the debate that will inform effective public policy decisions.

Physician Manpower

As noted earlier, three factors contributed to Canada's physician supply: the error by demographers in forecasting the Canadian population for the Royal Commission in 1964 that led to the expansion of existing medical schools and the creation of four new ones; the unanticipated increase in doctors immigrating to Canada; and the failure of the predicted exodus of doctors following the introduction of Medicare. The consequence, as we have seen, is a physician-population ratio of 1:467 in 1987. The World Health Organization has set an optimal target ratio of 1:650, lending credence to the perceptions of several provincial health ministries of a surplus in a number of metropolitan centers. Canada is not alone, however. A report by the Graduate Education Medical Advisory Council projected a surplus of 70,000 physicians in the United States by 1990 and a surplus of 120,000 by 2000.[6] The concern of provincial governments is the escalating volume of medical services provided by physicians—an average annual increase of approximately 2 percent—and their attendant costs.

Several provincial studies of medical manpower have been published, but, since it is basically a national problem, the Conference of Deputy Ministers of Health established the Federal-Provincial Committee on Health Man-

---

6. Eli Ginzberg, *From Physician Shortage to Patient Shortage* (London and Boulder: Westview Press, 1986), 3.

TABLE 8. Physician Supply, Requirements, and Surplus (Shortage), 1980 and 2000

Category	Physician Supply		Physician Requirements		Surplus (Shortage)
	1980	2000	1980	2000	2000
General practice	19,219	31,488	18,535	26,618	4,870
Medical specialties	9,368	14,978	9,322	12,483	2,495
Surgical specialties	6,506	7,225	6,286	8,219	(994)
Laboratory specialties	2,574	3,282	2,696	3,621	(339)

Source: Health and Welfare Canada.

power in 1982. Its report was released in 1985.[7] It divided physician man-power into four categories: general practice, medical specialties, surgical specialties, and laboratory specialties, including nuclear medicine (table 8). Physician requirements were established, taking into account the increasing population (age-sex adjusted for a more elderly mix) and an increasing pro-portion of female physicians in stock (as female physicians, on average, provide fewer services).

To reduce the surplus the advisory committee proposed a series of op-tions that governments could consider while emphasizing the short time available because of the numbers of students, interns, and residents already in the pipeline. The committee noted four areas in which policy options are available.

1. *Physicians from abroad.* Each year an average of about 380 landed immigrant physicians enter Canada. Of these about 138 are "selected" (filling a position that cannot be filled by a qualified Canadian), and the remaining 242 are sponsored relatives or refugee physicians. About 55 Canadian graduates of foreign medical schools per year return to Canada, and a further 183 foreign medical school graduates practice in Canada on temporary visas. The committee recommended that the number of selected immigrants be reduced from about 140 to 50 per year, that foreign medical graduates (including Canadian citi-zens) be reduced from 176 to 115 per year, and that the number practicing on temporary visas be reduced by 50 percent.

---

7. *Report of the Federal–Provincial Advisory Committee on Health Manpower* (Ottawa: Health and Welfare Canada, 1985). Mimeographed.

2. *Postgraduate training positions.* The committee recommended that the output from Canadian postgraduate training into a stock of general practitioners be reduced by encouraging trainees to proceed to surgical and laboratory specialties and that, in addition, there be a 20 percent reduction in output from Canadian postgraduate training of general practitioners and medical specialties. Even with such adjustments the committee foresees a continuing surplus by 2000.

3. *Medical school enrollment.* The committee recommended that by 1986 the annual output from postgraduate training of general practitioners be reduced by 125 per year and that this number be reduced by an additional 20 percent in output from Canadian postgraduate training in medical specialties by 1994.

4. *Distribution payments to physicians.* In this area the committee recommended that effective measures be adopted to insure that physicians be established only in areas of demonstrated need for medical services (in effect, the British Columbia policy of restricting billing numbers, which will be discussed).

These are drastic solutions with politically unattractive consequences: reducing opportunities for young people to pursue a medical career and reductions in medical training staffs, in internships, and, especially, in residencies, which would place more responsibility on busy specialists. But the alternatives are also unattractive, since each physician adds $150,000 to $250,000 annually to the provincial medical care bill for income, overhead, diagnostic tests, hospital admissions, prescriptions, and the like.

Only one province, British Columbia, has attacked the problems of physician oversupply and maldistribution head on (although several provinces have programs and incentives to attract physicians to rural and northern areas). In 1979 a committee, including members of the British Columbia College of Physicians and Surgeons and the British Columbia Medical Association (BCMA), recommended "that in certain areas restrictions concerning the number of physicians billing the Medical Services Plan be considered as a means to temper the supply and maldistribution of physician manpower."[8] No action was taken.

In 1982 a second representative committee recommended that billing numbers be restricted. In 1984 a Provincial Medical Manpower Committee was created, including representatives of the BCMA, the College of Physicians and Surgeons, the British Columbia Health Association (mainly hospitals), the Professional Association of Interns and Residents (PAIR), and the

---

8. W. Black, *Report of the Joint Committee on Medical Manpower* (Victoria: Ministry of Health, 1979).

Faculty of Medicine at the University of British Columbia. The committee issued a report, "Guidelines for Medical Manpower Plans," for use by local manpower committees (hospital based) and regional manpower committees (based on regional hospital districts).

Without legislative authorization the policy to limit billing numbers (i.e., the right to bill the British Columbia Medical Plan [BCMP] for insured services) was introduced in September 1983. Approximately one third fewer billing numbers were issued in the ensuing two years.[9]

On January 16, 1985, Mia Raza, a general practitioner, whose husband (a specialist) had settled in Kamloops, launched a suit in the Supreme Court of British Columbia challenging the B.C. Medical Services Commissions's decision to deny her a billing number. On March 21 the court ruled in her favor.

On May 5, 1985, the legislature passed the Medical Services Amendment Act, authorizing the commission to restrict billing numbers. On January 5, 1986, in another court challenge, the B.C. Supreme Court ruled that the law did not violate the Charter of Rights and Freedoms and was therefore constitutional. Justice Lysyk compared doctors to other workers, saying, "In the public sector no one suggests that any level of government is obliged to hire civil servants or contractually retain the services of others beyond its perceived needs."[10]

But that was not the end. The decision was appealed in the B.C. Court of Appeal, which overruled the Supreme Court and ordered the BCMP Commission to issue billing numbers to all applicants,[11] despite the government's request that no numbers be issued pending its appeal to the Supreme Court of Canada. In August 1988 and the first week of September over two thousand new numbers were issued, and the government has been deeply concerned about the additional costs that will occur.[12] Accordingly, the government appealed the decision to the Supreme Court of Canada, which, in December 1988, refused leave to appeal the decision.[13] The implications for a rational medical manpower policy are serious, indeed.

---

9. Personal communication from the Deputy Minister of Health.

10. *Globe and Mail,* January 6, 1986.

11. *P. S. Wilson and C. L. Mavson v. Medical Services Commission and Attorney General of British Columbia.* British Columbia Court of Appeal, Vancouver (April 5, 1988).

12. *Medical Post,* September 6, 1988.

13. *Medical Post,* December 14, 1988. Critical of this judicial intervention in the legislative process, Allan Hutchinson of York University's Osgoode Hall Law School said: "By intervening in the budgetary process of health care provision in such a partial way, the unelected judges blow their already tenuous cover. They not only invade the political terrain, but they usurp the function of our elected representatives in that area. Surely it is not the judges' business to second-guess legislators on the difficult choices in regulating health care costs." *Toronto Star,* December 30, 1988.

Shifting Emphasis from Sickness Care to Wellness

The enactment of the Hospital Insurance and Medical Care Insurance Acts in 1957 and 1966 represented the apex, in Canada, of the public's acceptance of the underlying foundation of modern medical practice, the biomedical disease model. As Norman White has defined it, the biomedical disease model "is a concept of sickness in which a strict linear causal sequence is followed from *cause* to *lesion* to *symptom* (or aetiology to pathology to outcome)."[14] People were to be taxed to remove the financial barriers to access to their medical doctors and their hospital-based armamentarium of high technology. The two parliamentary decisions were the most widely supported social measures ever passed in Canada. The expectation was that, after an initial rise in costs (to meet previously unmet needs), expenditures, like morbidity, would decrease. But, despite the many extraordinary successes of modern medicine, ubiquitous faith in the biomedical disease model has begun to decline as costs and morbidity continue to grow. Doubling the proportion of GNP allocated to the treatment system has not achieved a commensurate improvement in health status of the general population. To quote White again, "Despite increasing investment in evermore sophisticated delivery systems and technologies, our general health status is not improving as we believe it should."[15]

The last two decades have witnessed wide-ranging searches for alternative approaches. A major new thrust occurred in 1974 with the publication of *A New Perspective on the Health of Canadians,* issued by the Minister of Health, the Hon. Marc Lalonde, based on research by H. L. Laframboise, director general of the Long Range Health Planning Branch, Health and Welfare Canada. Trevor Hancock, a public health specialist, has written: "The Lalonde report was the first modern government document in the Western world to acknowledge that our emphasis upon a biomedical health care system is wrong, and that we need to look beyond the traditional health care (sick care) system if we wish to improve the health of the public. The Lalonde report was followed by similar reports in Britain, Sweden, and the U.S.A."[16]

The Lalonde report's main contribution was the outlining of a conceptual framework for the analysis and evaluation of the health field. It divided the field into four elements: human biology, environment, lifestyle, and health care organization. Based on extensive analyses of the causes of morbidity and mortality and of expenditures on facilities, professional education, and treat-

---

14. Norman F. White, "Future Models in the Health Field," paper presented to the First Global Conference on the Future, July 4, 1980. Mimeographed.

15. Ibid.

16. Trevor Hancock, "Beyond Health Care: From Public Health Policy to Healthy Public Policy," *Canadian Journal of Public Health* 76, supp. 1 (May–June 1985).

ment services, the report concluded that Canadians had placed too much trust in the biomedical disease model, thereby overextending their health services organization to the neglect of biological research, environmental cleanup, and life-threatening lifestyles.

The report has had an important, if not major, impact on attitudes and on the perspective from which the health care system is assessed. Although one cannot attribute recent advances directly to the report, there have been major legislative enactments at all levels of government, tightening up antipollution controls on industry directed especially to improving water quality and reducing acid rain. The inability to achieve a treaty with the United States on acid rain (it is estimated that 50 percent of acid rain falling on Canadian lakes, forests, and people originates in the United States) has been the Canadian government's most serious foreign policy failure. There has been a nationwide movement to regulate and curb smoking in public transportation, including airlines, and in public buildings and the workplace. (With a federal tax increase of $4.00 per carton of cigarettes in the April 1989 budget, the cost of a package of twenty-five cigarettes in most provinces is now over $4.00, indeed, in New Brunswick, as much as $6.25, or US$5.25.) And environmental issues were at the forefront in the national elections in 1988.

The move away from the biomedical disease model has received substantial support from the World Health Organization (WHO). Its strategy for attaining the goal of "Health for All by the Year 2000" is based upon the recognition that "health does not exist in isolation": "It is influenced by a complex of environmental, social and economic factors ultimately related to each other. . . . Action taken outside the health sector can have effects much greater than those obtained within it."[17]

"Healthy public policy," as the new approach is called, has been embedded more recently in the larger concept of health promotion. At a major international conference organized by WHO and Health and Welfare Canada in November 1986, the *Ottawa Charter for Health Promotion* was adopted. In it health promotion is defined as "the process of enabling people to increase control over, and improve, their health." Five main approaches were proposed: building healthy public policy; creating environments supportive of health; strengthening community action; developing personal skills; and reorienting health services.

Health promotion has now been incorporated in federal government policy. In a document entitled "Achieving Health for All: A Framework for Health Promotion," Health and Welfare Canada outlined a strategy that "com-

17. H. Mahler, "Health 2000: The Meaning of 'Health for All' by the Year 2000," *World Health Forum* 2, no. 1 (1981): 5–22.

plements and strengthens the existing system of health care."[18] The paper
outlined three *challenges:* (1) reducing inequities in view of the fact that
health status is directly related to economic status; (2) increasing the prevention effort, mainly by changing lifestyles; and (3) enhancing people's capacity
to cope with chronic conditions, disabilities, and mental health problems.

To meet these challenges the paper then proposed a set of health promotion *mechanisms:* (1) *self-care,* or the decisions and actions individuals take in
the interest of their own health; (2) *mutual aid,* or the actions people take to
help one another; and (3) *healthy environment,* or the creation of conditions
and surroundings conducive to health.

These mechanisms, in turn, lead to three major *strategies* for health
promotion: (1) fostering public participation to channel the energy, skills, and
creativity of community members into the national effort to achieve health; (2)
strengthening community health services that provide a natural focal point for
coordinating services such as assessment, home care, respite care, counsel-
ing, and the valuable services of volunteers; and (3) coordinating healthy
public policy. "All policies which have a direct bearing on health need to be
coordinated. The list is long and includes, among others, income security,
employment, education, housing, business, agriculture, transportation, justice, and technology." The paper concludes:

> The mutually reinforcing strategies taken together with the mechanisms,
> comprise the basic elements of the Health Promotion Framework. It is
> important to state that one strategy or mechanism on its own will be of
> little significance. Only by putting these pieces together, and setting
> priorities, can health promotion carry meaning and come alive. We be-
> lieve the approach we propose allows us to respond effectively and
> ethically to current and future health concerns.

The federal initiatives have been matched by complementary actions
among the provinces. In Ontario, for example, three separate task forces
issued reports in 1987. The first, chaired by John Evans (president of the
Rockefeller Foundation), issued a report entitled *Toward a Shared Direction
for Health in Ontario.*[19] The panel, which included representatives of the
professions, the public, and the government, was obviously impressed by the
concept of healthy public policy, for its main recommendation called for

18. Hon. Jake Epp, *Achieving Health for All: A Framework for Health Promotion* (Ottawa:
Health and Welfare Canada, 1986).

19. John R. Evans, *Toward a Shared Direction for Health In Ontario* (Toronto: Ministry of
Health, 1987).

the "integration of government policy for health as the shared responsibility of many different Ministries whose programs and policies in the areas of occupational and environmental health, social welfare, housing, manpower training and research have a fundamental impact on the health of Ontario's population over and above the formal health care system." To achieve the necessary coordination the panel recommended the establishment of a "Premier's Council on Health Strategy," saying:

> Such a prestigious agency would demonstrate the highest level of commitment to explore new ways of approaching health and health care. . . . The Premier's participation would also demonstrate the commitment of the government to a concept of health which goes beyond the formal management of the health care system by the Ministry of Health. It would acknowledge that the health of Ontario's residents is influenced significantly by the broader social, economic and environmental policies and priorities of government as a whole.

The Premier's Council was created in 1988. Its membership includes the premier, the ministers of seven departments, and fifteen other distinguished citizens, including health professionals.

The second panel, chaired by Robert Spasoff, was called the Panel on Health Goals for Ontario,[20] and it complemented the Evans report by citing a large number of specific goals for the province. The third panel, chaired by a former Olympic athlete, Steve Podborski, issued its report, *Health Promotion Matters in Ontario,*[21] after examining health promotion activities and potential in nine Ontario communities. The panel's perception of a "bottom-up" rather than a "top-down" health system anticipates new roles for the Ministry of Health and new local partnerships on health promotion issues.

The concepts of "wellness," health promotion, and healthy public policies are now well understood by all governments in Canada, but implementing them will be difficult. The Health and Welfare document, *Achieving Health for All,* observed: "Adjusting the present health care system in such a way as to assign more responsibility to community-based services means allocating a greater share of resources to such services." And there is the rub. Most of the needed resources must be allocated by provincial governments, which, in the current vernacular, find themselves between a rock and a hard place. On the one hand is the decrease in transfer payments from the federal government under (EPF); on the other hand is the inescapable financial com-

---

20. Robert Spasoff, *Health Goals for Ontario* (Toronto: Ministry of Health, 1987).
    21. Steve Podborski, *Health Promotion Matters in Ontario* (Toronto: Ministry of Health, 1987).

mitment to an overbuilt hospital system and the rapidly increasing supply of physicians. It should be emphasized that what the advocates of healthy public policy are proposing is not an abandonment of our current treatment system— that would be folly—but a shift in emphasis made possible, in fact, by the availability and the quality of the treatment system that Canada has built.

Innovations in the Delivery System

There is one other major subject on the continuing agenda, made necessary by both the desire for improved quality of care and the demands of cost containment. The Canadian medical profession and Canadian governments can no longer ignore the revolution in the organization and delivery of health services in the United States that gained momentum in the 1980s and is forecast to accelerate in the decades ahead. That is the burgeoning development of HMOs and of preferred provider organizations (PPOs) or, as they are sometimes called, independent practice associations (IPAs). The generic term used to encompass the various types is *alternative delivery systems* (ADSs).

The Canadian public medical care insurance system adopted the patterns of medical services delivery pioneered by the medical profession-sponsored prepayment plans—mainly solo practice and fee-for-service payments. It is a wasteful and unnecessarily expensive system, with built-in incentives for overservicing and unnecessary surgery and hospitalization.

Although there are many group practices in Canada, there is only one HMO based on the U.S. model, the Group Health Clinic in Sault Ste. Marie, Ontario. Launched by the United Steel Workers union before Medicare, its subscribers now constitute about one half of the Sault's population. It receives its funds from the Ontario Health Insurance Plan (OHIP) on a modified capitation plan called "capitation-negation." Like HMOs, it receives a monthly capitation payment for each member on its roster, but, if a member receives services (which the clinic could provide) outside the clinic, the clinic loses that month's capitation payment on behalf of that member.[22] There are two other comprehensive prepayment group practice clinics in Canada, both in Saskatchewan— the Prince Albert Community Health Center and the Saskatoon Community Health Center. But they are not paid by the capitation method.

In addition to the Sault Ste. Marie clinic there are twenty-four other health service organizations (HSOs) in Ontario, resembling HMOs in that they are paid by the capitation method but provide, essentially, only primary

---

22. Jonathan Lomas, *First and Foremost in Community Health Centres: The Centre in Sault Ste. Marie* (Toronto: University of Toronto Press, 1985). Obviously there is some confusion in Canada in the terminology used to describe these various types of organizations. Under new legislation the Sault Ste. Marie Clinic will become a "Comprehensive Health Organization" (CHO).

care. Total enrollment in Ontario HSOs in 1988 was just over 200,000. On average, Ontario HSOs use 16 percent fewer days of hospital care and the Sault's clinic 22 percent fewer than the population generally. They are eligible to receive an ambulatory care incentive payment (ACIP) in respect of this reduced utilization. There are also, in Ontario, thirteen community health centers (CHCs) with a total membership of 43,000. All are community sponsored, and their purpose is to provide primary care services in underserved, low-income communities. They are paid by OHIP on the basis of the programs they offer, rather than by the capitation method of the HSOs.[23]

But it is in Quebec that the most dramatic measures were taken to alter the system of providing primary care. The proposals were made in the first volume of the report of the (Castonguay) Royal Commission on Health and Social Welfare in 1967. With the election of the Liberals in 1970 Castonguay became the minister of health and began to introduce measures based on his own recommendations. Of chief interest here was the proposal to introduce local community service centers (CLSCs), where doctors, nurses, social workers, and community organizers, working together, were to try to develop the new (social) medicine and be responsible for all the social and health needs of the community. Some seventy CLSCs were created, but the Quebec Federation of General Practitioners encouraged the creation of over four hundred private, traditional poly-clinics in which physicians retained control. The results thus fell far short of the idealistic goals.[24]

In 1971 the Conference of (federal and provincial) Health Ministers requested a full investigation of CHCs under the direction of John Hastings of the University of Toronto. That report strongly recommended that payment systems alternative to the present form of fee for service be developed, the creation by the provinces of CHCs, and their funding through global or block budgets.[25] The Hastings report elicited much discussion but little action by the provinces.

In 1982 a second commission was appointed, this time by the new minister of health in Ontario, Larry Grossman. The chairman of the task force was J. Fraser Mustard, former dean of medicine at McMaster University.[26] It, too, endorsed CHCs and HSOs, and the minister stated that the ministry would support their development. As we have seen, not much happened.

---

23. Ontario Ministry of Health, *Annual Report, 1988.* (Toronto).

24. Marc Renaud, "Reform or Illusion? An Analysis of the Quebec State Intervention in Health," in David Colburn et al., eds., *Health and Canadian Society* (Toronto: Fitzhenry and Whiteside, 1987).

25. *Report on the Community Health Center Project* (Hastings Report) (Ottawa: Health and Welfare Canada, 1972).

26. *Report of the Task Force to Review Primary Health Care in Ontario* (Mustard Report) (Toronto: Ministry of Health, 1982).

But there are now welcome signs that the Ontario Ministry of Health is moving forward. Speaking to the Ontario Hospital Association in April 1989, the (Liberal) minister of health, Elinor Caplan, announced that the government would launch approximately six projects a year over the next three years. These would take the form of nonprofit corporations to be known as comprehensive health organizations (CHOs) and would provide medical and other health services, including hospital care, and would be paid by the ministry on a capitation basis. Enrollment would be voluntary. She also announced that the Ontario Medical Association was cooperating fully with the ministry and that inquiries had come in from over thirty interested communities.

It has been posited that there are two times when change is possible. One is when there is a budget feast; then change can be "bought." The other is when there is a budget famine, when change becomes inevitable. Perhaps, in this era of restraint, improvements in our health services delivery system—as good as we believe it to be—can be made. Vision, political will, and cooperation among all the participants are the basic requirements.

CHAPTER 12

Public Decision Making in Public Health Care Systems: The Quebec Experience

Lee Soderstrom and Luciano Bozzini

The high cost of the health services has generated much concern in Canada; central issues include the efficiency of the ten provinces' public health systems and the ability of the governments to continue financing them. A variety of strategies for dealing with this problem has been suggested, including changing the financial incentives confronting users and providers of services, privatizing some aspects of the systems, increasing utilization review, and increasing prevention programs. Another possible strategy is to improve public decision making.

Public decision making plays a pivotal role in a public health care system. In theory there are good reasons for public involvement in the financing and management of a health system (Evans 1984). In practice, however, the actual effects of public involvement depend on the quality of the decisions made by government and other public agencies regarding the financing, operation, and structure of the system. The actual effects of public financing of hospital services certainly depend on the government's funding decisions for hospitals' operating and capital costs.

The focus here is on public decision making in Quebec, although the situation with respect to decision making is the same in all Canadian provinces. Certainly much has been accomplished through extensive public involvement in Quebec's public health system during the past thirty years. Yet more could be accomplished through better public decision making. Significant financial and organization problems persist, in part because of public decision-making difficulties.

The quality of public decisions depends on the characteristics of the people making decisions and on the organization of decision making. The latter includes a variety of factors. The focus here is on two, which are currently receiving attention in Quebec: the extent to which decision making is decentralized; and the information available to decision makers and other people interested in health policy. It is argued that Quebec's health system would perform better if decision making were more decentralized and information available improved.

Similar decision-making problems exist in the other provinces. All are searching for the appropriate balance between provincial (i.e., centralized) and local decision making, and all have insufficient information about their health systems. Quebec has already done at least as much as the other provinces, however, to decentralize decision making and improve information.

Americans are now debating whether to increase public financing of health services. The analysis presented here implies that they should also consider carefully the organization of the public decision making that is an inevitable part of any public financing program. Attention should be given to the adequacy of information available. And, whatever role government eventually does have in a reformed American system, attention should be given to the division of decision-making responsibilities and powers between the national, state, and local governments.

In the following section the factors that shape public decisions are sketched, and the concepts of "decentralization" and "information" are discussed. Next, Quebec's health care system is described and its current performance summarized. This is not a comprehensive discussion; only information needed to understand the analysis that follows is provided. Then it is argued that decision making is too centralized and that the information available is inadequate. Finally, current efforts to decentralize decision making are discussed, and a way to improve information is proposed.

Determinants of Public Decisions

A simple public health system indicates the meaning of "public decision making." Let one government agency be involved in the system and let the providers of services be self-employed physicians and nonprofit, community-operated hospitals. Then public decision making refers to decisions made by the government agency with respect to the financing of the system (e.g., fees for physicians and budgets for hospitals), the current operation of the system (e.g., distribution of available resources and the functioning of hospitals and physicians), and the future structure of the system (e.g., resources available, existence of particular programs, extent of public financing, and internal organization of the hospitals).[1]

The domain of public decision making depends on a system's design. In

---

1. In reality, public decision making involves various public organizations. There can be several provincial government agencies. Some decision making may be delegated to local health councils, which are public organizations (e.g., Quebec's twelve regional health councils). Some may also be delegated to other nongovernmental public agencies (e.g., Quebec's Professional Corporation of Physicians and Surgeons, which oversees the quality of physician manpower).

Quebec, as indicated below, this domain is large; there is extensive public involvement in the financing and management of the system. In the United States the domain is much more limited. Although the idea of reducing the domain of public decision making has been discussed in Quebec during the past six years, little privatization has actually occurred.[2]

Decentralized Decision Making

Within the domain of public decision making four groups of factors shape the actual decisions made. The first one is the structure of public decision making. This refers to the public organizations involved, the division of responsibilities and decision-making powers among them,[3] and the division of responsibilities and powers within each organization.

The aspect of this structure discussed here is decentralized decision making. It refers to the division of financial and managerial responsibilities and powers between the central government and regional agencies. It can take various forms, depending upon the nature of the regional agencies and their responsibilities and powers (Turgeon 1983; Gow et al. 1987). In terms of their nature they could merely be branch offices of the central government's health ministry, so that the local decision makers are only ministry employees. Alternatively, the agencies could be regional health councils or boards, organically distinct from the government. Council members would be local residents popularly elected, appointed by the central government, or selected by various local organizations (hospital associations, local governments, etc.).[4] Although functioning according to some centrally determined norms, each council would have some autonomy from the ministry and some accountability to the people living in its region. In Quebec discussions of decentralization involve some sort of regional council; the debates relate to how the members should be selected and the functions of the councils.

---

2. There are several reasons for this. Extensive public financing has been very popular. Quebec health planners have been impressed by the performance of the public health system. And strong evidence that privatization would improve the system's performance has been lacking (Stoddart and Labelle 1985; Quebec 1988; Soderstrom 1988).

3. This division is largely established by statute and regulation. They can be viewed two ways. They can be taken as a given and decision making viewed in the context of a given legal environment. This is appropriate for a short-period analysis. Alternatively, the law can itself be viewed as a result of public decision making. One must then find more fundamental explanations of the decisions that are taken. Both views are used here.

4. Organizationally, a regional council consists of a policy-making administrative council (or board of directors) plus an administrative staff, headed by an executive director, which carries out functions assigned to it by the administrative council or the government. The selection of council members refers here to the selection of administrative council members, and the council's managerial resources refers to the administrative unit's resources.

In principle decentralized decision making has at least five advantages, proponents argue. First, regional decision makers can better tailor policies and programs to local resources, problems, and priorities, which vary among regions. They can better integrate programs too. Local decision makers should be better informed about local conditions than the more distant central officials, thus reducing the problem central decision makers always face in dealing with regional diversity, that of imperfect information. Decisions can also be made more promptly, because time is not required for communicating between the center and local establishments and for adapting central decisions to local conditions.

Second, regional decision making can involve smaller, more efficient bureaucracies, although this argument ignores the possibility of economies of scale for some functions. For example, it is more efficient to have one agency reimburse all Quebec physicians than one agency in each region doing that. Similarly, it is more efficient having one provincial agency responsible for some areas of research; having twelve regional councils evaluating the same new technology is unnecessary.

Third, decentralized decision making can provide more encouragement for local providers and the population to participate in program development and operation. Efforts to improve the coordination among different providers have greater chance of success when the providers are meaningfully involved in developing and operating them.

Fourth, centralization can limit experimentation, whereas decision makers in different regions may try different approaches to similar problems. Given the uncertainty about appropriate solutions for many problems and the fact that individual decision makers do err, this diversity can be desirable (Sah 1991). Finally, regional decision makers may be more accountable to the people in their region than the more distant central government officials. Accountability can be affected, however, by the way regional council members are selected (i.e., election versus appointment) and the attention local residents give to their council's activities. The extent to which these councils serve the public interest also depends on the influence that provider groups have on them.

On the other hand, centralized decision making also has important advantages. Health-related programs of various government ministries are better coordinated centrally. And central decision making facilitates national standards. Central financing avoids interregional differences in the ability to finance services. Central norms can provide uniformity with respect to objectives and availability of services. Of course, the extent to which national standards are desirable is a matter of social values.

Thus, the appropriate balance between central and regional decision making depends on efficiency considerations and social values. This helps explain why health care is largely in the provincial domain in Canada. For many functions this promotes efficiency, given Canada's size and diversity. And, equally important, given Canadians' attachment to the province in which they live, social values are such that there is more concern that people have comparable access to services at the provincial than at the national level. Within each province there is considerable agreement that the provincial government should, in principle, facilitate comparable access to services for all provincial residents. But the same degree of social concern does not exist nationally, so the federal role is more limited.[5]

Information

The second factor shaping public decisions is the information available to decision makers and other interested parties. Information has four aspects. One is the data available describing the actual performance of the system (e.g., the population's health status, its utilization of services, the use of available resources, and the cost of services). The second aspect is the evaluative information available. This includes evaluations of specific services, of particular organizational features of the system and public policies, and of possible reforms of existing services, programs, and organizational features. Evaluations made in Quebec itself and elsewhere can be relevant. Quebec can learn from evaluations made elsewhere of surgical procedures, home care programs, and methods of remunerating physicians.

Information involves more than numbers. Its third aspect is the interpretation available of the descriptive and evaluative data. A mountain of tables describing services used and research reports is of limited usefulness for most people. The tables and reports must be distilled and interpreted. Key findings and policy implications must be highlighted and key issues needing further research identified.

The final aspect is the extent to which available data and interpretation are disseminated among relevant policymakers as well as interested parties, the media, and the public. The information available shapes what policymakers

---

5. There is certainly some concern in each province that people across Canada should have access to "necessary" hospital and physician services, so the federal government has helped the provinces finance their hospital and physician insurance programs. And, to qualify for Ottawa's dollars, a provincial program must satisfy certain federal standards: It must cover all provincial residents for all inpatient hospital and medically required physician services; there can be no user charges; when residents are in other provinces its benefits must be "portable"; and the program must be publicly administered. Although these national norms are important, the provinces still have great latitude in how they organize their respective health systems, the number of doctors and hospitals they have, and the extent to which they finance other health and social services.

know about the issues involved in their decisions, and it influences discussions among people interested in health policy. Access to good information can facilitate good public debate, providing decision makers with better indications of social priorities. Good information and public debate can also point to issues not previously considered. Although information can facilitate better decisions, it does not guarantee them. Information can be ignored.[6] Other factors also influence decisions. And simply having more data and research reports is not always desirable. The accuracy of the data, its relevance, and the cost of obtaining additional information must also be considered. Researchers outside of government as well as government officials shape the information available. But government is responsible for information, because it is responsible for the performance of the health system.

Two Additional Factors

Two other factors also shape public decisions. One is the financial constraints and incentives confronting government and other public organizations involved in decision making. The other factor is the nature of the public decision makers themselves. This refers to the quality of the decision makers, which depends on their ability, training, and experience. It also depends on the resources available to them—the quantity and quality of their staffs and their available tools (i.e., knowledge, analytic and managerial techniques, access to computers, etc.). The nature of the decision makers also refers to the values they allow to influence their decisions. These values can reflect the values of the decision makers themselves, the public (electoral considerations), and political pressure groups.

The Quebec Health Care System

Constitutionally, health services in Canada are largely a provincial matter, so Canada has ten distinct provincial health care systems. The relevant government for each system is its provincial government, not the federal government. Thus, in this analysis *government* refers to the Quebec government.

The idea that health and social problems (i.e., problems of social integra-

---

6. Looking at the state of the U.S. health care system, the value of good information might be questioned. The United States has better information about its health system than does any other country, yet the U.S. system is beset with access and cost problems. But decisions depend on more than just the information available, and in the U.S. information has in fact had an important role in clarifying the existence and nature of the problems. Moreover, the argument developed here is that, given the present state of Quebec's health system and the relative paucity of information in Quebec, the performance of Quebec's system can be significantly improved with better information.

tion, deviance and social misadaptation, and personal violence) are often inextricably bound together has been taken very seriously in Quebec. Considerable effort has been made to create an integrated health and social services system. The government agency primarily responsible for this system is the Ministry of Health and Social Services (MSSS).[7] And "the establishments" in the system include acute-care hospitals, local community service centers (CLSCs),[8] rehabilitation centers, long-term-care centers, nursing homes, and youth protection centers.

Public Involvement

Health and social services are largely government financed in Quebec as well as in the other provinces. In 1987, 77 percent of Quebec's health costs were publicly financed (Canada 1990b). Medical services and acute-care hospital services are almost entirely publicly funded; these programs are universal and comprehensive, and no use is made of user charges.[9] The Quebec Health Insurance Board (RAMQ),[10] a provincial agency, reimburses the physicians, and the MSSS the hospitals. The government negotiates physicians' fees and salaries with their four federations and wages and working conditions in the hospitals with a number of unions. It also sets annual global budgets for each hospital. The four medical schools and new facilities are largely publicly financed.

The government is not an important provider of services. Physicians are largely self-employed, and almost all establishments are operated by non-profit, public organizations. The 155 nonprofit, community-operated, MSSS-financed CLSCs are a significant source of primary medical and social services as well as preventative services (Bozzini 1988).

Government is deeply involved in system management. The situation in Quebec, in this respect, is no different from that in the other provinces. The Quebec government oversees the system's operation. Although it does not run the establishments, no facet of their operations is untouched by government regulation. In addition, the government evaluates programs and services. It also shapes the system's evolution (e.g., resources available, existence and organization of particular programs, extent of public financing, and the establishments' internal organization).

---

7. Ministère de la Santé et des Services Sociaux.

8. Centres Locaux de Services Communautaires (CLSCs).

9. There is also much public funding of convalescent care, chronic care, and nursing home services. In addition, optometric services, prostheses, social services, dental services for children and welfare recipients, and prescription drugs for the aged and welfare recipients are publicly funded.

10. Le Régie de l'Assurance-Maladie du Québec (RAMQ).

In addition to the government agencies and the establishments there are twelve regional health and social services councils. These are public agencies, which receive small annual budgets from the MSSS. The councils' role in system management has been very limited, though there has been much more regional involvement in system management in Quebec than in the other provinces. In addition, there are thirty-two Community Health Departments (DSCs),[11] each attached to an acute-care hospital. Financed by the MSSS, the DSCs are responsible for public health services within their assigned localities. The MSSS also periodically assigns them program evaluation and planning tasks.

This extensive public involvement started in the late 1950s, in response to public concern about access to health services and the financial burden borne by users of services. Public financing increased the availability of these services and then reduced the financial barriers to them.[12]

By the late 1960s it became clear that government in Quebec and in the other provinces should not limit its activities to paying bills passively. Access to some services remained a problem for some people, and costs were beginning to mount. In 1971 Quebec's Castonguay Commission urged a major overhaul of the system, including increased public management, more concern about social services, and a major restructuring of the system (e.g., introduction of CLSCs, reorganization of the establishments, extensive decentralization). Many of its recommendations were implemented. As a result, a situation in which health and social services were financed publicly and privately, and in which providers had much autonomy, was transformed into a largely publicly financed and centrally steered public health and social services system. Similar reforms were introduced in other provinces at the same time.

As the 1970s progressed, costs continued to increase rapidly in all provinces. Concerns mounted that services were being produced inefficiently, that some were being produced excessively while access to others was inadequate, and that providers' incomes were rising too fast. In response, the government worked harder to curb spending. Increasingly, constraints were imposed on establishments' budgets and the fees, wages, and the salaries of people working in the system. This further increased government's role in the system.

Throughout the 1980s these budget constraints continued. Pressure mounted, however, to find other ways for improving the system's efficiency and to improve access to various services. As a result, Quebec's Rochon

---

11. Départements de Santé Communautaire (DSCs).

12. Hospital facilities were expanded in the 1950s and 1960s; public funding of hospital services started in January 1961 in Quebec. Then, beginning in the mid-1960s, the supply of physicians was increased; public financing for physician services started in November 1970.

Commission was established in 1985 to make a thorough evaluation of the system. Its lengthy report, published in 1988, sparked a major debate over system reform, culminating in recent legislation making sweeping reforms of the system (Quebec 1988).

Performance of the System

In the aggregate, access to health services in Quebec and in the other provinces, particularly hospital and physician services, is widely viewed as being very good; good quality services are available and equitably financed. This is generally attributed to extensive public involvement in the system. Government has done much to guarantee the availability of services; in general, services are now as readily available in Quebec as they are in the wealthier provinces.[13]

Public financing has largely eliminated financial barriers to hospital, physician, and other health services (Broyles et al. 1983; Enterline et al. 1973, McDonald et al. 1974; Manga et al. 1987). Public financing is very popular. Being universal, people do not worry about losing coverage if they become unemployed or about financial hardship if they have serious illness. Equally important, people appreciate having convenient and humane financing arrangements: they can obtain services without being hassled about who will pay the bill, and they do not have to endure a lot of red tape to get their bills paid.

Yet access problems still exist in Quebec and elsewhere. The availability of certain health services remains a problem. For example, the residents in rural areas have trouble obtaining doctors' services, particularly those of specialists. Although access to social services has also been greatly improved during the past twenty years, their availability and financing also remain a problem. Services for particular groups of people are inadequate (e.g., the aged, youth, women in difficulty, handicapped, alcoholics, drug addicts, native people). Preventative programs are also underdeveloped. Finally, the debate over the adequacy of government funding has led many observers to believe that some desirable acute-care services are in short supply while others are produced excessively (i.e., they are ineffective or their benefits do not justify their costs).

In addition, the cost of services continues to generate much concern. Quebec's control of its health costs has received much attention (Quebec 1988, 1990a). The fraction of its income devoted to health services is only slightly higher than the national average and significantly less than is spent in

---

13. For example, the number of physicians per one thousand population in Quebec exceeds the national average (2.05 versus 1.94 in 1989) (Canada 1990a).

the United States.[14] There is, however, considerable debate over whether current spending is adequate, in light of new technological developments and the needs of the aging population and other groups. Providers frequently claim services are underfunded, while other observers claim current funding is adequate. Moreover, there is growing debate about the ability of government to continue its extensive funding of services. Although the Rochon Commission rejected user charges, the government now wants to introduce them for hospital, physician, and other services (Quebec 1990b).

The poor integration of many health and social services also creates access and efficiency problems. The Rochon Commission stressed that social services are not well integrated with health services. It was very concerned that the system has become a "prisoner of innumerable interest groups . . . [and that] the common good has been dominated by the interests of these groups."[15] This has resulted in the poor integration of services as well as duplication, lack of continuity, and needed services not being developed. The commission was also concerned about the poor coordination of various government ministries' programs affecting health and social well-being; this has been a significant obstacle to developing preventative programs.

Finally, a variety of other problems persists, including overcrowded emergency rooms, inadequate mechanisms to deal with users' complaints, shortages of nurses, and deteriorating working conditions for managers and other health care workers.

Excessive Centralization

There is considerable agreement that public decision making has been excessively centralized. This was a key conclusion of the Rochon Commission, which stated, "the Minister cannot manage 900 establishments from Quebec City." Providers, socioeconomic groups, and the minister of health and social services agree with this conclusion. Quebec is not the only province in which this problem has been recognized. For example, in British Columbia a royal commission on health services has just reported that there is excessive centralization there too.

Excessive centralization is an important reason for the problems currently confronting Quebec's health and social services system. The MSSS devotes most of its resources to overseeing the hundreds of establishments in

---

14. In 1987 Quebec spent 8.86 percent of its gross domestic product on health and social services, while the national average was 8.71 percent. At the same time, Canada devoted 8.98 percent of its GNP to health, while the United States devoted 10.8 percent (Canada 1990b). Quebec and the other provinces spend less than the United States because their financing arrangements result in lower administrative costs and provide a much better framework for controlling costs (Evans 1990; Woolhandler and Himmelstein 1991).

15. Quebec 1988, 407.

the system, responding to specific problems as they arise in order to avoid their becoming political problems, and dealing with the Treasury Board. As a result, the MSSS has little time for evaluating programs, resolving persistent problems, or coordinating programs with other ministries. At the same time, the establishments feel overwhelmed by the steady flow of detailed government directives, decrees, and regulations. This is discouraging for managers. And the establishments' efficiency is compromised and their ability to resolve problems limited.

The MSSS is preoccupied with the affairs of individual establishments and particular associations of providers, each one competing vigorously with the others for available resources and each concerned about provincial norms affecting it. Consequently, the MSSS gives insufficient attention to the integration of services, and it has been slow to delegate responsibility for integrating them to the regional councils. One result has been poorly integrated mental health services. When the regional council for the Outaouais Region was asked to deal with this problem, however, the result was a major improvement in service integration in that region. The parties involved there wanted to integrate the services and had the responsibility, power, and time to do it. They knew the problem as it existed in the region, and they knew what resources were available there. The regional council provided a good framework within which they could discuss the problem and find a mutually satisfactory solution.

The difficulty in pursuing local priorities in a centralized system is illustrated by an incident at a CLSC in a region with much unemployment and other social problems. The CLSC felt priority should be given to these problems, but the MSSS insisted the CLSC devote its available resources to a ministry-developed, provincewide antismoking program.

The lack of accountability in a centralized system is illustrated by the long-standing shortages of various services in rural regions. People there have long complained. But they are a minority of Quebec's population and elect only a small fraction of the legislature. As a result, they have had limited influence on provincial officials who determine the regional distribution of resources.

On the other hand, there are instances of excessive decentralization. For example, the failure of the government to provide planners at the various DSCs with appropriate terms of reference and tools has resulted in undue duplication of effort among DSC researchers and program analysts.

Explanation

Regional councils were established in the early 1970s to facilitate decentralized decision making. But the councils' responsibilities and powers have been very limited by the government (Gosselin 1984; Quebec 1988; Turgeon

1983). There are various explanations for this. One relates to the early history of the regional councils. In the early 1970s government and other health planners believed the new councils were not ready for major decision-making responsibilities; managerial resources and experience were too limited. Over the past ten years, however, the councils' managerial resources and competency have greatly improved. In addition, there was also much concern in the early 1970s that the existing political structures and culture did not facilitate significant decentralization. The regional councils represented a new level of decision making, which did not correspond to existing political institutions, then existing only at the provincial and local levels. Regional identities were also not well developed in most parts of Quebec. Thus, there was little support for elected councils with taxing powers. It is now widely believed, however, that regional institutions and identities are much better developed. Finally, planners were concerned—rightly or wrongly—that decentralization could raise costs; this concern persisted into the 1980s. As a result of these concerns, the councils became largely advisory bodies for the ministry.

A second reason for limited decentralization is that in the early 1970s no blueprint was prepared detailing the future development of the councils. Decentralization was left an ill-defined concept. Thus, when policymakers' focus shifted to rising health costs in the mid-1970s, there was no mechanism in place to facilitate the councils' further development. Their evolution from mere advisory bodies has been very slow as a result.

Third, some providers (e.g., physicians, hospitals) have opposed significant decentralization, fearing that it would erode their power (Turgeon 1983). They have preferred negotiating directly with the government. Similarly, the MSSS has been reluctant to give up power. As the problems with central decision making have become clearer to government officials and other people, however, the current government has warmed to the idea of more decentralization.

Finally, socioeconomic groups with particular problems as well as providers have recognized the weakness of the regional councils and have often bypassed them, appealing directly to the ministry through administrative, political, and media channels. This has tended to demoralize and further weaken regional authorities and to reinforce the tendency of the government not to delegate additional powers to the councils.

Does the actual performance of the regional councils during the past ten years suggest that they could successfully handle significant new power and responsibility? This question is hard to answer. Little serious effort has been made to evaluate the councils' performance. Yet various observers, including the Rochon Commission, have given a positive answer to this question. Performance has varied among the councils (Bherer et al. 1986), but there have been enough good experiences to make these observers think that expanding the councils' roles is justifiable. Councils have sometimes provided a useful forum for providers to discuss common problems and negotiate regional plans (e.g., the integration of mental health services in the Outaouais Region). They have also had some success developing and implementing some preventative and primary-care programs as well as organizing and managing some common services (e.g., group purchasing) (Gosselin 1984). Observers also believe the councils would perform better if changes were made in their structure, particularly their membership. Providers have had undue influence on the councils.[16] The general public has played only a minor role on the councils and in their activities. The Rochon Commission concluded that the majority of the councils have not provided an effective means by which the population could influence either providers or the ministry.[17] The providers have often fought among themselves, rather than pursue the public's interest. In addition, the lack of a local political base has placed the councils in a weak position when dealing with the government and individual establishments.

Available Information Insufficient

It is very difficult to obtain readily a comprehensive, up-to-date picture of the system's performance and emerging trends. Data describing the health status of the population are limited.[18] Much administrative data describing the utilization of services, resource use, and health service costs are generated by providers and government agencies in the normal course of doing business. But only limited administrative data relating to hospital and physician services are readily available to policymakers and even less to the public.[19] Data

---

16. One reason for this is that establishments have had a large number of council seats. Currently, the councils have fifteen members, six of whom represent providers. The hospitals, the CLSCs, and two other provider groups each has one representative, who typically has been an executive director in one of the establishments. The chief executive officers of the establishments and physicians also have one representative each. In addition, the universities, community colleges, and community service organizations have one representative each. The mayors of the region elect two members, and the minister appoints three. Although the latter three might be viewed as public representatives, they are frequently perceived as being government representatives.

17. Quebec 1988, 169.

18. Standard mortality data and hospital morbidity data are available annually from Statistics Canada. But comprehensive pictures of the population's health status have been scarce. The federal government conducted a national household health status survey in 1950–51 and another in 1978–79. The Quebec government sponsored a similar survey in 1987.

19. The Quebec Health Insurance Board annually publishes much data describing the use of physician services and certain other publicly financed, nonhospital services. Statistics Canada provides some data describing hospital utilization and performance, though only with considerable time lag.

relating to other important sources of services are very scarce (e.g., nursing homes, CLSCs, dental services).

Better descriptive data are certainly possible.[20] Perusing such data can answer policy questions about the performance of the system and help identify health and organizational problems. Better data would also facilitate evaluating system performance. The value of good descriptive data is well illustrated by the attention given by the public and the Quebec government to the idea that health costs will rise substantially in the coming years as the fraction of the population aged sixty-five and over rises. This attention is misplaced. Researchers elsewhere in Canada calculate that the aging of the population should have only a modest effect on health costs (Hertzman and Hayes 1985). A much more important source of future cost increases, these researchers warn, would be the continuation of the large increases in services per capita for the aged that have occurred during the past fifteen years (Hertzman et al. 1990). If people in Quebec during the past ten years had paid more attention to data describing trends in the per capita use of services by different age groups in Quebec, the real nature of future cost problems would now be much better understood.[21]

Evaluative information has also long been insufficient in Quebec. The Castonguay Commission in 1971 and the Rochon Commission in 1988 noted the need for much more evaluation. Attention has focused on the lack of evaluation of health technologies. Although agencies mandated to evaluate them have existed in the United States since the late 1970s, the establishment of similar agencies in Canada only began in the late 1980s. Quebec's Council for the Evaluation of Health Technologies (CETS) was established in 1988.[22] Although its resources are limited, this council has prepared a series of useful literature reviews regarding specific medical technologies.

Evaluations of public policies are also scarce. Most strikingly, no serious

---

20. One important step toward better description data would be to guarantee that each resident has a unique health care identification number, which is recorded whenever a service is provided, and that each resident's address is known. This would allow planners to determine service utilization according to the region in which people live and to develop comprehensive profiles of services used by people in different sociodemographic and health status groups. Such data can greatly facilitate analysis of system performance. Using such data, Leslie and Noralou Roos in Manitoba and their collaborators have provided a great deal of useful analysis of the performance of the Manitoba health care system.

21. For example, between 1978 and 1985 the per capita use of physician services in Quebec increased by 24.5 percent among men sixty-five and older, while it increased by only 2.7 percent among men twenty to fifty-four. This represents an increase of 302 acts per 100 men sixty-five and older and an increase of 14 per 100 men aged twenty to fifty-four.

22. Conseil d'Evaluation des Technologies de la Santé (CETS). Several other provinces are developing similar programs. In addition, a Canadian Coordination Office for Health Technology Assessment was established in Ottawa in 1989.

evaluation of the budget constraints in Quebec or in the other provinces has been made, even though these constraints have been the central policy issue for fifteen years.[23] Wise decisions about hospital finance cannot be made without good information about the constraints' effects on service use and people's health. Nevertheless, even now very little is known about these effects.

The funding debate has been based largely on anecdotal evidence (Detsky et al. 1990). When constraints were first introduced, it was widely agreed that there was much "fat" in the system. Anecdotal evidence provided sufficient guidance then for good policy. But the situation has changed. Much inefficiency has been eliminated, new health problems have emerged, and important new technologies have been developed. In order to assess the funding implications of these changes, better information than is now available is needed.

Some planners argue that continued constraints are justified because resources could be better used by putting more emphasis on prevention and because many health services are ineffective (Quebec 1990a). Expanding prevention programs and eliminating ineffective services are desirable. But this argument does not justify the failure to evaluate the utilization and health effects of the constraints, which may in fact have had negative health effects. Quebec has been constraining resources for acute care, without shifting them to preventative care. It is also uncertain whether hospitals have eliminated only excess laundry soap and ineffective clinical services. At the same time, the people who argue that there is underfunding point to waiting lists, but the significance of these lists has not been evaluated. They also point to the greater spending in the United States, but it is not apparent that this spending is socially warranted (Evans 1990).

Better information about the health effects of budgetary policies is possible, as demonstrated by the rapid growth of analyses of the effects of the prospective payment system (PPS) in the United States. Seven years after PPS was introduced, substantial information about its utilization and health effects is available (Kahn et al. 1990). But, after fifteen years of constrained funding in Quebec, there is still no comparable evidence of the constraints' effects.

Finally, little effort has been made to interpret and widely disseminate available information. Occasionally, interpretations relating to particular is-

---

23. The budget constraints are not the only important health policy that has not been properly evaluated. Little effort has been made to evaluate the CLSCs (Bozzini 1988), though Quebec is now planning to expand the roles of the CLSCs. There is also much interest in expanding home care services. But Quebec's home care programs have not been subjected to a proper evaluation, despite the overwhelming American evidence that such programs—at least as presently organized there—neither reduce costs nor improve health (Soderstrom 1988).

sues are published.[24] But the report of the Rochon Commission in 1988 provided the first comprehensive assessment of the system since the report of the Castonguay Commission in 1971. The MSSS does not publish regularly an analysis of the state of the system.

Better interpretation and dissemination of available information are feasible. This is well demonstrated by the Prospective Payment Assessment Commission (ProPAC) in the United States. This small, independent commission provides Congress, the administration, and other interested parties with substantive information about the financing and use of hospital services covered by Medicare and about other issues relating to PPS. Its annual reports are based largely on data gathered by other agencies and researchers. In them ProPAC reviews hospital performance, the utilization of hospital and other services by Medicare beneficiaries, and the available evidence regarding quality of care.

Possible Explanations

The explanation for this information insufficiency is not fully clear.[25] One possibility is that the problem has not been fully recognized. Quebec researchers and health planners have not emphasized the problem. Moreover, it has not received a lot of attention elsewhere. The Castonguay Commission, however, did stress the need for better descriptive and evaluative information twenty years ago (Quebec 1971). The attention the problem has received in Quebec has related primarily to the need for more evaluations of services. But Quebec did not move rapidly to deal with even this aspect of the problem; the CETS was only established in 1988. Moreover, Quebec still does not attach much urgency to improving information.

Another possible explanation is that research resources are scarce. But this is not a complete explanation; there is a sizable research community with considerable funding in Quebec's six major universities. Moreover, this argument does not explain the lack of good descriptive information.

A third explanation is that government has preferred having insufficient information. The interests of society and those of governments may not coincide: Although better information would improve social well-being, the inter-

---

24. Special commissions examine particular facets of the system (e.g., the commission on CLSC's in 1987). Various agencies publish reports on particular topics (e.g., the Social Affairs Council). And researchers publish analyses of particular health problems and aspects of the system.

25. The need for more technology assessment and the reasons for the unduly rapid diffusion of new technology have been discussed for many years by health planners in Quebec and elsewhere. But there is little discussion in the literature of the reasons why government and researchers have generated insufficient information in either Quebec or the other provinces.

ests of government may be better served if information is limited. There are at least two possible reasons for this. One is that there are various political pressures on government to limit information. The government of the day may fear better information will fuel criticism of its policies, though the opposite may also happen.[26] Providers of services and manufacturers of drugs, equipment, and appliances pressure government to constrain the development of information.[27]

Second, information is expensive, and government officials question the value of better information. Evaluative research is certainly difficult, methods for answering some questions are not well developed, and the results are often hard to understand, ambiguous, and controversial. Research can also take years, while some problems require immediate attention, and politicians have short time horizons.[28] Such thinking can lead government to undervalue research, the result being insufficient information. But the actual return on health services research seems high. This is research with considerable social relevance. The results provide important new information for policy-making and continue to have an important impact on health planners' thinking and the development of health services.

Reforming Public Decision Making in Quebec

Stimulated by the Rochon Commission, many facets of the system are now being reformed. The government outlined its reform plan in a White Paper in early December 1990 (Quebec 1990b). A week later it presented the enabling legislation (Bill 120), which was approved in August 1991. Now the plan is being implemented. The wide-ranging reforms touch patients' rights, establishments' administrative structures, the availability of various health and social services (e.g., the regional distribution of physicians), the introduction of user charges, etc. A key reform involves decentralization, but little is being done about information problems. The Rochon Commission reaffirmed the social value of extensive public involvement in Quebec's health and social services system. These reforms are widely viewed as an attempt to improve this public involvement. The introduction of user charges, however, is a serious threat to the system.

---

26. In the words of Detsky et al. (1990), "It may be in the interest of all parties, including government, institutions, and clinicians, to have the facts remain unknown; in that way rhetoric and 'orchestrated outrage' can be freely used without fear of being proven wrong."

27. Linton and Naylor (1990) hint at this problem in their recent discussion of efforts to improve information in Ontario.

28. A related problem is that government officials change positions frequently. This can make it difficult for particular officials who recognize the need for more research to develop permanent research programs.

Decentralization

The government's decentralization plan has two key features. First, additional responsibility and power are supposed to be shifted to sixteen regional boards, which will replace the existing twelve regional councils. The boards will determine regional priorities, develop programs, allocate operating funds to establishments, oversee the operation of establishments and programs, and integrate various providers' activities. In all their activities, however, the boards will be constrained by provincial norms.

The boards' funding will come entirely from the MSSS. The ministry has indicated it will divide its budget among a series of programs and then give each board a share of each program's budget, a board's share being determined in the next several years by the current budgets of the region's establishments.[29] The board will then allocate each program's funds among the region's providers in order to meet the program's centrally determined objectives. There is one exception: funding for physician services. Under pressure from the physicians the government dropped the idea of having prospectively determined regional budgets for these services.

The MSSS will continue to be a major decision maker. At minimum it will determine the system's general objectives, aggregate funding for each program, and norms for system operation. It will also oversee the boards closely and will be responsible for overall planning and evaluation.[30] The philosophy underlying the division of responsibilities and powers between the MSSS and the boards is that there should be Quebec-wide norms regarding the availability of services and financing but that the operation of the system should be managed regionally.

Second, the membership of the new boards will be different from that of the councils. The government is trying to prevent the boards from being dominated by providers, while at the same time having people serve who are informed about health and social services, and to strengthen the boards' political roots within their respective regions. The Montreal Island and Montérégie Boards will have twenty-five members and the others twenty-three. In all regions twenty members will come from four different community-based groups, including eight who are members of individual establishments' administrative councils. A two-step selection process will be used;[31] it is hoped

---

29. According to current plans, each board's share of available funds will eventually be determined by the demographic characteristics of the board's region.

30. Fees and salaries for physicians as well as wages and salaries for other health care workers will continue to be set at the provincial level, largely through collective bargaining.

31. Each region will have a general assembly, with at most 150 members elected by four community groups in the region. The establishments will elect 40 percent of the assembly's members; those so elected must be people who are members of individual establishments'

that this will result in board members who represent more than just the interests of their particular constituency. There is one exception: Under pressure from physicians the government agreed that physicians can have one representative on each board.

Thus, meaningful decentralization could be under way. The regional boards are supposed to have significant new managerial responsibilities and powers. And the boards have been strengthened. Yet the actual effects of the reforms once implemented remain unclear; much depends on how the government implements its plan. There are two sources of uncertainty.

First, though some responsibilities and powers will undoubtedly be transferred to the boards, the extent of this transfer is uncertain. The new legislation gives the government great discretion to determine the boards' role: It must set norms that will guide their decision making, approve the boards' plans, and decide how much money to give them. If the norms are very detailed, the reviews of the boards' plans very stringent, and funds limited, the boards' new roles will also be limited.[32] Proponents believe a significant shift of power is under way; critics are doubtful. MSSS officials claim the boards will be given a major role in decision making. Various interest groups now expect that will happen, so there will be political pressure on the government to make a significant transfer of power. Provincial politicians and MSSS bureaucrats, however, may prove reluctant to give up their power, and hospitals and physicians still appear lukewarm about a significant shift of power.

The boards' latitude will be affected by agreements negotiated between the government and providers. Here decentralization has gotten off to a rocky start. Quebec physicians, unhappy with several aspects of the initial plan, threatened in June to strike unless changes were made. As a result, the government backed away from several ideas.[33] Yet the extent to which pro-

---

administrative councils. In addition, the municipal councils will elect 20 percent of the assembly members; all must be elected council members. Finally, the socioeconomic groups and the community organizations in the region will each elect 20 percent of the members. Then this general assembly will elect twenty of its members to sit on its regional board's administrative council. Eight must be assembly members elected by the establishments, four assembly members elected by the municipal councils, four elected by socioeconomic groups, and four by the community organizations. In addition, physicians will have one representative on the council. The executive director of the board will also be an ex officio member. Finally, these twenty-two council members will name three more board members in the Montreal Island and the Montérégie regions and one more member in the other regions.

32. It also remains to be seen how much effort the ministry will make at developing good working relations with the boards and how tolerant it will be when the boards make mistakes.

33. As already noted, it eliminated regional budgets for physician services and added one physician to each regional board. It also has agreed to set aside its plan to require new physicians to practice in rural areas as long as shortages persist there; it is now negotiating with physicians a

vider groups influence decentralization depends on the government's willingness to negotiate with them. It also remains to be seen whether the government will continue to permit some establishments to negotiate special arrangements with it, bypassing their regional boards.

A second uncertainty is the performance of the boards themselves. MSSS officials indicate that the boards will be given more managerial resources. Impressed by the performance of some of the existing regional councils, some observers believe the prospects for the boards are good. But critics predict the boards will become another system-stifling bureaucracy, because the MSSS will give the boards much busywork, requiring providers in turn to do more busywork, and because the boards' staffs will develop their own bureaucratic practices. But it will not be easy for such bureaucracies to develop. Provincial officials and various interest groups recognize the potential danger here. And, given the scarcity of public dollars, the MSSS should be reluctant to finance regional bureaucracies. The bigger danger is that the boards will have insufficient resources.

Another source of this uncertainty is the extent to which the boards will look after providers' interests as opposed to those of the public.[34] This was a problem with the old councils. And the history of regulatory bodies in North America warns that the regulated often unduly influence their regulators. At least nine board members will have direct links with providers, and there are other ways the providers can also influence the boards.[35] But providers are a diverse group; the concerns of hospitals and CLSCs are different. At least it will be harder for providers as a group to dominate a new board than an old council; the members of the new boards who are not directly linked to providers will come from a wider array of community organizations, and the majority of members will have stronger ties with the general public and users in their communities.

One factor that could strengthen the performance of board members is the information available to them. Information is power, and people not closely linked to providers or other interest groups are often handicapped by their lack of relevant information. Unfortunately, the government has shown little interest to date in improving information.

---

scheme involving a variety of financial incentives to get more physicians into those areas and into public organizations.

34. The government will certainly have less direct influence on the boards than it had on the old councils because it will no longer appoint any board members.

35. As in the past, employees of establishments in a region are eligible to serve on the region's board. Also, people friendly to the providers could be encouraged to run for election, providers could engage in lobbying activities, and providers will be represented on the boards' advisory committees.

Information

The need for better information has not gone unnoticed. Both the Rochon Commission and the minister in his 1990 White Paper proposed that the MSSS should do more program evaluation, though neither offered a concrete plan for doing this. Both also proposed increasing outside research on health and social services. And the minister proposed creating a special research center to assess the state of health and social well-being.

Though reasonable, these proposals are insufficient. Aside from the proposal to gather more health status information, no improvement in descriptive information has been proposed. In addition, the MSSS will continue to have a large number of responsibilities for the day-to-day functioning of the health system under the new plan, so it may well continue to neglect program evaluation. It is not clear that additional resources will be committed to internal MSSS evaluations or external research.[36] Finally, there is nothing in these proposals providing for the interpretation and distribution of the available descriptive and evaluative data.

Thus, more should be done to overcome the information problems. It would be useful if the MSSS would publish an annual assessment of the state of health and social services. But an independent "arms-length" assessment would be even better. Government might unduly limit information; as already indicated, an important reason for current information deficiencies is that government has an incentive to do this. The ministry being a key party in policy debates, there would also be concern that its assessments could be "one-sided." Finally, the results of independent assessments should be useful for MSSS and other public decision makers.

Although the MSSS should have primary responsibility for generating and providing data, a small independent information agency—a Health and Social Services Council (HSSC)—should be established. This council could be patterned after ProPAC in the United States. As already indicated, the information and advice provided by this small commission have had a positive impact on government decision making with respect to hospital services covered by Medicare, particularly its prospective payment system.

The HSSC would assemble available data describing the performance of the health care system as well as evaluations of specific programs and public policies relating to health and social services. It could also undertake some

---

36. MSSS officials have indicated that, as power is transferred to the boards, there will be a corresponding transfer of MSSS staff to them. If this happens, there may well be few additional resources in the ministry for program evaluation.

small research projects itself. It should, however, be primarily concerned with gathering the results of work done by other government agencies and outside researchers in Quebec and elsewhere.[37] In addition, this council would identify important, remediable deficiencies in the descriptive and evaluative information available.

Equally important, this council would provide thoughtful interpretation of the available information, pointing out important policy implications and identifying issues requiring further investigation. The data gathered and this interpretation would be the basis for an annual or biannual report on the state of health and social services. It would be sent to the minister of health and social services and would be made widely available to other interested groups. The council might also publish detailed reports on pressing issues.

This council should not simply be a forum for government or providers. Its members—appointed by government—should be thoughtful, independent-minded experts in matters relating to health and social services, health administration, health economics, health care evaluation, etc. Their knowledge should enhance the quality of the council's work. CETS provides an attractive model; its members are experts in a variety of fields relevant to the evaluation of health care technologies. One reason for ProPAC's success is that its twenty commissioners are thoughtful people with experience in health economics, hospital finance, and health care.

Discussion

The performance of a public health care system can be significantly affected by the quality of the public decision making, as Quebec's experience indicates. Its public system has been hampered by problems with the organization of decision making, including excess centralization and inadequate information. The problems created by the former, however, have been recognized. And, under the leadership provided by the Rochon Commission and the government, steps are being taken to decentralize decision making. This is a significant accomplishment. But reform is difficult and imperfect. There is much uncertainty about what will actually emerge from this decentralization. And there is little pressure to improve information.

Quebec is not alone in having problems with public decision making. The performance of the other provincial health systems has also been hampered by problems similar to those in Quebec. Moreover, none of the provinces are moving rapidly to eliminate their information deficiencies. Yet

---

37. The MSSS would be responsible for program evaluations and CETS for the evaluation of specific health care technologies. If the center proposed by the minister were established, it would have primary responsibility for gathering information on health status.

Quebec is the only province thus far to attempt significant decentralization of management functions. Others are now thinking about decentralization (e.g., British Columbia). And all will be watching the Quebec experience closely.

Americans are showing interest in health system reform, with attention focused on how to expand health insurance coverage and better control health costs. Such reform will inevitably mean increased reliance on public decision making. And the results of any reform will depend in part on the quality of public decision making. Thus, Americans should give careful thought to the way this public decision making is organized. Quebec's experience does not imply, however, that the reform of U.S. financing arrangements must wait until adequate information and decentralized decision making can be properly developed. Quebec's universal, comprehensive public financing programs have significantly improved social well-being, despite problems with decision making. The point argued here is that even more could be accomplished by reforming public decision making in Quebec.

The United States does not necessarily need to decentralize decision making to the same extent that Quebec has done. The appropriate structure for public decision making will depend in part on the specific form of the health insurance reforms adopted. The structure appropriate for a reform patterned after the proposals of Enthoven (1989) is probably different from that for a reform patterned after Canada's universal public plan. In addition, as already indicated, the appropriate degree of decentralization depends on social values as well as efficiency considerations.

Finally, the political culture as well as the existing political-administrative structures probably limits the extent to which decentralization is now feasible. Even if a public health insurance plan patterned after the Canadian plan were adopted, it may only be feasible now to have the states assume substantial managerial functions, with the federal government providing some financing and setting some national norms. Although more decentralization might yield better system performance, such a universal, publicly financed, state-managed plan probably would perform better than the present American system (Fein 1986). The key message from Quebec is not that only its model can succeed but, rather, that careful thought should be given to how public decision making is organized.

It is frequently argued that the federal and state governments are now too weak to be entrusted with more managerial responsibilities for health care. The Quebec experience suggests this argument is not necessarily correct. If careful thought is given to the organization of decision making, good-quality public decision making is feasible. Consider the issues that have been discussed here, information and decentralization.

Whichever reform is implemented, the information available will influence the quality of decision making. It is feasible to have better information in the United States than is now available in Quebec. The descriptive data now available in the United States seem more complete and up to date than that available in Quebec. Furthermore, American researchers are actively generating more useful evaluative information than their Canadian counterparts. In this regard, the contrast noted between the significant American research on the effects of PPS and the paucity of evaluations of hospital budget constraints in Canada is very striking. Finally, U.S. reformers can draw upon the experience with ProPAC. This small advisory organization provides them with a good model upon which to build a more complete information system.

The wisdom of decentralizing decision making is also questioned. It is argued that the states are incapable of properly managing their respective health care systems. But they are now in a better position to undertake the management of their health systems than any of the provinces were when they introduced public financing. The state governments have had experience managing health care under Medicaid; the Canadian provinces had had little comparable experience. The full extent of the task facing the state governments is now clear; when public financing was introduced in Canada, there was little recognition of the need to control health care costs. Finally, the states now have better access to key managerial tools than the provinces had. Information available should certainly be better. Experienced health care administrators are certainly more readily available today in the United States than they were even in the 1970s in Quebec. State governments can draw upon a large pool of capable, experienced people now working in government agencies, hospitals, and the insurance industry.

Two other factors shaping public decisions have not been discussed because of space limitations: the financial constraints and incentives confronting decision makers; and the nature of the decision makers themselves. Both involve important issues for public decision making. Much has been said about constraints on the government's ability to finance services. But the situation is more complicated than has been widely perceived. The real problem is not the lack of resources; Quebec spends only 9 percent of its income on health. Rather, the problem is the scarcity of information about the system's performance. People in Quebec are understandably reluctant to pay higher taxes for more health and social services because they are unsure whether the value of the additional benefits would justify the higher taxes. If it could be shown that more spending would yield valuable benefits, people would probably be willing to pay higher taxes.

The nature of the public decision makers refers in part to the values that shape decision making. Public decision making in Quebec has been shaped by two contradictory value systems. On the one hand, people want public authorities to finance services and guarantee that services are available. This requires extensive government involvement in system financing and management. On

Public Decision Making in Public Health Care Systems 269
t>

the other hand, people are reluctant to have government intervene too extensively in society; the idea that people should have freedom of choice and be responsible for their own affairs is deeply rooted in North American culture. This has constrained the degree of government involvement in Quebec's health and social services system. For example, while people want services to be available and well integrated, they also are reluctant to allow public decision makers the necessary tools and powers, because this would constrain the freedom of choice of providers and users. To make further improvements in the performance of Quebec's health and social services system, it will be important to find ways of accommodating the structural contradiction between these two value systems.

REFERENCES

Bherer, Harold, et al. 1986. *Le miroir magique de la décentralisation.* Quebec: Ministère de la Santé et des Services Sociaux, Rapport de recherche, 239.
Bozzini, Luciano. 1988. "Local Community Services Centers (CLSCs) in Quebec: Description, Evaluation, Perspectives." *Journal of Public Health Policy* 9 (1): 346–75.
Broyles, Robert W., et al. 1983. "The Use of Physician Services under a National Health Insurance Scheme. *Medical Care* 21:1037–54.
Canada. 1990a. *Health Personnel in Canada, 1989.* Ottawa: Health Information Division, Department of National Health and Welfare.
———. 1990b. *National Health Expenditures in Canada, 1975–1987.* Ottawa: Health Information Division, Department of National Health and Welfare.
Detsky, Allen S., et al. 1990. "Containing Ontario's Hospital Costs under Universal Insurance in the 1980s: What Was the Record?" *Canadian Medical Association Journal* 142 (6): 565–72.
Enterline, Philip E., et al. 1973. "The Distribution of Medical Services before and after 'Free' Medical Care—The Quebec Experience." *New England Journal of Medicine* 289 (22): 1174–78.
Enthoven, Alain C. 1989. "A Consumer-Choice Health Plan for the 1990s: Universal Health Insurance in a System Designed to Promote Quality and Economy." *New England Journal of Medicine* 320 (1): 29–37 and 320 (2): 94–101.
Evans, Robert G. 1984. *Strained Mercy: The Economics of Canadian Health Care.* Toronto: Butterworth.
———. 1990. "Tension, Compression and Shear: Directions, Stresses and Outcomes of Health Care Cost Control." *Journal of Health Politics, Policy and Law* 15 (1): 101–28.
Fein, Rashi. 1986. *Medical Care, Medical Costs.* Cambridge: Harvard University Press.
Gosselin, Roger. 1984. "Decentralization/Regionalization in Health Care: The Quebec Experience." *Health Care Management Review* 9 (1): 7–25.
t>

Gow, James I., et al. 1987. *Introduction à l'administration publique: une approche politique*. Montreal: Gaëtan Morin.

Hertzman, Clyde, and M. Hayes. 1985. "Will the Elderly Really Bankrupt Us with Increased Health Care Costs?" *Canadian Journal of Public Health* 76 (6): 373–77.

Hertzman, Clyde, et al. 1990. "Flat on Your Back or Back in Your Flat?: Sources of Increased Hospital Services Utilization among the Elderly in British Columbia." *Social Sciences and Medicine* 30 (7): 819–28.

Kahn, Katherine, et al. 1990. "The Effects of the DRG-based Prospective Payment System on Quality of Care for Hospitalized Medicare Patients: An Introduction to the Series." *JAMA* 264 (15): 1953–55.

Linton, Adam L., and C. David Naylor. 1990. "Organized Medicine and the Assessment of Technology—Lessons from Ontario." *New England Journal of Medicine* 323 (21): 1463–68.

McDonald, Alison D., et al. 1974. "Effects of Quebec Medicare on Physician Consultation for Selected Symptoms." *New England Journal of Medicine* 291 (13): 649–52.

Manga, Pran, et al. 1987. "The Determinants of Hospital Utilization under a Universal Public Insurance Program in Canada." *Medical Care* 25 (7): 658–70.

Quebec. 1971. *Health: Vol. III, The Health Plan (Continuation)*. Report of the Commission of Inquiry on Health and Social Services. Quebec: Quebec Official Publisher.

———. 1988. *Rapport de la Commission d'Enquête sur les Services de Santé et les Services Sociaux*. Quebec: Les Publications du Québec.

———. 1990a. *Financement des services de santé: défis pour les année 90*. Conseil des Affaires Sociales. Montreal: Gaëtan Morin.

———. 1990b. *Une réforme axée sur le citoyen*. Gouvernement du Québec. Quebec: Ministère de la Santé et des Services Sociaux.

Sah, Raaj K. 1991. "Fallibility in Human Organizations and Political Systems." *Journal of Economic Perspectives* 5 (2): 67–88.

Soderstrom, Lee. 1988. *Privatization: Adopt or Adapt?* Synthèse critique 36, Commission d'Enquête sur les Services de Santé et les Services Sociaux. Quebec: Les Publications du Québec.

Stoddart, Greg, and Roberta Labelle. 1985. *Privatization in the Canadian Health Care System: Assertions, Evidence, Ideology, and Options*. Ottawa: Health and Welfare Canada.

Turgeon, Jean. 1983. *Evaluation du processus de décentralisation administrative vers leniveau régional en affaires sociales*. Gouvernement du Québec, Ministère des Affaires Sociales, Direction de l'Evaluation des Programmes, Evaluation des Programmes no. 12.

Woolhandler, Steffie, and David U. Himmelstein. 1991. "The Deteriorating Administrative Efficiency of the U.S. Health Care System." *New England Journal of Medicine* 324 (18): 1253–58.

Conclusion

Jonathan Lemco

In both the United States and Canada health care reform is high on the agenda. The American system is perceived as broken and in need of massive repair. The Canadian system is functioning adequately, for it offers access with less costs than its U.S. counterpart, but it too could be improved. In both cases the issue is what remedies will work best.

President Clinton has been explicit in his call for a health care plan that is affordable, offers universal coverage, is comprehensive, provides greater efficiency, and is of the highest quality. Virtually all Americans and Canadians would agree that these are noble goals. Finding a reform package that can successfully accommodate these demands, however, has been extremely difficult. We do not yet know how to combine immediate access and the best high-tech medicine without incurring a high price. If we focus on cost containment, as many politicians in both countries have done, access and/or quality will suffer.

Although the Canadian system is less culpable than the American one, preventative medicine is woefully underfunded. In the long run greater emphasis on prevention could substantially cut costs as it saves lives and prevents disease. So, we need thoughtful reform prescriptions as quickly as possible. Implementation must be quick, for the longer reform takes the more expensive it will be.

But this is a very tall order. In the United States the public and health care experts have very different expectations of health reform. If everyone agrees that large-scale change is needed, much of the public strongly resists the sacrifices the experts assume will need to be made. Both experts and the public agree that escalating costs are required. But the former calls for slowing the growth in national spending on health care to reduce the deficit and boost productivity. On the other hand, consumers want to spend less of their own money while enjoying lifetime access to the highest standard of care.

In addition, many health care analysts insist that extending coverage to the uninsured will require higher taxes for all Americans. But much of the public either does not fully appreciate this or isn't willing to make the necessary financial sacrifices. Cutting costs might also lead to hospital closings and layoffs, and these will be particularly hard to take.[1]

Nevertheless, there will be reform in the United States. If it is to be some form of national health care, certain conditions will have to be introduced. It must be understandable to the public. It will be administered, in large part, by public authorities and available to all citizens. Benefits will be comprehensive. Cost sharing, in the form of deductibles, coinsurance, and copayment provisions, will be minimized. Funding for a national health care plan will be paid for by progressive taxes. An emphasis will still be placed on reducing costs wherever possible.[2]

Reform will not be easy. Implementation of a Canadian-style health care system will be very expensive in the short run. Opposition from the health insurance industry, the American Bar Association, and the American Medical Association will be daunting. The American public may not accept the level of government involvement that would be required to make the reforms work.[3]

The Canadian system is also under strain. In the next few years we can expect public expenditure cutbacks. Provincial governments are expected to reduce their spending, and it is possible that direct public payments will increase. Provincial health ministers are also proposing 10 percent cuts in medical school enrollments, and more doctors are being pressured to accept flat salaries rather than fee for service. The fee schedules themselves are examined more carefully than ever before for excess or fraud.

Hospitals will be forced to better track their procedure costs. Fewer patients will stay in the hospital overnight as a cost-saving measure. Resources will be transferred to lower-cost day surgeries and home care services. Duplication of specialized services by hospitals in a single geographic area will be reduced. Other cost-saving measures are likely.

The Canadian system of national health care remains effective, but it is second in cost only to the U.S. system. The level of dissatisfaction with the health care system in Canada is dwarfed by that evident in the United States, but it is there and it is growing. National health care is not a panacea for the United States. But it is certainly an improvement over the existing system.

1. For a discussion of some of the sacrifices that might be required to finance meaningful reforms, see Miriam K. Mills and Robert H. Blank, eds., *Health Insurance and Public Policy: Risk, Allocation and Equity*. Westport, Conn.: Greenwood, 1992.

2. These points are discussed in Rashi Fein, "National Health Insurance: Telling the Good from the Bad," *Dissent* (Spring 1992): 157–63.

3. For a fuller discussion of the constraints associated with implementing national health care in the United States, see Robert P. Huefner and Margaret Battin, eds., *Changing to National Health Care: Ethical and Policy Issues*. Salt Lake City: University of Utah Press, 1992.

The difficult task before American policymakers is to devise a system that is more efficient, cost effective, comprehensive, and universal while remaining sensitive to the desire by most Americans for a system that is consistent with their values and unique culture. It will be a formidable task.

Contributors

Morris L. Barer is Director of the University of British Columbia Centre for Health Services and Policy Research.

Luciano Bozzini is Associate Professor in the Department of Health Administration at the University of Montreal.

David W. Conklin is Director of the Office of the Institute for Research on Public Policy, Director of the Centre for American Studies, and Adjunct Professor in the Faculty of Social Sciences, University of Western Ontario.

Raisa B. Deber is Professor in the Department of Health Administration, University of Toronto.

Robert G. Evans is Professor of Economics at the University of British Columbia.

David U. Himmelstein is Assistant Professor of Medicine at Harvard University, Director of the Division of Social and Community Medicine at the Cambridge Hospital, and National Coordinator of Physicians for a National Health Program.

Jonathan Lemco is Research Director of the Canadian-American Committee and a Senior Fellow at the National Planning Association, Washington, D.C. Dr. Lemco is also the Managing Editor of *North American Outlook* and an Adjunct Professor at the Johns Hopkins University. He has written or edited ten books and numerous scholarly articles on topics such as the implications of the NAFTA, the costs and benefits of health care reform in the United States, energy and environmental policymaking, Canadian and U.S. policy interests in Central America, and the implications of Quebec's sovereignty movement for Canada and the United States.

Theodore R. Marmor is Professor of Politics and Public Policy at the School of Organization and Management, Yale University, and a fellow of the Canadian Institute for Advanced Research.

Jerry L. Mashaw is Gordon Bradford Tweedy Professor of Law and Organization at Yale Law School.

Edward Neuschler is Deputy Director of Policy Development and Research for the Health Insurance Association of America.

Frank W. Puffer is Professor of Economics at Clark University.

275

Bert Seidman is a consultant to the National Council of Senior Citizens, a board member of the National Council on the Aging, a vice president of the National Consumer League, and advisory director of the International Foundation of Employee Benefit Plans.

Lee Soderstrom is Associate Professor in the Department of Economics, McGill University.

Paul W. Sperduto is Assistant Professor of Radiation Oncology and Director of Stereotactic Radiosurgery at the University of Minnesota Hospital.

Malcolm G. Taylor is Emeritus Professor of Public Policy at York University.

Steffie Woolhandler is Assistant Professor of Medicine at Harvard University, Director of Inpatient Services at the Cambridge Hospital, and National Coordinator of Physicians for a National Health Program.

Index